6/92-

282.

Gore Vidal

GORE VIDAL
Writer Against the Grain

EDITED BY JAY PARINI

COLUMBIA UNIVERSITY PRESS
NEW YORK

COLUMBIA UNIVERSITY PRESS

NEW YORK   OXFORD

Copyright © 1992 Columbia University Press

The essays and reviews in this collection appear by permission of each author.

Several of the essays or reviews appeared, in earlier form, elsewhere. Thanks are due to the editors of the following publications:

The New York Review of Books (Harold Bloom, Louis Auchincloss, Richard Poirier), *The Nation* (Thomas M. Disch), *New Statesman* (Stephen Spender).

"Imagining Vidal" by Italo Calvino first appeared in English in *The Threepenny Review.*

"*The City and the Pillar* as Gay Fiction" by Claude J. Summers appears, in different form, in Summers' *Gay Fictions: From Wilde to Stonewall* (New York: Continuum, 1990).

"The Vidalian Manner" is reprinted from *Gore Vidal* by Robert F. Kiernan (New York: Frederick Ungar, 1982).

"Gore Vidal: The Entertainer" is reprinted from Bernard F. Dick, *The Apostate Angel: A Critical Study of Gore Vidal* (New York: Random House, 1974).

"Vidal as Playwright: In Gentlest Heresy" is reprinted from *Gore Vidal* by Ray Lewis White (Boston: Twayne, 1968).

The essays by David Price, Alan Cheuse, William H. Pritchard, Samuel F. Pickering, Robert Boyers, Catharine R. Stimpson, James Tatum, and Donald E. Pease were commissioned especially for this volume.

Heather Neilson's essay on *Messiah* is adapted from her Oxford University D.Phil. thesis.

Book design by Jennifer Dossin

PRINTED IN THE UNITED STATES OF AMERICA

c 10 9 8 7 6 5 4 3 2 1

CONTENTS

GORE VIDAL: A CHRONOLOGY
OF HIS WORKS

1946 *Williwaw*
1947 *In a Yellow Wood*
1948 *The City and the Pillar* (rev. ed., 1965)
1949 *The Season of Comfort*
1950 *Dark Green, Bright Red* (rev. ed., 1968)
1950 *A Search for the King: A Twelfth-Century Legend*
1952 *Death in the Fifth Position* [Edgar Box pseud.]
1952 *The Judgment of Paris* (rev. ed., 1965)
1953 *Death Before Bedtime* [Edgar Box pseud.]
1954 *Death Likes It Hot* [Edgar Box pseud.]
1954 *Messiah* (rev. ed., 1965)
1956 *A Thirsty Evil: Seven Short Stories*
1956 *Visit to a Small Planet and Other Television Plays*
1957 *Visit to a Small Planet: A Comedy Akin to Vaudeville*
      [Broadway version]
1960 *The Best Man: A Play About Politics*
[n.d.] *On the March to the Sea: A Southern Tragedy*
1962 *Rocking the Boat*
1962 *Romulus: A New Comedy, Adapted from a Play by*
      Friedrich Dürrenmatt

Gore Vidal

1

Gore Vidal: The Writer and His Critics

Jay Parini

I.

When the dust settles on this half of the twentieth century, Gore Vidal may well assume the place among his contemporaries denied to him throughout a long and various life of writing. His vast, almost Trollopian, productivity spans five decades and includes over twenty novels, collections of essays on literature and politics, a volume of short stories, successful Broadway plays, television plays, film scripts, even three mystery novels written under the pseudonym of Edgar Box. One has to wonder at the lack of serious critical response to this extraordinary body of work.

Vidal has in fact been written about a good deal. The problem is with the quality, not the quantity, of this attention. Much of the writing about him takes the form of light magazine profiles and ephemeral reviews, since Vidal has been a celebrity from the beginning. And the reviews of Vidal's work have been remarkably uneven, often presenting a reviewer's assumptions (usually second-hand) about the man instead of offering something like an objective viewpoint. Harold Bloom, among others, has noticed this; he observes in his essay-review on *Lincoln*, included here, that Vidal's "achievement is vastly underestimated by American academic criticism." It has been one of my tasks in editing this volume to attempt to rectify this slight of sustained critical attention as well as to uncover some of the best writing that has already been published about Vidal.

One of the curiosities in surveying the critical scene around Vidal is his relation to academe, which has been troubled from the outset. And one quickly sees the price Vidal has paid for this stubbornness. His contemporaries—Mailer, Updike, and Bellow, among others—have been the source of minor cottage industries in the academy, whereas Vidal has been pretty much ignored. A good example is Frederick R. Karl's comprehensive study of postwar American fiction, *American Fictions: 1940–1980;* Karl dismisses Vidal in a single, rather lengthy, footnote.[1] He writes that

> Gore Vidal's *Williwaw* (1946), as one of the first war novels, was a fine performance for a nineteen-year-old author; similarly, *The City and the Pillar* (1948), as one of the first American novels to touch directly on homosexual themes, was a fine performance for an only slightly older author. I have, however, omitted Vidal from this study. By assiduously separating himself from modernism and the modern novel, he has produced a large body of work that rejects the new.

He goes on to compare Vidal to Louis Auchincloss, who has also made "literary choices that—despite trendy themes—look back, not forward." This assumption, that Vidal is somehow old-fashioned and has failed to confront modernism, has been turned frequently against him; being "old-fashioned," he is rarely mentioned in academic studies of the postwar novel. Even a fine critic like Elizabeth Dipple, whose *The Unresolvable Plot* is among the best recent books on contemporary fiction, refers slantingly to the "intemperate anti-academic American novelist, Gore Vidal" on the very first page of her book.[2]

Yet Dipple is forced to turn to Vidal in her chapter on Italo Calvino. For it was Vidal who brought Calvino to the attention of American readers, partly because he has understood Calvino's postmodern pyrotechnics better than anyone. What seems to have been missed by critics of Vidal is that he has not only understood but absorbed a good deal of postmodernism himself; in many ways he can be seen as one of its founders in such novels as *Myra Breckin-*

ridge and *Duluth*. Calvino himself says in a little-known essay called "Imagining Vidal" (included here) that "one cannot speak of the revival of the novel's form in the last fifteen years without turning back to what may be his most famous novel, *Myra Breckinridge*. That satirical and grotesque burlesque, made up of a collage of the language and myths of the mass-culture, inaugurated a new phase in the way to present our era, which is comparable to pop art, but much more aggressive and with an explosion of expressionistic comedy."

So what's going on here? Is Vidal a rather old-fashioned realist? Is he anti-modern? Why has this perhaps postmodern prototype been put on the shelf before he has, indeed, been taken off the shelf? Such questions have many answers, and I can do no more than suggest a few obvious reasons for such a miserable state of affairs.

One straightforward reason is that Vidal's unusual productivity, already alluded to, has gotten in his way. A writer like Saul Bellow, by contrast, is easy to assimilate and talk about; his dozen or so novels and two story collections are all of a piece. And it's a smallish piece. The same could be said for Pynchon, Barthelme, and many other fictionists whose work has been the focus of critical tomes. But laziness on the part of critics isn't the only obvious thing that's gotten in Vidal's way. Norman Mailer has a lot of books on *his* bibliography, but critics—especially in the sixties and seventies— flocked to Mailer, eager to dissect every paragraph. Such a fate for Mailer has something, I think, to do with the fact that his work could easily be discussed in existential terms; Mailer offered critics the terms by which he wished to be judged, and they all bit. In short, he was critically popular when macho versions of the existential hero still had some appeal.

The feminist revolution essentially knocked Mailer out of his own self-constructed ring, and he has, it seems, gone up in his own smoke. This has forced critics to look elsewhere—to John Updike, for instance, a writer who has been a favorite of critics (though a substantial group of dissenters exists). Only slightly younger than Vidal, Updike is, if anything, even more prolific. But his corpus— however remarkable—is fairly uniform, even predictable, and this is comforting to a critic trying to organize a book or an essay.

Vidal has been anything but predictable. The novels and plays focus on subjects ranging from World War II (*Williwaw*) to the ancient world (*Julian, Romulus, Creation*), to the postwar gay scene in America (*The City and the Pillar*), to the politics of Central America (*Dark Green, Bright Red*), to apocalyptic religion (*Messiah, Kalki*), to the sexual revolution (*Myra Breckinridge, Myron*), to the great march of American history (*Burr, 1876, Lincoln, Empire, Hollywood,* and *Washington, D.C.*). His Swiftian satire, *Duluth,* has the whole of American pop culture in its deadly aim.

But it's not just the bulk and variety of Vidal's oeuvre that befuddles or annoys his critics. Some of the prejudice against Vidal has to do with the author's characteristic approach to literary representation, which in some respects might be considered anti-*post*modern if not anti-modern. In postmodern fiction, the reader is expected to do a good deal of the work of mental reconstruction: as in a game of connect the dots. The writer puts in the points of demarcation, but the reader draws the lines. Even Vidal, in his elegiac retrospective on Calvino, points out that in Calvino—the quintessential postmodern writer—one has the uncanny sense that one is writing the text as well as reading it. This is true of Nabokov, Beckett, Borges, Robbe-Grillet, and other writers of the postwar era. But it is distinctly not true of Vidal.

Consider, for instance, the opening paragraphs of *Empire:*

> "The war ended last night, Caroline. Help me with these flowers." Elizabeth Cameron stood in the open French window, holding a large blue-and-white china vase filled with roses, somewhat showily past their prime. Caroline helped her hostess carry the heavy vase into the long cool dim drawing room.
>
> At forty, Mrs. Cameron was, to Caroline's youthful eye, very old indeed; nevertheless, she was easily the handsomest of America's great ladies and certainly the most serenely efficient, able to arrange a platoon of flower vases before breakfast with the same ease and briskness that her uncle, General Sherman, had devastated Georgia.
>
> "One must always be up at dawn in August." Mrs. Cameron sounded to Caroline rather like Julius Caesar, reporting home. "Servants—like flowers—tend to wilt. We shall be thirty-seven for lunch. Do you intend to marry Del?"
>
> "I don't think I shall ever marry anyone." Caroline frowned with pleasure at Mrs. Cameron's directness. Although Caroline thought of herself as American, she had actually lived most of her life in Paris

and so had had little contact with women like Elizabeth Sherman Cameron, the perfect modern American lady—thus, earth's latest, highest product, as Henry James had not too ironically proclaimed.[3]

As in *Portrait of a Lady* or *Middlemarch*, there is little left for the reader to do her but sit back and enjoy the scenery, the exchange of witticisms, the development of characters, the accumulating sense of a many-layered social and political world. The mandarin tone (which is typical of Vidal) relates not only to the sense of the world as a fait accompli; it exists in every aspect of the actual content. This is a fictional world where French windows and china vases and people with connections to the likes of General Sherman or Del Hay (the son of John Hay, who had been President Lincoln's personal assistant) are taken for granted. In "high" art of the postwar era, only shabby best-selling writers deal with such things, not serious writers. Let Danielle Steele or Geoffrey Archer deal with the Rich and Famous. "Real" writers deal with characters like Moses Herzog or Harry Angstrom: figures from the common—or commoner— world.

The "tone" of Vidal's prose is also troubling to many critics: his attitude toward his subject matter. He writes, always, as an insider himself, and he communicates this feeling. This aspect of his mandarinism is present in most of the fiction and all the essays. The tone *is* the essays; it gives them their wonderfully acerbic edge and their vitality. Vidal, in his best essays, somehow invites the reader to participate in the "knowingness" of it all (see Stephen Spender's splendid review-essay on Vidal as essayist—included here). But a strain of critics—represented in this collection by Robert Boyers in "On Gore Vidal: Wit and the Work of Criticism"—recoils from the typical Vidalian stance. "One never feels that Vidal will allow himself to learn much from his encounters, that his stance will in any way be affected, or that he will be moved to confess an important change of heart," Boyers writes. "His determination to look down on things guarantees that he will master what comes before him without ever submitting to it in a way that makes for genuine intimacy."

Boyers has chosen a very interesting word here: intimacy. Vidal is not an "intimate" writer. This is simply true. Updike and Bellow both, in their various ways, invite the reader to share their obsessions, their verbal sprees, everything. Vidal holds the reader at some distance. Especially in the essays, he is like a rather formal host but definitely *not* a relative. We learn from him, we admire his turns of phrase, the illuminations that occur and occur. But we are not going to come away from a Vidal essay feeling cozy or wanting to call him on the phone.

One aspect of Vidal's critical writing that immediately strikes the reader is his ability to describe a text. He does so with an acute eye and attentive ear, as when he writes about John O'Hara's stories:

> *The Hat on the Bed* is a collection of twenty-four short stories. They are much like Mr. O'Hara's other short stories, although admirers seem to prefer them to earlier collections. Right off, one is aware of a passionate interest in social distinctions. Invariably we are told not only what university a character attended but also what prep school. Clothes, houses, luggage (by Vuitton), prestigious restaurants are all carefully noted, as well as brand names. With the zest of an Internal Revenue man examining deductions for entertainment, the author investigates the subtle difference between the spending of old middle-class money and that of new middle-class money. Of course social distinctions have always been an important aspect of the traditional novel, but what disturbs one in reading Mr. O'Hara is that he does so little with these details once he has noted them. If a writer chooses to tell us that someone went to St. Paul's and to Yale and played squash, then surely there is something about St. Paul's and Yale and squash which would make him into a certain kind of person so that, given a few more details, the reader is then able to make up his mind as to just what that triad of experience means, and why it is different from Exeter-Harvard-lacrosse. But Mr. O'Hara is content merely to list schools and sports and makes of cars and the labels on clothes.[4]

This is absolutely right, and it is typical of Vidal at his best, whether describing the theory of the French "new novel," introducing Italo Calvino to an American audience, rethinking the importance of Henry James or William Dean Howells, or rediscovering a "lost" writer like Dawn Powell. But Vidal is not just a superb literary critic. He is a shrewd social critic, although his attitudes and opinions have won him few friends except on the extreme left of the political spectrum. Again, it's the tone that critics find troubling as much as the content. Writing in *Esquire* in one of his periodic

"State of the Union" mock-speeches—each a tour de force of radical intelligence and lively wit—Vidal says:

> Fascism is probably just a word for most of you. But the reality is very much present in this country. And the fact of it dominates most of the world today. Each year there is less and less freedom for more and more people. Put simply, fascism is the control of the state by a single man or by an oligarchy, supported by the military and the police. This is why I keep emphasizing the dangers of corrupt police forces, of uncontrolled *secret* police, like the FBI and the CIA and the Bureau of Narcotics and the Secret Service and Army counterintelligence and the Treasury men—what a lot of sneaky types we have, spying on us all![5]

Some critics would, I dare say, quarrel with Vidal's technique of generalization. The Wildean influence is registered boldly in the tendency to formulate an aphorism rather than argue, in the creation of overly neat parallels for the sake of argument, and in the underlying note of contempt for those who do not agree. It's a rhetorical mode with a long history, alas, and Vidal is simply a vivid current example of the genre. But he has, for all his generalizing, been largely correct in his descriptions and assessment of what he calls the National Security State. Like Noam Chomsky, whom he has always admired, Vidal has consistently refused to "tone it down." He describes what he sees, and if what he sees looks to him like fascism, he calls it fascism.

Vidal's deadpan approach can be devastating, as in the beginning of his essay on "The Real Two-Party System."[6] "In the United States there are two political parties of equal size," he writes. "One is the party that votes in presidential elections. The other is the party that does not vote in presidential elections." Behind all this wit lies Vidal's firm conviction that America is a country run *by* the rich and *for* the rich, that America's pretence of being a great "democracy" is a sham, and that we as a nation have caused a good deal of pain, misery, and danger in the world by continuing the practice of imperialism begun by our forefathers, such as Teddy Roosevelt. In particular, Vidal has focused a good deal of his critical attention on the media (which he has known well from firsthand experience) and their obeisance to those in power. The world he describes is one of folly and arrogance, a world drawn rather sharply in caricature but one that seems all too true. Vidal is, as Thomas M. Disch says in a brilliant little review included here, "one of our best essayists," an heir to the tradition that includes Mark Twain, H. L. Mencken, Edmund Wilson, and few others.

II.

Probably no American writer since Hemingway has lived his life so much in the public eye. While most writers cannot tolerate this kind of attention, Vidal has apparently thrived on it. It began in 1926, when he was born into a family with high political and social connections. His father, Eugene L. Vidal, was a pioneer in the American aviation industry who held a subcabinet-level position in the Franklin D. Roosevelt administration as Director of Air Commerce from 1933 until 1937. His maternal grandfather was Senator Thomas P. Gore of Oklahoma, a commanding figure in Washington politics for many decades. Vidal grew up in the company of people like Huey Long and Eleanor Roosevelt, and he learned from the inside how life in the upper echelons of society was conducted. His mother, Nina Gore Vidal, divorced his father when he was a child and married the well-known financier Hugh D. Auchincloss, who in turn divorced *her* and married Jackie Kennedy's mother, thus establishing a connection between Vidal and the Kennedy clan that persisted through the presidency of JFK. (Vidal's witty response to the Bouvier sisters occurs in one of his least-known works, *Two Sisters*, a novel that appeared in 1970).[7]

Vidal was largely raised by his grandfather, whom he idolized (and about whom he later wrote and narrated a moving television documentary).[8] Because Senator Gore was blind, he often asked his grandson to read to him; this, in effect, was the beginning of Vidal's education. In the fall of 1940, he entered the Phillips Exeter Academy in New Hampshire, where his career as a writer began with poems and stories in the *Phillips Exeter Review*. (Vidal's life at Exeter has been fictionalized by John Knowles, who apparently based the character of Brinker Hadley in *A Separate Peace* on him, though it would be foolish to assume that Vidal's life at Exeter was much like that described by Knowles.) According to Vidal, at least, these were happy years. He graduated in June 1943 and entered the Enlisted Reserve Corps of the U.S. Army.

The fall of 1943 was spent at the Virginia Military Institute, where he briefly studied engineering. He joined the Army Transportation Corps as an officer that winter and was immediately sent to the Aleutian Islands. In December 1944 he began his first novel, *Williwaw*, during a run between Chernowski Bay and Dutch Harbor. Suffering a bad case of frostbite, Vidal was sent back to the States, where he finished the novel in less than a year. Published in 1946, *Williwaw* focused on a rivalry between two maritime officers; in style and movement, it owed something to Hemingway and Stephen Crane. For a writer barely out of his teens, the book was an extraordinary achievement, and it retains a certain luster. Writing in the *New York Times* about *Williwaw*, Orville Prescott said that "the Aleutian climate and scenery, the Army talk and Army thought are all palpable and real."[9] Prescott, perhaps the most influential reviewer of the day, judged this novel "absolutely authentic" as a whole—an assessment that was commonly shared by reviewers at the time and recapitulated by John W. Aldridge in his famous study of postwar fiction, *After the Lost Generation* (1951). In this collection David Price reconsiders *Williwaw*; his elegant reading of that novel concludes that, while not a masterpiece, the novel is a "candid, revealing, provocative, and psychologically realistic" novel in the great tradition of war fiction.

Vidal worked briefly in New York after the war, for the publishing firm E. P. Dutton, before turning to full-time writing. Having little money, he moved to Guatemala, where the living was cheap. There he bought an abandoned fortress—the first of his many unusual (and often) grand dwellings. One of his closest friends in Guatemala was Anaïs Nin, who wrote a good deal about Vidal in her diaries of that period. By any standard, the postwar years were amazingly productive ones for the young Gore Vidal, who published eight novels in quick succession between 1946 and 1954. While some of these novels are slight and only occasionally rise above what one might call "workmanlike" writing, there are nevertheless three important novels (not including *Williwaw*) of the period: *The City and the Pillar* (1948), *The Judgment of Paris* (1952), and *Messiah* (1954).

The City and the Pillar is remarkable for many reasons. It is, to begin with, a compelling story written in elegantly spare prose. Vidal's hero is Jim Willard, and he is sitting in a New York bar in the postwar period recalling the years 1937 to 1943 as his fingers trace islands and rivers in the water spilling on the tabletop from his drink. What he visualizes through the watery haze is the time he first made love to Bob Ford—an American as prototypical as his name. The pursuit of Ford by Willard across the waters of the world gives the novel a wonderfully mythic shape, though Vidal is ever the satirist, ready to send up any convention that stumbles into his path.

Jim's quest takes many fascinating turns; among these is a tour of the postwar homosexual demimonde of California, which Vidal writes about with reportorial cool. The quest ends, tragically, in a reconciliation scene that quickly becomes a nightmare. In the 1948 version of the novel, Jim strangles Bob and walks out into the morning air, having taken himself beyond the bounds of morality and the possibilities of love.[10] In a later (1965) revision, Vidal eliminates the melodramatic quality of the first version, changing the murder to a rape—a more believable ending altogether. But the change of endings goes beyond mere verisimilitude, as Claude J. Summers notes in *"The City and the Pillar* as Gay Fiction," which he has adapted especially for this collection from his book on gay literature.[11] The "conclusion of the 1965 revision is altogether more satisfying," he writes. "Here, when Jim makes a pass at the sleeping Bob, the latter initiates the violence. A menacing Bob, his fists ready, attacks Jim, and Jim, overwhelmed by an equal mixture of rage and desire, responds by overpowering and, finally, raping his dream lover."

Summers' important essay places *The City and the Pillar* in the context of postwar gay fiction: "Prime among the novels that challenge the widespread Anglo-American contempt for homosexuality and homosexuals is Vidal's pioneering work, which is one of the first explicitly gay fictions to reach a large audience. Emphasizing the normality of gay people, *The City and the Pillar* traces the coming out process of a young man as ordinary and American as apple pie. Coming at the beginning of the postwar decade, the novel is an important and exemplary contribution to the emerging popular literature of homosexuality." While this may well be so, Vidal's brave entry into the world of gay fiction did nothing to help his burgeoning career as a novelist.

Indeed, Vidal's next five novels were largely dismissed by the mainstream press, and one can feel the hostility to him in the period reviews of those novels. The reaction of John W. Aldridge is typical: "His writing after *Williwaw* is one long record of stylistic breakdown and spiritual exhaustion. It is confused and fragmentary, pulled in every direction by the shifting winds of impressionism. It is always reacting, always feeling and seeing; but it never signifies because it never believes."[12] Aldridge just could not forgive Vidal for failing to blossom into the Hemingway who seemed to be lying there, dormant, in *Williwaw.*

A few of the best critics did, of course, see merit in Vidal's post–*City and the Pillar* work. Leafing through Robert J. Stanton's invaluable bibliography of Vidal criticism,[13] one finds a scattering of intelligent and laudatory reviews. Edward Wagenknecht, for instance, reviewed *A Search for the King* (1950) with care and insight, calling Vidal "just the man to redeem the historical novel from the lushness and bad taste into which it is always in danger of falling."[14] In *The Saturday Review,* Samuel Putnam said that Vidal "happens to be perhaps the most delicately sensitive of all" young postwar American writers.[15] For the most part, however, critics turned away from Vidal during this period. (Bernard F. Dick surveys this era in Vidal's fiction in an excerpt, included here, from his book-length study of Vidal.)[16]

Among the best of Vidal's novels in the postwar decade was *Messiah,* a book that—according to Heather Neilson in her essay "The Fiction of History in Gore Vidal's *Messiah*" (published here for the first time but part of a larger study of Vidal in progress)— "depicts the period of the 1950s, in which it was composed, as an age of anxiety and superstition, of supernatural phenomena, ripe for a new object of worship." This highly inventive novel makes deft use of the modernist technique (pioneered in this century by André Gide in *The Counterfeiters*) of the journal within the memoir—a form that Vidal would exploit to good effect in later novels. *Messiah's* memoirist is Eugene Luther, who is writing about the 1950s from around the year 2000. He recalls the spread of a strange religious cult based on the figure of John Cave, whose message to the planet is terribly simple, if not simple-minded. Cave preaches the goodness of death and encourages suicide among his followers (those who adhere to "Cavesway")—shades of Jonestown, of course —but he is not exactly willing to practice what he preaches; so he is murdered, and his ashes are spread across the country. In a manner that seems eerily and especially American, Cave is merchandised to the hilt; indeed, the selling of Cave can hardly fail to remind a latter-day reader of television preachers like Jim Bakker and others who have used evangelical religion as a platform for naked self-promotion. The religion that evolves in Cave's wake is fiercely hierarchical and bound to the literal "Cavesword" created by his Pauline apostles, and it is all brilliantly satirized by Vidal. Alan Cheuse, in the "Note on Vidal's *Messiah*" written for this volume, says that this novel is "the book in which Vidal first seems to turn away from conventional narrative romanticism and shine his light on broader matters, whether they be the continuation of his investigation into theological mania (as in *Kalki*, which with *Messiah* stands as the second part of a de facto diptych on the religious impulse in the modern world), or the Washington sequence, in which he attempts to turn his nonconventional view of American history into an entertaining series of novels that persuade as they amuse." Cheuse rightly calls *Messiah* "an authentic American novel of ideas."

Vidal was determined to live by his pen, and since he has never been one to live meagerly, the failure of his post–*City and the Pillar* novels to sell lots of copies put him in a very awkward situation. After a period of wandering in Europe with his friend Tennessee Williams in 1948 (in Paris he was greeted by André Gide as a prophet of the sexual revolution), Vidal settled along the Hudson River Valley. There—in 1950—he bought Edgewater, an impressive Greek revival mansion built in 1828 by a former New York governor. Among other projects of this period was the writing of *The Judgment of Paris*, one of his most compelling early novels, described by Bernard F. Dick as "a novel on the order of *Tom Jones*" and a book in which "a sensuous but decent lad journeyed through a world of seducers eager to ensnare him in their fine meshes."[17] The ghost of Henry James hovers over this elegant novel, but it is written in a style that looks forward to the later Vidal: dryly witty, sonorous, crisply ironic—a kind of dry run for the style that makes *Burr* the great book it is. But *The Judgment of Paris* is a lovely novel in its own right, even though it did not win a larger audience at the time of its publication in 1952.

Vidal, sitting in Edgewater—the great house on the Hudson—needed money. With ferocious single-mindedness, he set about to make himself financially independent as quickly as he could. Under the pseudonym of Edgar Box, he wrote three conventional but extremely witty mystery novels: *Death in the Fifth Position* (1952), *Death Before Bedtime* (1953), and *Death Likes It Hot* (1954). These clever thrillers, which play off the conventions of the genre with typical Vidalian gusto, have never been out of print, although they apparently did not solve their creator's financial problems. Prompted by his agent, he decided to try his hand at writing scripts. The so-called Golden Age of television had begun, and Vidal took naturally to the new medium, producing nearly a hundred scripts in the course of the next decade. Among his large number of adaptations were William Faulkner's "Barn Burning" and Henry James' *Turn of the Screw*. His best original teleplay was "Visit to a Small Planet," televised on May 8, 1955.

Not surprisingly, Vidal soon turned to Hollywood and Broadway to expand his outlets for scripts. He wrote a full-length stage version of *Visit to a Small Planet* that opened in 1957 and ran for an amazing 338 performances. In a recent essay on the American writer Dawn Powell, Vidal recalls the opening night of his first play on Broadway:

> One evening back there in once upon a time (February 7, 1957, to be exact) my first play opened at the Booth Theatre. Traditionally, the playwright was invisible to the audience: One hid out in a nearby bar, listening to the sweet nasalities of Pat Boone's rendering of "Love Letters in the Sand" from a glowing jukebox. But when the curtain fell on this particular night, I went into the crowded lobby to collect someone. Overcoat collar high about my face, I moved invisibly through the crowd, or so I thought. Suddenly a voice boomed-tolled across the lobby. "*Gore!*" I stopped, everyone stopped. From the cloakroom a small round figure, rather like a Civil War cannon ball, hurtled toward me and collided. As I looked into that familiar round face with its snub nose and shining bloodshot eyes, I heard, the

entire crowded lobby heard: *How could you do this?* How could you *sell out* like this? To *Broadway!* To *Commercialism!* How could you give up *The Novel?*"[18]

Vidal knew exactly what he was doing. The plot of *Visit* is irresistible and concerns a visitor from outer space who arrives in Virginia with the fond hope of viewing the Battle of Bull Run in 1861. Being about a century too late, he becomes a houseguest of a family called Spelding. When the federal government learns that this visitor, called Kreton, is about to start World War III, panic breaks loose. But Kreton isn't a vicious fellow. He wants a war because he adores the primitive aspects of men, and he considers war the greatest achievement of this curious race. Eventually, Kreton is recalled by his fellow planeteers, who explain apologetically that he is a mentally (and morally) retarded child. It's a brilliant play that recalls Oscar Wilde and George Bernard Shaw, though it reverberates with Vidal's own unmistakable tone. In a laudatory review in the *New York Times*, critic Brooks Atkinson said that the play "makes us look ridiculous in a low-comedy carnival that has its own insane logic and never runs out of ideas."[19]

What Vidal wrote about himself as a playwright in 1957, shortly after the success of *Visit to a Small Planet*, seems true of his relation to the drama in general: "I am not at heart a playwright. I am a novelist turned temporary adventurer; and I chose to write television, movies, and plays for much the same reason that Henry Morgan selected the Spanish Main for his peculiar—and not dissimilar—sphere of operations."[20] In short, Vidal was never completely won over by playwrighting; as a result, he did not develop as a dramatist. He did, however, manage to write a remarkably good political play, *The Best Man*, which indeed outran *Visit to a Small Planet* on Broadway (520 performances); it was also made into a 1964 film with a script by Vidal. That play, set at a political convention, feels somewhat dated, but it still works brilliantly on the stage. Two other plays for Broadway, neither of which attracted much in the way of favorable comment, were *Romulus* (1962), adapted from Friedrich Dürrenmatt's *Romulus der Grosse*, and *An Evening with Richard Nixon and . . .* (1972). Vidal's career as a playwright is discussed in detail here by Ray Lewis White in an excerpt from his book-length study of Vidal.[21]

Vidal entered into contract with MGM in the mid-1950s, and he has since remained active as a screenwriter. His numerous early credits include *The Catered Affair* (1956), *I Accuse!* (1958), and *Suddenly, Last Summer* (1959). He also worked on the script of *Ben Hur* (1959). More recently, he wrote a television version of *Dress Gray* (1986; based on a novel by Lucian K. Truscott IV) that received an Emmy nomination, and adapted his own early teleplay, *Billy the Kid*, for Turner Network Television in 1989. For ABC, he recently adapted his novel *Burr*. As ever, Vidal is a thorough professional; his scripts are invariably put together with skill and a firm sense of what must be done to hold the attention of a diverse audience.

Vidal was not content just to write novels, short stories, plays and screenplays, essays, and reviews. For along time now he had watched the political world from the sidelines, having been raised in a family where politics and life were inseparable. When he threw his hat into the ring in 1960 and ran for Congress as a Democrat-Liberal in New York's traditionally Republican 29th District, it was simply a natural move. Vidal-the-candidate stood for many wildly controversial things, including the recognition of Red China, limiting the Pentagon's budget, and increasing federal aid to education. Not surprising, he lost the election, but he won a significant number of votes for a man running on a liberal platform in such a traditionally conservative district. In 1982, he ran in the Democratic primary for the U.S. Senate in California, where he finished just behind Jerry Brown.[22]

How seriously are we to take Vidal's bids for public office? One can't imagine a man of his literary energies content to sit, day after day, in the House or Senate. Still, one has to admire the fact that he has engaged the issues of his day with such fervor, that he has ventured farther afield than almost any American writer of this century into nonliterary regions. The experience of actually running for office can only have helped him when he began the series of novels about American politics that begins with *Washington, D.C.* (1967) and continues through *Burr* (1973), *1876* (published in 1976), *Lincoln* (1984), *Empire* (1987), and *Hollywood* (1990). Reading these "political" novels, one quickly senses that Vidal knows the world he is writing about. Sitting at dinner with his grandfather, with JFK (whom he knew quite well), with endless politicos and business people, he acquired an inward sense of how the "real" world operates. That sense of the world, which is—as Wallace Stevens might have added—Vidal's own supreme fiction, animates the novels in this remarkable sequence.

The 1960s were, for Vidal, a watershed period. He stepped back, a little, from the bustle. Most importantly, he decided to leave the United States and moved, in the early part of the decade, to Italy—which he has often referred to (rather impishly) in interviews as a "pre-Christian country." Italy was, I suspect, coincident in his mind with a highly personal notion of the civilized life; there he resumed his primary vocation as a novelist. In Rome, with the library of the American Academy available to him for research, he worked on *Julian* (1964), a novel that Robert F. Kiernan has shrewdly judged "the first novel of his artistic maturity."[23] But, in his heart, Vidal did not leave the United States. As William Vance notes in *America's Rome*, his marvelous two-volume study of Americans in Rome, Americans continue abroad to "labor as Americans for America."[24] James Tatum expands upon Vance's insight in his essay on "The *Romanitas* of Gore Vidal," commissioned for this volume (*Romanitas* being, says Tatum, "a word the Christian Tertullian used in disparaging reference to Rome's cultural legacy"). Tatum writes: "By returning to the source of all *Romanitas*, Vidal recovered the original model for our Second Rome, as well as a characteristically Roman way of attacking it. In Rome he knew he would find the original version of what the artists and founding fathers of the Capitol in Washington had labored so hard to imitate."

Julian was the magnificent first fruit of Vidal's reinvention of himself as a Roman. Ever a ventriloquist, he enters into the mind of the Emperor Julian with an eerie nonchalance. Vidal tracks Julian as he renounces Christianity and embraces paganism. His transformation from philosopher to soldier follows, then his elevation to emperor. The well-researched period details of the book are fascinating, enhanced by Vidal's clever embellishments. One little example is when Vidal, writing as Julian, comments on the strange voices of the eunuchs (who were very much a part of the imperial scene). He relates this voice—and its childlike tones—to their position of power over Constantius: "In actual fact," says Julian, "the voice of a eunuch is like that of a particularly gentle child, and this appeals to the parent in both men and women. Thus subtly do they disarm us, for we tend to indulge them as we would a child, forgetting that their minds are as mature and twisted as their bodies are lacking," Vidal's authority here, as everywhere in this strong novel, makes the tapestry of history ever more radiant.

Reviewers were apprehensive about *Julian*, which seemed to come out of nowhere. *Newsweek*, for instance, called it a "metaphysical costume drama,"[25] while in Britain the anonymous reviewer in the London *Times* felt that the novel lacked coherence, that it needed a wider scope "than the hero's idiosyncratic vision of his times."[26] But the best reviewers were sympathetic. Walter Allen, for example, said that *Julian* "brings together and dramatizes more effectively and with much greater authority than ever before preoccupations that have been present in his fiction almost from its beginnings."[27] Anthony Burgess said that Vidal "handles his huge cast well, achieves a triumph in his portrait of . . . Constantius and makes his hero perhaps more sympathetic than the tradition of bitter aggressiveness would approve."[28] My own feeling is that *Julian* ranks high among Vidal's creations, a novel in all ways equal to *Burr*, *Lincoln*, *Myra Breckinridge* and *Duluth*. As an historical novel about the ancient world, it is every bit the equal of anything by Mary Renault or Robert Graves; in fact, Vidal as a writer is generally more sophisticated than Renault and less cranky than Graves.

It has often been noted that Vidal twins his novels. *Messiah* is a prelude to a later apocalyptic novel, *Kalki* (1978). *Myra Breckinridge* has its sequel, *Myron* (1974). And *Julian*, in its way, beckons *Creation* (1981) into being. The latter poses as the autobiography of an aged diplomat, Cyrus Spitama, who is half Persian and half Greek. This memoir becomes a panoramic minihistory of the ancient world in the fifth century B.C., taking in the Persian-Greek wars as well as visits to India and China. Spitama, in over thirty years of service to the Persian empire, has been everywhere and seen everything. He was there when Zoroaster was assassinated, has met the Buddha as well as Confucius, and he has even (almost accidentally) bumped into Socrates, whom he hires to repair (badly) a masonry wall. The conceit is startling, of course. The novel, ambitious as it is, was, nevertheless, a critical failure. Novels on such a broad scale have rarely worked.

The oddity is that *Creation* often does work, though it lacks the aesthetic tightness of *Julian* (a tightness borne of Julian's own idiosyncratic voice, which is pure Vidal). Spitama, however, is just too global, and his voice often seems too much the disembodied voice of History. Spitama is endlessly knowledgeable and a trifle weary of the great world he knows so well, as in the following passage from near the end of his wanderings:

> During the next weeks I dealt with the various merchants and guilds who wanted to do business with Persia. I was by now something of a merchant myself. I knew what could be sold at Susa; and for how much. I quite enjoyed the hours of haggling in the tents that are set up in the central market. Needless to say, whenever I found myself in the company of an important merchant or guild treasurer, the name of the Egibis would be mentioned. In a sense, that firm was a sort of universal monarch. Wherever one goes in the world, its agents have already been there, and done business. [29]

Reading *Creation*, one is struck by the staggering amount of sheer information that Vidal has assimilated and transformed into fiction. And even when Spitama is being somewhat overly didactic, telling us more than we might really want to know about the philosophical theories of Democritus or specific protocol at the court of Darius, there is always the pleasure of the prose. Kiernan puts it well: "Vidal's sentences . . . glimmer through any amount of dust and through the most overbearing and unnecessary amplitude. Classically graceful, totally poised, and brimming with quiet intelligence, they are the masterstrokes in all his fictions." [30] Spitama has a gift for the memorable phrase, and this gift redeems *Creation*— one of those Vidalian books that has tended to slip between the critical cracks in spite of what remains a wide readership. [31]

In 1968, Vidal took satire into new realms of outrageousness and produced what some critics regard as his masterpiece: *Myra Breckinridge*. Again, the memoir form proved the ideal vehicle for Vidal's novelistic talents. This time we hear from Myra, formerly (via a sex change) Myron, nephew of Buck Loner, a retired horse opera star. Myra has returned to Hollywood to reclaim her inheritance, owed by Buck to Myron; he appeases her by making her a teacher at the

Academy of Drama and Modeling—an astute appointment since Myra is, among other things, the prototypical couch potato, a cinema junkie of the first order who celebrates "celluloid, *blessed* celluloid." She is also a proto-feminist who repeatedly warns, "No man will ever possess Myra Breckinridge." One of the kinkiest, funniest, and most shocking scenes in any Vidal novel is Myra's subjection, through seduction, of a strapping young student called Rusty Godowsky, who is anally raped with a dildo by the triumphant Myra. Again, the voice is everything, as *Myra* begins:

> I am Myra Breckinridge whom no man will ever possess. Clad only in garter belt and one dress shield, I held off the entire elite of the Trobriand Islanders, a race who possess no words for "why" or "because." Wielding a stone axe, I broke the arms, the limbs, and balls of their finest warriors, my beauty blinding them, as it does all men, unmanning them in the way that King Kong was reduced to a mere simian whimper by beauteous Fay Wray whom I resemble left three-quarter profile if the key light is no more than five feet high during the close shot.[32]

I dare say there has never been such an opening in the history of literature, and there may never be again. In "My O My O Myra," written specifically for this volume by Catharine R. Stimpson, Vidal's blazing originality is put in postmodern perspective; Stimpson observes the novelist as he "picks over the various narrative forms available to the twentieth-century writer: the *nouveau roman*; the memoir, written or taped; the client's confession to the therapist/ analyst; the Hollywood star biography/autobiography; the Hollywood novel; and the female impersonator's monologue, which both pays lavish tribute to traditional femininity and tosses acid at the world." Vidal's catalogue of narrative possibilities is seen to be "a tough-minded elegy for literary culture." Memorably, Stimpson concludes: "If we are to believe her creator, in a post-Gutenberg age our most popular gods and goddesses will be born and borne from celluloid, not paper. Our new interpreters of signs and symbols will huddle around television or movie screens. For those of us who still read, there yet remains the glow of pleasurable embers that Vidal throws on his pages—the occasional graffiti, the provocations of satire, and the risible comfort of the Myra/Myronic cult figures."

Myron follows *Myra* as the night the day. Published in 1974, it picks up the story about five years later. In many ways, *Myron* is a novel of restoration, or a parody of restoration. The splintered psyche of Myra/Myron is fused in the narrative. Swinging backward and forward in time, blending celluloid "reality" with everyday reality, Vidal in *Myron* actually pushes beyond the mock-realism of *Myra Breckinridge* into something utterly strange yet resonant. And Myron's rhetoric, which might be called "American square squared" presents a terribly funny contrast to Myra's decadently baroque ebullience.

In one minor vein of *Myron*, Vidal explores the links between Hollywood-style fantasy and American politics as Richard Nixon appears on the scene in various guises. At one point, for instance, Nixon turns up at MGM on the back lot and wants to know if 1948 has an extradition treaty with the future. This link between the twin capitals of Washington and Hollywood will become a dominant theme in the later novels of Vidal's American sequence, *Empire* and *Hollywood*, where these links are explicitly and (as opposed to *Myron*) realistically invoked.

This American chronicle may well be seen as Vidal's main achievement by future historians of literature. The author, however, had nothing like a sequence in mind when he wrote *Washington, D.C.* (1967). That fairly conventional novel begins in 1937 at a party where the defeat of FDR's bid to enlarge the Supreme Court is being celebrated by a group of political insiders. The two main families whose lives are chronicled over a decade of national events are those of Senator James Burden Day and Blaise Sanford, who owns the *Washington Tribune*. Clay Overbury is a protégé of Senator Day, and he serves as a link between the two families by marrying Enid Sanford, daughter of the newspaper baron.

The novel turns on a bribe that is ultimately the senator's undoing. While nothing in the plot would surprise anyone familiar with the traditions of political fiction, there is always the Vidalian style to redeem the moment. The language of *Washington, D.C.* is remarkably imagistic; one quickly senses that Vidal is writing about a world that he has known quite intimately. The foibles and obsessions of the late 1930s and 1940s are skillfully summoned. As an observer of American political life, Vidal has few peers. He knows how these people talk—or, at least, he is able to make us believe that this is how people in power talk (which, for a novelist, is what actually matters). Vidal also has a firm sense of the way the machinery of power works, as in his description of The Club to which senators either belong or don't:

> No one was ever quite sure who belonged to The Club since members denied its existence but everyone knew who did not be-long. The Club was permanently closed to the outside personality, to the firebrand tribune of the people, to the Senator running too crudely for President. Members of The Club preferred to do their work quietly and to get re-elected without fanfare. On principle they detested the President, and despite that magnate's power to loose and to bind, The Club ruled the Senate in its own way and for its own ends, usually contrary to those of the President.[33]

While there is much to admire in *Washington, D.C.*, nobody could have guessed how Vidal's American chronicle would unfold from this modestly unexceptional beginning. *Burr*, the next to appear (in 1973), is among the richest of Vidal's works, a mature novel that brings into play virtually all the author's various talents. It was finished about the time Vidal moved from Rome to Ravello, an idyllic town perched on a cliffside overlooking the Mediterranean Sea between Salerno and Naples. (The villa that Vidal and his companion, Howard Austen, moved into is called "La Rondinaia," meaning "Swallow's Nest." It has remained Vidal's base of operations since 1972, though he has retained an apartment in Rome and a house in Hollywood Hills, California.)

The narrative voice in *Burr* belongs to Charlie Schuyler, a young law clerk and journalist who works for Aaron Burr, the man who killed Alexander Hamilton in a duel in 1804 and who, two years later, initiated a secessionist conspiracy that challenged the assumptions of America's founding fathers, all of whom Burr knew well. Too well, as *Burr* suggests. In "America and the Vidal Chronicles," an incisive study of the Vidal sequence written for this collection by Donald E. Pease, the latent intent of the chronicles is discussed in challenging ways. Pease links the six novels in the American chronicle in a previously unimagined scheme, connecting Vidal's revisionist approach to American history with the New Historicist effort to revitalize literary studies by plunging into the archives. "When construed as the historical consciousness missing from the counterculture, Vidal's chronicles can be understood to historicize the New Historicists' project," Pease writes. He argues that Vidal has succeeded in undermining the separation of fact from fiction, using the traditions of the historical narrative to revitalize both history and literature by insisting on their parity and permeability. As a leading voice of the countercultural revolution of the late 1960s, Vidal has worked with incredible diligence to rethink the past, to create a new sense of historical consciousness that was simply missing during the sixties.

Vidal's essays have always been published at regular intervals between the novels, and collections such as *Matters of Fact and Fiction* (1977), *The Second American Revolution* (1982), and *At Home* (1988) attest to the historical and political preoccupations that set the various novels of each period in motion. Vidal's "Note on Abraham Lincoln" in *The Second American Revolution*, for instance, might be read as the author's working notes for *Lincoln*, which appeared in 1984. The essay called "Hollywood!" in *At Home* is obviously a spin-off of the work that went into the writing of *Hollywood*, the novel. Reading back and forth between the essays and the novels, one is inevitably struck by the continuity of voice, the blending of fiction and fact into a kind of metanarrative in which literal and imaginative truth merge.

The novel *1876* soon followed *Burr*, continuing the story of Charlie Schuyler, who returns to New York on the eve of America's centennial year. It's a brilliant sequel—a form that Vidal has perfected; Vidal sketches the Gilded Age with an acid pen, scanning that gaudy and energetic period in American history with an eye for the kind of idiosyncratic detail that marked *Creation*. We hear about the building of new churches in Brooklyn, about goats trotting down East 24th Street, about the beginnings of Chinatown and the European idea of a city park as the origins of Central Park. Schuyler is the panoptical observer, taking in everything from a discreet distance. He sees but is rarely seen—the ideal Vidalian hero.

It is nearly axiomatic that good historical novels provide a kind of resonance with contemporary affairs, and *1876* is no exception (indeed, it was published in America's bicentennial year of 1976). Vidal cleverly aligns his echoes, so that Samuel J. Tilden reminds one of the idealistic yet ineffective George McGovern, while Rutherford B. Hayes recalls the stumbling and bumbling Gerald Ford. Mark Twain (in his white suit) comes off as a Tom Wolfe figure, a bright-winged insect buzzing in society's ear. Vietnam and the Civil War are eerily drawn into parallel rows of absurdity and cruelty, while the Lincoln assassination reminds one inevitably of JFK. The Babcock break-in might be taken as a dry run for Watergate. And so forth. Violence, low-mindedness, greed, and corruption form the constants of American political life—a view not designed to instill total admiration in Vidal's critics, who remain inclined to view America as the greatest (or at least the most well-intentioned) show on earth.

As usual, Vidal's blend of cynicism with old-fashioned storytelling elicited mixed reviews, with some critics complaining that the novelist often wrote with scorn for his own characters. Edwin Morgan, for instance, suggested that "Vidal's Laodicean ironies, clever and devastating as they are, in the end fail to satisfy on any deeper level."[34] The most thoughtful of the reviewers this time out was Peter Conrad, who wrote a lengthy review of the novel in the *Times Literary Supplement*.[35] He regarded Vidal's political novels in general as "the result of a precarious, dazzling partnership between Gore the researcher and Vidal the frivolous meddler with history." Vidal's work was seen not as straightforward history but as a playful version of the same, with Shakespeare's Roman plays as his natural precursor. "America is Rome reborn," said Conrad. "The decadent comedy of ancient history happens a second time as coarse, uncultivated farce [in *1876*]."

Surveying the reviews of *1876* and virtually every other book by Vidal, it becomes clear that English reviewers have almost always understood him better than his compatriots. This is partly, I suspect, because of the ironic mode that Vidal has cultivated, which has affiliations with the English novel from Henry Fielding to Evelyn Waugh and Kingsley Amis. The English have also been more able to appreciate Vidal's mandarin style, with its controlled ironies, its neatly balanced syntactical parallelisms, and its occasional baroque flurries of eloquence. The American novel has, by contrast, been either seemingly without style in the manner of Dreiser and Mailer or, like Crane or Hemingway, somehow "beyond" style. There have been important exceptions, of course, such as Henry James and F.

Scott Fitzgerald, although both of these writers suffered a kind of exile. James could not live comfortably in America, where his style and manner clashed with those of his contemporaries. Fitzgerald found the United States an alien place as well, however much he loved it; he was quickly shut out by the culture that briefly embraced him, and he ended up in one of the most unreal places on earth— Hollywood. While Vidal does not consider himself an "ex-patriot" (even though he has lived much of his life abroad in the past few decades), one does find Jamesian echoes in his work (and, indeed, he has written about James with astonishing perspecuity); the Fitz-geraldian side is there, too: the lure of Hollywood, the shimmering prose style, the stylish affect and preoccupation with "style" in its many guises, the concern with "success."

Vidal's readership, as I have said, expanded notably after *Julian*; yet *Lincoln* went beyond almost anything else in the historical vein when, in 1984, it appeared to a din of praise and spectacular sales. In many ways, however, *Lincoln* is Vidal's least Vidalian novel. The prose contrasts rather severely with that of *1876*, being much less ornate and flashy. The subject, for once, takes center stage. The very weight of the historical material pushes the author to one side (and it is to Vidal's credit that he knew enough to stay in the background here).

Reviewing the novel on the front page of the *New York Times Book Review*, Joyce Carol Oates said that *Lincoln* was "not so much an imaginative reconstruction of an era as an intelligent, lucid and highly informative transcript of it, never less than workmanlike in its blocking out of scenes and often extremely compelling. No verbal pyrotechnics here, nothing to challenge a conservative esthetics biased against the house of fiction itself. By subordinating the usual role of the novelist to the role of historian-biographer, Mr. Vidal acknowledges his faith in the high worth of his material."[36]

The most comprehensive and influential discussion of *Lincoln* was Harold Bloom's essay-review in the *New York Review of Books* (reprinted here).[37] Bloom describes Vidal as "a masterly American historical novelist, now wholly matured, who has found his truest subject, which is our national political history during precisely those years when our political and military histories were as one, one thing and one thing only: the unwavering will of Abraham

Lincoln to keep the states united." Bloom discusses *Lincoln* in the context of Vidal's developing career, turning at the end of his essay to "the still ambiguous question of Vidal's strength or perhaps competing strengths as a novelist." Adamantly, Bloom concludes: *"Lincoln,* together with the curiously assorted trio of *Julian, Myra Breckinridge,* and *Burr,* demonstrates that his narrative achievement is vastly underestimated by American academic criticism, an injustice he has repaid amply in his essayist attacks upon the academy, and in the sordid intensities of *Duluth."*

Vidal continuously draws a contrast in *Lincoln* between Salmon P. Chase and Lincoln. Chase is presented as the archetypal Republican abolitionist who is nevertheless endlessly jealous of the President, selfish in almost comical ways, conniving, and crudely pious. Lincoln comes across as bizarrely single-minded, ready to sacrifice anything—including the Constitution and human rights—to preserve a theoretical ideal. Chase, it seems, is genuinely concerned about the slaves, while Lincoln clearly does not care; abolition is merely an issue he can use to defend his notion of union. That Lincoln was willing to go to any end—a dreadful and terrible end, as it were—to perpetuate an idea that appears, in retrospect, curiously abstract, is Vidal's underlying theme. One senses, throughout, Vidal's admiration for Lincoln's Machiavellian aspects; at the same time, Vidal's judgment of Lincoln is severe in its way, and the novel—as a whole—offers a unique and gripping portrait of the man who is clearly the most important figure in U.S. history.

The originality of *Lincoln* has not been overly discussed or even noticed. Most critics in fact treated the novel as one of Vidal's most conventional. In conventional historical novels, however, such as those by Walter Scott or, more recently, Paul Scott, history is really nothing more than a backdrop to a fictional melodrama that takes center stage. Vidal, by placing Lincoln at the fictional center of his novel, has in effect reversed the traditional method, creating what may well become a new genre.[38]

The last two novels in the American chronicle, *Empire* and *Hollywood* (published in 1987 and 1990), in many ways constitute one novel appearing in two installments. Both novels are written self-consciously in anticipation of *Washington, D.C.*, drawing on the Sanford family as key figures. Louis Auchincloss, in the essay-review included here, sees the progression from *Lincoln* to *Empire* to *Hollywood* as a direct one, focused on the "grim, dramatic story of the forging, for a good deal worse than better . . . of the American empire and its ultimate conversion into the celluloid of the moving picture."

Vidal is uncanny in the way he links his various heroes and heroines to History and to each other. Caroline Sanford, for instance, is being pushed at the beginning of *Empire*—as we have seen—to marry Del Hay, son of John Hay, who had been Lincoln's private secretary. Another major character who emerges from "real" life is William Randolph Hearst, who takes on Caroline Sanford's half brother, Blaise Sanford (who reappears in *Washington, D.C.*), as a protégé. Other historical figures—Theodore Roosevelt, McKinley, William Jennings Bryan, Henry James, and Henry Adams—mingle with Vidal's creations. Fact and fiction become, once again, permeable; the world, recast by Vidal, is given the kind of marvelous unity that only fiction can generate. One sees history—the chronology of public events—unfold and made sense of in the private lives of "real" and imagined figures. As Richard Poirer notes in an essay about *Empire* (included here): "Vidal manages inextricably to mix the fictive and the historical, the social and the legendary. These elements are so fused in his style that none can be differentiated from the others. All partake of the same issues of inheritance, legitimacy, rivalry, deception, and ambition."

The connections between Hollywood and Washington have been of interest to Vidal from the beginning, but it wasn't until the 1980s that history served up on a platter the presidency of Ronald Reagan, thus bringing the two worlds into fantastic juncture. Responding to history's little gift, Vidal began—in essays as well as novels—to explore these connections, finding Woodrow Wilson there at the beginning, fully aware of the infinite propaganda potential represented by Hollywood. With his intimate knowledge of the history of the movies and the history of American politics, Vidal was perfectly situated to explore these links. Against the continuing sage of the Sanford family, the rise and fall of presidents from McKinley to Wilson and Harding is heard like the beating of waves on the shore throughout *Empire* and *Hollywood*; the parallels with the present become increasingly shocking and converge like infinite railroad tracks into the not-so-imaginary future, where Ronald Reagan stands with arms folded, his smile in place. He is, as Vidal memorably puts it, "our first Acting President."

Writing in the New York Times Book Review, Joel Connaroe noted that "reviewers have tended to greet each installment of Mr. Vidal's saga with hyperbole, suggesting that he regularly manages to outdo even his previous outdoings, as if he were involved in some sort of novelistic Olympics."[39] He continues: "My own sense is that with the exception of Washington, D.C., which lacks both the trenchant wit and the historical players of the other works, the novels are pretty much of a piece, huge chapters in a continuing opus rather than self-contained entities." There is merit to this viewpoint, but while one must sometimes strain to find much narrative connection between, say, Burr and Hollywood, all the novels have in fact the unifying theme of Vidal's approach to certain revisionist aspects of American political history.

There is also, of course, the capital itself: Washington, D.C.—which serves to yoke these novels in a geographical plane that is both social and sociological (if not pathological as well. Writing in the TLS, Michael Wood notes that "Washington for Vidal is like some Jacobean court, a city where even the smallest movement is interesting and dangerous, and where strokes and suicide have taken the place of poison."[40] Then again, the novels widen out so dramatically from Washington—especially in Hollywood—that one hesitates to place too much emphasis on this point. (And, in 1876, Vidal is just about as good on New York as he is on Washington.)

Perhaps the point is not to look for more unity in the sequence than exists but to let the novels live where they do, in a kind of daisy chaining of historical moments and history-based conjurations that interlock in a rather delicate way. Louis Auchincloss, discriminating among the novels, says that the six novels "do not form a true constellation," suggesting—as I have done—that Vidal never even thought of them as a sequence until he had finished Lincoln. (William Faulkner, of course, did not think of his Yoknapatawpha novels as a "sequence," per se; what bound them together was the land and culture they issued from.)

Apart from the American chronicle, Vidal's more recent satirical novels—Kalki (1978) and Duluth (1983)—reach back to Messiah through *Myra Breckinridge* and *Myron*. Written almost as a pause between *1876* and *Lincoln*, they are Vidal's darkest creations. John Simon called *Kalki* a "diabolically clever" novel, and he is right.[41] An apocalyptic thriller about a man who would take over the world, and full of satirical jibes at religious gurus who create satanic cults to screen their egotistical and greedy sensibilities, the novel wheels through contemporary culture making fun of everything. As usual, Vidal's interest in the transmogrifications of celluloid are crucial: "This was a commonplace in that era," says Vidal's narrator, a bisexual aviatrix and feminist called Teddy Ottinger. "Events were only real if experienced at second hand, preferably through the medium of the camera."

In his essay on the Vidalian manner (included here), Robert F. Kiernan regards *Kalki* as a failure, which, he writes, suggests that Vidal's genius is for the quick effect, not the sustained technique, for the clothesline, not the story line." Possibly, then, this writer's imagination is better suited to books like *Burr* and *Julian*, where plot is not terribly consequential. "Perhaps this is why," Kiernan speculates, "Vidal's first-person narratives are generally more successful than his third-person narratives and why the imaginary journal, requiring so little in the way of plot, has proven his most successful narrative form, *Kalki* excepted."

Duluth has been both praised and disparaged by critics. It is certainly Vidal's bleakest (but also, in many ways, his funniest) book, an utterly Swiftian rant against what life in America has become. Angela McRobbie, writing in the *New Statemen*, said: "Just imagine what Derrida might do with *Dallas*. Consider what might be Gore Vidal's relationship to each of these, dare I say it, signifiers. *Duluth* ('Love it Or Loathe It, You Can Never Leave It Or Lose It') could well be seen as an answer. Both Vidal and Barthes before him have commented on the practice of summarizing a text as a kind of re-writing: not a claim most critics in their modesty would make. In any case, *Duluth* almost denies the possibility of its own summary."[42] McRobbie went on: "I find this book one of the most brilliant, most radical and most subversive pieces of writing to emerge from America in recent years."

The conceit of the novel is dazzlingly postmodern: the novel is purportedly the property of one Rosemary Klein Kantor, the Wurlitzer Prize winner who, like the infinite number of monkeys in a room who manage to type out *Hamlet* by accident, creates the novel *Duluth* (as well as the TV series *Duluth*) out of a word processor that contains the plots of ten thousand previously published novels. Full of outrageous wordplay, endless gags, whims of iron, sleights of thought, and baroque fictional whirligigs, *Duluth* is Vidal's most open assault on the excesses of American mass culture. In many ways a novel designed to deconstruct before our very eyes, *Duluth* can be thought of as a cultural maze in which the endless free-floating signifiers of a culture with no definite frame of reference coalesce and swirl in the polluted stream of contemporary life. The novel brings into harsh focus the same obsessions with politics as with the celluloid and video culture that are dealt with more realistically in the American chronicle. One might think of *Duluth* and *Kalki* together as fiendish midnight cackles occasioned by Vidal's prodigious day-laborings on *1876* and *Lincoln*.

III.

One steps back from Gore Vidal's vast opus—surely one of the largest and most intellectually and artistically substantial of any American writer in our time—with mingled awe and exhaustion. Most writers at his level of productivity withdraw utterly from public life, but Vidal has refused to do this. Almost perversely, he has thrown himself into the stream of events by running for office, debating William F. Buckley, Jr., and Norman Mailer, and responding in quick journalistic pieces to events of the moment.[43] Interpreters of Vidal from Mitchell S. Ross[44] and Joseph Epstein[45] on the right to Russell Jacoby[46] on the left have tried to put a finger on Vidal, seeing him variously as a "detoured politician" (Ross) or Edmund Wilson-like "last intellectual" (Jacoby). But no single tag is going to explain this unusual career.

Vidal is, most centrally, a writer. One of the premier essayists this nation has produced, he is also one of its most gifted novelists. His best work, from *The City and the Pillar* through *Julian, Burr, Lincoln, Myra Breckinridge* and *Duluth*, is steeped in an intimate acquaintance with American history and culture, with the twin capitals of Washington and Hollywood, with the ways that Americans have chosen to conduct their lives. A satirist at heart, Vidal's work recalls that of Mencken as an immediate precursor and Swift as a long-distant ancestor. In a country not known for (or kind to) its satirists, Vidal stands out as something of a national treasure in this regard.

But comparisons are, as they say, odious, and while Vidal himself keeps drawing parallels (with Henry James, in particular), one must nevertheless aver. Vidal is sui generis—an American original. One can never say which writers will survive the winnowing of time, but Vidal has—I would argue—as good a chance as any writer of his generation of lasting. His reenvisioning of American history (including the history of film in *Myra / Myron*) will perhaps be even more important in the future than it is now. This is, after all (to quote Vidal), "the United States of Amnesia."

2
Imagining Vidal

ITALO CALVINO

Celebrating Gore Vidal here in Ravello, I find myself in a strange, multitrack situation. I think of Gore in his house here, suspended over a dazzling and sheer cliff, or I see him in the main square seated at the cafe where I met him this morning, while at the same time I feel myself transported to a backdrop, one of a huge city on a lake which is encircled by skyscrapers and neon lights.

The fact is that I've just finished reading Vidal's latest novel, *Duluth*, to continuous amusement and stimulation to the imagination. It is a novel in which contemporary life seems to have been completely taken over by fiction, with the world being nothing but episodes of TV serials, with characters who switch their roles, dying in one of the series only to reappear in another. Or else life is a criss-crossing of plots from cheap novels, published in installments, or issued in massive volumes destined for the masses.

One cannot tell where real life, or that which Vidal calls "life, or nonfiction," ends and where the intricate jungle of imaginary stories, with episodes which alternate and overlap, thanks to the combinations of a word processor (whose memory has been fed the plots of all the world's novels), begins.

Therefore, inspired by the recent reading of *Duluth*, in which the things which happen do not conform to Vidal's principle of "absolute uniqueness," I must ask myself if we are indeed in Ravello, or in a Ravello reconstructed in a Hollywood studio, with an actor playing Gore Vidal, or if we are in the TV documentary on Vidal in Ravello which we were to have seen tonight and which mysteriously vanished, or whether we are here on the Amalfi Coast on a festive occasion, but one in 1840, when, at the end of another Vidal novel, *Burr*, the narrator learns that the most controversial of America's Founding Fathers, Colonel Burr, was his father. Or, since there is a spaceship in *Duluth*, manned by centipedes who can take on any appearance, even becoming dead-ringers for American political figures, perhaps we could be aboard that spaceship, which has left Duluth for Ravello, and the E.T.s aboard could have taken on the appearance of the American writer we are gathered here to celebrate.

The key to all those mysteries may lie in the book's finale, when we learn that the world exists only in the mind of a tireless woman novelist who has the power to erase houses, hills, existences, until the invasion of the centipedes from the spaceship creates hundreds of Ravellos in time and in space, complete with all the municipal dignitaries and the guests here tonight, and with a Gore Vidal in each Ravello, all that much more multiform and gifted with ubiquity, and thus that much more "absolutely unique" and faithful to himself.

As for the ubiquity of Vidal, I believe that we can gather that right here in Ravello, because when we read or listen to Vidal it seems that he has never left America even for one second. His passionate and polemical participation in American life is without interruption. What we see in Ravello is someone living a tranquil, parallel life. Is it Vidal or his double? Or is there a satellite circling over the Amalfi Coast which keeps him informed of all that is happening in America?

Certainly, in today's world where distance has been erased, where everything is present, Vidal has initiated a new way of staying in Italy. For many generations, American writers saw our country as a picturesque background, exotic, mysterious, and anyhow a world opposite to America. Their sojourning in Europe and above all in Italy of those days, so archaic, distant from America in time and in space, signified a symbolic breaking-away almost like going to the great beyond. Not for nothing were they called then "exiles" or "expatriates."

Gore, here, does not feel himself an exile anywhere. He lives with the same ease and assurance on the Mediterranean as on the Pacific or on the Atlantic. In fact, he manages to keep one foot on each shore, which must require some fast footwork as his feet are two and his shores three. That could be the reason why he has never felt the need to give us his Italian novel, his *Marble Faun*, his *Daisy Miller*, his *Across the River and Into the Trees*.

I would be very pleased, now that he has become an honorary citizen of one of our cities, if he should feel himself authorized to write that Italian novel. And I'm sure that unlike those of his il-lustrious predecessors, it would be entertaining from beginning to end. But I must admit that so far, we also may have been luckier than we realize! When I think of the ferocious glee with which Vidal rips apart the American reality with a transfiguration both grotesque and truculent, and what could come forth if he were to turn his powers on *our* manners and morals, I experience a foretaste of enjoyment and at the same time an attack of cold sweat. I can already see the Furies of his fantasy hungrily turning on the public and private image of Italian society, with all the gusto of *Duluth*'s women-police corps when they force "illegal aliens" to undergo body searches. I can already see all of us in some of his hilariously cruel pages. Which can take their place in the great *humour noir* tradition from Swift onward.

Vidal knows us well. In his essays and interviews about Italy he is right on target. He once defined Italian society as being that which "combines the less attractive aspects of socialism with practically all the vices of capitalism." Staying in Italy for Vidal is, to be sure, a less problematic adventure than it is for us. It is rather a way of keeping that little distance from America which permits him to observe it better. And being American is his problem. His passion for what America is or is not dominates his thoughts. It is not true that this enfant terrible respects nothing and no one. His point of departure can be found in the fundamental principles of the Decla-ration of Independence, which, from the first lines, defines as the inalienable rights which all men have received from their creator the rights to life, liberty, and the pursuit of happiness. With these very simple principles as his strength, Vidal fires point-blank at everything which contradicts them. His view is one of absolute pessimism. In *Duluth*, no social stratum is spared, nor any institution. But he always leaves a door ajar for a harmonious ideal. In this case it is proclaimed by the centipedes from the spaceship (which, however, does not preserve these E.T. visitors from getting caught up in disastrous stock market speculation).

This polemical passion for America's public affairs, and for everything which could be called the anthropology of that country's mass-culture, is the nucleus of the "absolute uniqueness" which binds together the many Gore Vidals who are acting contemporaneously and taking on diverse forms. There is the essay form, of which he is one of the contemporary masters, incomparable for his sincerity, agility, and concreteness. There is the contemporary novel form as a grotesque transfiguration of the language and myths of the mass media. There is the historic novel which brutally presents the past in a way which alarmingly resembles our present. (This is as true in his interpretations of the American past, in *Burr* and in *1876*, as when he evokes the more remote past in *Creation*.) There is the theater form, where Vidal's instinct to make a drama of everything he does or says converges. And there is the conversationalist, or TV personality, form, which made his senatorial campaign so different from any others. As a political animal, he delivers what he calls his Discourse on the State of the Union. We also know what some of the average Americans' reactions to those discourses are, as Vidal has recorded them as well.

I chanced to hear one of these discourses before a public of his co-nationals, though probably not typical of the average American, inasmuch as no one was scandalized and everyone greeted his *jeu de massacre* (or, "hit the baby," a game at a fair or carnival) with a sense of complicity and fun was had by all. But what was the reaction of the foreign listener?

It led me to reflect that the strength of a country can be measured by its capacity to swallow the most radical criticism, to digest it, and to draw from it nourishment. And I found myself saying—"only in a society sure of itself, of its stability and good health could a polemicist like Gore Vidal be born! That is the difference between the United States and our fragile Italy! What Italian has ever done a satire so radical of our political world, or of our social mores? Only when we shall have writers capable of merrily and mercilessly attacking our government, parties, and institutions, can we be certain of having become a great power."

Vidal also can be a lethal literary critic, but here I must mention one exception. That is when he writes about Italian writers, when his criticism is full of *simpatia*—and coming from a temperament like his, that can only be sincere. Not that the polemicist is nodding on those occasions. He always has a critical attitude toward other American critics which leads him to present our works in the most favorable light. The link between Vidal and the Italian writers he has introduced to the American public is that most of them are of his generation. They began writing after the war, and Vidal never forgets coming to a still-devastated Italy in 1948 with Tennessee Williams. In other words, there is a sense of some shared experiences which he wants to perceive on this side and on the other side of the Atlantic.

Vidal's bêtes noires are the writers and critics in the United States and in France who want to experiment with or theorize new forms of the novel. Is there, then, a conservative Vidal? It would be difficult admitting to that, since one cannot speak of the revival of the novel's form in the last fifteen years without turning back to what may be his most famous novel, *Myra Breckinridge*. That satirical and grotesque burlesque, made up of a collage of the language and myths of the mass-culture, inaugurated a new phase in the way to present our era, which is comparable to pop art, but much more aggressive and with an explosion of expressionistic comedy.

Vidal's development along that line, from *Myra* to *Duluth*, is crowned with great success, not only for the density of comic effects, each one filled with meaning, not only for the craftsmanship in construction, put together like a clockwork which fears no word processor, but because his latest book holds its own built-in theory, that which the author calls his "*après*-poststructuralism."

To be sure, Vidal's explicit intention is to parody the current university vogue for "Narratology," but his mythology seems to me to be no less rigorous and his execution no less perfect. For that reason, I consider Vidal to be a master of that new form which is taking shape in world literature and which we may call the hyper-novel or the novel elevated to the square or to the cube.

As for Vidal's wars against new experiments in novels, I don't share his views toward that general tendency because I hope always that some good will come out of it all to bring more life into a pallid scene. But there is a point where I share Vidal's concern: that is the risk today that literature is being reduced to subject matter for universities. The fact that there are books being written today in the United States exclusively for internal consumption on the campus does not offer a happy prospect. (Complementary to that tendency is the spread of novels prefabricated for an undemanding public: the fashionable lady novelist who does not know either how to write or read and who uses ghost writers is a character that appears both in Vidal's *Kalki* and in *Duluth*.)

Anyhow, you may rest assured, dear Mr. Vidal, that *Duluth* is one of those novels upon which the universities will base courses and seminars, producing theses and tracts bristling with diagrams. It is a fate which cannot be avoided. The important thing is the spirit which you have put in the book and which races nonstop throughout its pages.

With this observation, I want to close my salutations to Gore Vidal. He belongs to that group of writers of our times who, precisely because they always have kept their eyes open to the disasters and distortions of our age, have chosen irony, humor, comedy—in other words, the whole range of literary instruments belonging to the university of the laugh—as their means of settling accounts.

That is the terrain where literature can reply to history's challenge. In an epoch of tragic mystifications, in which language serves more to conceal than to reveal, the only serious discourses are those delivered as if for laughs.

3

Williwaw: *Gore Vidal's First Novel*

DAVID PRICE

> After such knowledge, what forgiveness?
> —T. S. Eliot, "Gerontion"

In "Gore's Wars," an essay/interview in *Vanity Fair* in June 1987, Stephen Schiff had this to say about Gore Vidal's first novel:

> In 1943, Vidal enlisted in the Army Reserve Corps and soon became warrant officer on a transport ship in the Aleutian Islands. There he began what would become his first published novel (he had been scribbling unpublishable ones since childhood), a Hemingwayesque men-against-the-sea saga called *Williwaw*, which appeared to considerable acclaim in 1946. Vidal was all of twenty.

Not surprisingly, *Williwaw* is about a warrant officer commanding an army transport ship in the Aleutian Islands sometime after 1943. Vidal's actual experience obviously informed his fiction here; but mere experience may indeed engender, without necessarily sanctifying, a literary account: in any event, as Joseph Conrad put it in his Preface to *"Typhoon" and Other Tales*, "experience in these stories is but the canvas of the attempted picture."

The "attempted picture" in *Williwaw* is what might surprise us; or perhaps we might be surprised, over four decades later, by the "considerable acclaim" with which the novel was greeted when it first appeared.[1] In 1946 the United States, essentially unscathed by the Second World War and at the peak of its political and industrial travel under unaccustomed physical and social conditions, like enforced obedience, bad food, and absence of baths.

Martin, the first mate of the transport ship in Williwaw, reflects at one point on his military service:

> He thought of the three years he had spent in the army, and, of those years, only a few things stood out in his memory: certain songs that were popular when he had left for overseas, the waiting in line for almost everything. . . . The rest of his army career came to him only as a half-feeling of discomfort.

Leonard Woolf noted in a letter written during World War II the feeling of "negative emptiness and desolation of personal and cosmic boredom" of the war. Early in Williwaw, Evans, the skipper of the transport ship, is lying in his bunk, nursing a hangover:

> Someone turned on the radio. A deep sterile radio voice staccatoed in the air for a moment and was gone. The air was filled with static, and then the voice came back again. Evans could not make out what the voice was saying but he could guess from the tone that our "forces were smashing ahead on all fronts": the usual thing. He was bored by the war.

In the Vanity Fair article "Gore's Wars," Vidal is quoted as saying to Schiff:

> "The great untold story is what those of us who were in the army from seventeen to twenty-one in the Second World War, what we are really like . . . " I ask him whether he's talking about the damaged gift for intimacy that commonly afflicted the veterans of Vietnam, and he replies, "Well, now you're coming to it—the problems of young soldiers. We missed our youth . . . which we then over compensated for later."

This is an odd exchange, even allowing for the inevitable nonsequiturs of interviews. In the first place, it is tempting, even if smug and self-righteous, to point out that for many participants in the more active theaters of the war, the loss of youth coincided violently with massive physical or mental trauma or the actual loss of life. When James Jones was asked by an interviewer long after the publication of From Here to Eternity if "the men resented the war," he replied, "Well, yes, they did. They resented getting their asses shot off." In relation to the world represented in *Williwaw*, then, this loss or "missing" of youth must take on another coloration: but what? What were those young men in the army "really like"? The interviewer, as happens so often, does not ask Vidal to elaborate on his remark, but instead provides him with a combined question and formulaically glib and topical answer, to which he need only assent. Instead, Vidal sidesteps the ready-made answer and answers another question which was not asked.

What can we salvage from this teasing and frustrating exchange that will help us to understand the truly frightening world of *Williwaw*, frightening, despite the implications of its title, not in its measure of nature's malice or violence or destruction, but in its sense of human disconnection, alienation, cynicism, drift, and failure?

To begin to answer this question, we should turn to the humans in this novel. Evans, the skipper, is about twenty-five, though "he looked much older." He is seriously hung over at the beginning of both chapters 1 and 2. He keeps a bottle of bourbon in his cabin and nips at it when the going gets tough. He is a competent seaman, but his morale is strikingly low. In his private moments, he thinks he might be going crazy. At a critical point, one of his mates asks him if they should set to sea again from a safe shelter:

> "What do you think, Skipper?"
> "I don't know. I'll have to think about it. I don't know." Evans suddenly felt inadequate. He wished that he did not have to make this decision. He wondered for a moment what would happen if he got into his bunk and refused to get out.

Once at sea again, Evans, feeling sick, walks out on deck:

> The air was cool and moist. There was no wind and no sign of wind. Dark clouds hung motionless in the air. He felt the vastness of the sea and the loneliness of one small boat on the dividing line between gray sky and gray water. They were quite alone out here and he was the only one who realized it. This was very sad, and feeling sad and lonely he went back into the wheelhouse.

Evans has not seen his family for seven years, though his mother writes once in a while. He was married once, and it lasted a month.

> Evans thought about his wife. She was a nice girl. If he had met her at any other time than during a war they might have been happy. He

did not know her very well, though. He could not decide whether their marriage would have been any good or not.

Under the circumstances, it is hard to be sanguine about Evans' postwar plans: "Evans thought of Seattle. He would get married again. That would be the first thing he would do."

Martin, his first mate and one year younger than Evans, had been a hack actor in a New England stock company. The narrator tells us that "He knew nothing about being a mate," and even Martin himself has come to this conclusion:

> He had fought constantly with Evans and he had known all the time that Evans was right: that he was no seaman. Martin had drifted into boat work in the army. After two years he had been made a Warrant Officer and assigned to this Freight-Passenger ship. The whole thing was unreal to him, the Bering Sea, these boats, the desolate stone islands . . . the thought that he would be at least another year in these islands was maddening.

After reading a letter from a girl back home,

> Martin folded the letter and put it in his pocket. Her letters were always the same but she was a nice girl and he would probably marry her and be bored. He felt sorry for himself. He looked at the bleak sky and saw that it suited his mood.

Bervick, the second mate, "was an old seaman at thirty"; but his painful naïveté and inexperience with women and intimacy is revealed in his response to Olga, a Norwegian waitress in Big Harbor, a larger port further west.

> Because she had let Bervick sleep with her for nothing, he had decided that it must be love and he had almost decided to marry her. Then one day he discovered that she was also seeing Duval and accepting his money and a great many other people's money, too. He had asked her to stop but she was a thrifty girl, supporting her mother in Canada. She had told him that it was none of his business. Duval had laughed at him because of this and he come to hate Duval and feel that it was his fault that Olga had changed.

Duval, the Chief Engineer, is fifty, a "Frenchman" from New Orleans, coarse and insulting to the crew and greasily confidential with any passengers of rank. He seems especially to enjoy baiting

Bervick on the subject of Olga at every opportunity, the more public the better.

Smitty, the ship's Indian cook, might be said to lend some comic relief to this group, with his pained refrain of "I seen everything now," were it not for the fact that his constant cursing, his complaining, his china-smashing, his transcendentally horrible cooking, and his unremitting focus on himself and his own problems, not to mention his race, all combine to create a palpable distance between himself and the men he feeds so badly.

Major Barkison is a West Pointer, about thirty-one, and a reluctant representative of the prematurely aged look so ubiquitous in this novel: "He was not old and did not like to be thought old, but because he was bald and his face was lined, people took him to be older than he was. He did not like that." He is a master of the truism, the cliché, and the platitude; and the narrator snipes at his Walter Mitty-like fantasies, in which the Major imagines himself to be the Duke of Wellington or General Chinese Gordon. In fact, he is an entirely unimportant petty functionary in the vast and inefficient administrative bureaucracy of the army; and he can't even see the irony in his rush to file a report that the Andrefski Bay base, working port of the transport ship, should be dismantled and shut down:

> "It is imperative that I get back to Headquarters."
> "The war would stop if you didn't get back, wouldn't it, Major?" The Captain said this jovially but Evans thought there was malice in what he said.
> "What do you mean, Captain?" said the Major stiffly.
> "Nothing at all, sir. I was just joking. A bad habit of ours here." Evans smiled to himself. He knew that the Captain did not like regular army men.

In the novel's cleverest example of a symbolism based on realistic conditions, Major Barkison receives an expected if not especially deserved promotion to Lieutenant Colonel just after he steps off the ship at Arunga near the end of the novel, and the Colonel who brings him the news tries to pin on his new insignia on the spot:

> The Colonel searched in one of his pockets and brought forth two silver Lt Colonel's leaves. "I'll pin them on," he said. He managed to

get the Major's insignia off but his hands got cold before he could pin the new insignia on.

"Oh, hell," said the Colonel, handing the leaves to Barkison. "Put them on later."

Barkison is left momentarily with no insignia at all. Given who he is, the effect is the same as if he had suddenly disappeared.

Lieutenant Hodges is a "pink-faced" young career officer who acts as Barkison's assistant. At the start of the novel, he seems relatively untouched by the conditions that seem to have afflicted everyone else. He looks even younger than he is, which is twenty-one. He admires Barkison, he likes the army, he is charmingly embarrassed by pinups, he tries to act like a human being with the men, and he unself-consciously enjoys the storm at sea, as a good young romantic should. But by the end of the novel, he has inadvertently created the conditions in which Duval dies, he is troubled—one might even say haunted—by his suspicions about Bervick and by his sense of a tacit conspiracy to cover up any wrongdoing, and he concludes that Barkison is a poseur and a phony. It seems only a matter of time before he begins to look as old as everyone else.

The Chaplain of the Andrefski Bay base, O'Mahoney, is middle-aged and awkward, as if understanding that he doesn't quite fit in. "He had been a monk in a Maryland monastery," the narrator comments, "and now, in the army, he acted as if he were playing a part in a bad dream, which perhaps he was." Martin, the first mate, says to him before they board ship:

> "You'll be ready for bad weather, won't you?"
>
> "Bad weather? Is that the report?"
>
> "Well, yes, but it's also a joke of ours that whenever we haul a Chaplain we have bad weather."
>
> O'Mahoney chuckled uneasily. "Well, that's the way those things go, I suppose."
>
> "Yes, it's probably just an invitation for you to talk on the water."
>
> "What? Oh, yes." Mahoney was not quite sure if this was blasphemy or not. He decided it was not. "Are you Catholic, Mr. Martin?" he asked. He usually asked that question.
>
> Martin shook his head. "I'm not much of anything," he said.

Chaplain O'Mahoney is the one man who tries to connect with everyone, but on such an embarrassingly spiritual or inanely fatuous level that everyone either shuts him out or, at best, politely tolerates him. Vidal chose deliberately to include a chaplain in this ship of fools, mean spirits, simple suffering souls, and half-crazed malcontents, for the sake of the multiple ironies it would generate. It would be churlish to diminish or to ridicule the innumerable beneficent and sometimes heroic ministrations of U.S. military chaplains in and out of combat theaters in the Second World War; but as a general rule, borne out during my own several years of service in the Marine Corps, the chaplain is uneasily accommodated as one who, though a formal part of the military structure, serves no particular warlike purpose and is regarded by many with "manly" suspicion as belonging to a softer and unmilitary world. In my units, if a man complained of a problem, the advice snarled by sergeants everywhere, with undisguised sarcasm and contempt, was "Tell it to the chaplain." In Samuel Hynes' recent memoir *Flights of Passage* (Naval Institute Press, 1988), he relates how he and his fellow Marine aviators would steal jeeps to go joyriding on Pacific Islands, and how they always, out of consideration for obvious priorities, tried to steal a chaplain's jeep if they could.

O'Mahoney's well-meant but fussy and mawkish attempts to socialize with the crew and passengers focus largely on his spiritual revelations and his seasickness. His connections with God are not sufficiently powerful to prevent the storm. He has a "presentiment" that no one will be hurt on the voyage, just before a man is lost overboard; and he comes into his own only when reading the service for the dead, which he clearly relishes, regretting only that he is not properly robed:

> The Chaplain nodded gravely. "I wish," he said in a low voice, "that I had my, ah, raiment."
> "It's in the hold," said Evans. "I don't think we could get it."
> "Perfectly all right."

Several other unnamed characters play minor supporting roles, all of which contribute to the sense of an authentic service atmosphere. We might expect the ship itself to function as a character, as ships do in so many sea stories, but she is nameless, unnumbered, and undescribed, as anonymous as the men who labor on the docks, loaf in warehouses, busy themselves at desks, or invisibly drive jeeps and trucks up and down the desolate roads of the base.

The narrator sparsely scatters some descriptions of the natural surroundings throughout the novel, but there is so little to describe:

> No trees grew on the island. The only vegetation was a coarse brown turf which furred the low hills that edged the bay. Beyond these low hills were high, sharp, and pyramidal mountains, blotched with snow.
>
> Evans looked at the mountains but did not see them. He had seen them many times before and they were of no interest to him now. He never noticed them.

The Aleutian chain stretches out for hundreds of miles, island after island, large and small, as separate and as barren as the men themselves seem to be: "In these islands there was no odor of earth and vegetation in the wind, only the scent of salt and stone." When human purpose intrudes on such a landscape in the form of warehouses and Quonset huts, it alights like a thinly distributed leprosy. In a realistic description that also functions as an ironic pun, the narrator explains that "All the buildings of the port were, for the sake of protection, far apart."

If there is little to observe and even less to talk about when looking at the land, the weather is another story. "You know that sailor habit of referring to the weather in every context," remarks the narrator in Joseph Conrad's *Lord Jim*. *Williwaw* presents no exception. In it, weather is the alpha and the omega. There are almost thirty references to, guesses about, questions concerning, and predictions of the weather in the first twenty-seven pages of the novel, uttered by a dozen different characters, all of whom contradict or qualify each other and even themselves, sometimes in the same breath. This is a firm and sustained pattern throughout the novel, and the obsessive and compulsive concern with the weather takes on a nearly insane character of its own. To be so dependent on, so ruled by, so much at the mercy of something so utterly out of your control suggests a natural equivalent for the service experience itself:

They watched the snow swirling over the water; they watched for signs of change. That's all this business was, thought Evans. Watching the sea and guessing what it might do next.

Later, after getting testy with one of his mates, Evans recognizes in himself a sort of weather-induced combat fatigue:

> Gloomily Evans looked at the sky again. He knew that he must be acting strangely. He had never let them see him nervous before. Weather was beginning to get on his nerves after all his years in these waters.

The plot of the novel can be simply rehearsed. The action takes place over six consecutive days, the first while the ship is at port at Andrefski Bay, the next four partly at sea and partly in harbor, expedient shelter, and, for a time, on the rocks, and the last after she makes port at Arunga, her destination. She carries a light cargo of insignificant machinery. Her passengers include Major Barkison, who is the General's Adjutant on Arunga, and who has just visited Adrefski Bay in order to write a report recommending that the base there be closed down. The weather will not permit flying, and so he insists on being transported to Arunga by sea, to make his report. He is accompanied by his young assistant, Lieutenant Hodges; and the base chaplain, O'Mahoney, also comes along to attend a meeting of chaplains at Arunga.

The ship makes Big Harbor in a day and moors for the night. Bervick heads into town to see Olga, and is rebuffed by her in favor of Duval, who has more money. He consoles himself by getting drunk and sleeping with a truly repulsive prostitute, whose favors he nevertheless also has to compete for. The next morning the ship puts out to sea again and runs into a bad storm by evening. Late at night they run for shelter into a small bay of Ilak, an uninhabited island, and anchor there. In the morning Evans decides to head to sea again; and that afternoon, off Kulak, another uninhabited island, the much-anticipated williwaw strikes without warning. The ship, out of control, is driven toward the shore and wedges between two rocks inside a reef. The big wind dies down, the crew manages to get the ship clear, and they continue west. That night, Bervick and Duval argue about fixing a leaking ventilator, and the helpful Hodges suggests that they both fix it. While they are doing this, in a stunning sequence of events Duval falls overboard and is lost. Bervick pretends not to know what happened, but the crew almost to a man assumes that Bervick killed Duval deliberately, and even Barkison and Hodges are puzzled and disturbed by the circumstances of Duval's sudden disappearance. It is soon made clear, however, that no one wants or intends to cooperate with any investigation which assumes that anything other than an accident may have caused Duval's death. The day spent in Arunga represents a restoration of the petty, egotistical, rank-conscious bureaucracy that was temporarily subsumed at sea; but finally everyone tacitly agrees that convenient cover-up is to be preferred to messy truth-seeking, and the sun shines on the happy prospect of the ship heading south to Seattle for repairs.

The style of narration, as I have suggested and tried to illustrate, is laconic, characterized by brief exchanges of dialogue which are, I assume by intention, frequently dull, boring, or inane, and by economical descriptions that use modifiers and figurative language sparingly. There is a certain studied flatness or suppression of tone throughout, as well as a fastidiousness with respect to representing the ritual profanity with which all service discourse is saturated. We also don't see any of the current mannerism of dumping unintegrated blocks of technical information into the text; and the very lack of technical specificity, the sparseness and bareness of the style and structure, lends a somewhat allegorical quality to the narrative. The novel seems delivered to us in a style that mimetically enacts the stunting or arresting of development.

The williwaw, or big storm, may be the manifest subject of the novel, from the title to the constant and obsessive references to the weather, to the premonitory and foreboding mood and atmosphere of the first half of the novel. Indeed, given all the narrative preparation and foreshadowing, even the crudest and least demanding sense of organic form would require that the storm take place, and of course it does.

The storm scenes are competently written, though the narrator's laconic and only tentatively figurative style does not serve him particularly well in conveying the sense of a cataclysmic force seemingly bent on destroying the ship and annihilating the men:

The wind became more powerful every minute. The big wind was at its height. Great streams of wind-driven water battered the ship.

It might be instructive to compare Joseph Conrad's somewhat more baroque style in "Typhoon":

> The wind had thrown its weight on the ship, trying to pin her down amongst the seas. They made a clean breach over her, as over a deep-swimming log; and the gathered weight of crashes menaced monstrously from afar. The breakers flung out of the night with a ghostly light on their crests—the light of sea-foam that in a ferocious, boiling-up pale flash showed upon the slender body of the ship the toppling rush, the downfall, and the seething mad scurry of each wave.

Finally, though, the storm in *Williwaw* is no more than an incident which the men endure and survive, not even through any remarkable exercise of courage or skill:

> "How did Evans manage to get us on the rocks, I wonder?"
> "He didn't," said Bervick. "Just fool's luck that we got out of this thing this well."
> "You mean so far," said the Chief sourly.

I can't feel that the storm is the novel's crisis, or even that it is very important. As I see it, the most powerful events, the most powerful writing, and the most provocative effects and implications take place after the actual storm itself has subsided.

Along with other damage to the ship, the storm has broken a deck ventilator, which is leaking on one of the engines below. Bervick agrees to fix it, forgets, and is reminded of it hotly by the Chief. They trade spirited insults in front of Hodges, who, somewhat out of his depth, suggests that they fix the ventilator together.

> "Why," said Hodges, "don't you do it together?" At Officers' School they had taught him that nothing brought men closer together than the same work.
> "That's a fine idea," said Bervick, knowing that Duval would not like it.
> "Sure," said the Chief, "sure."

Out on deck, Bervick and Duval continue to goad one another. Bervick gets a hammer and nails and tries to repair the ventilator, while Duval harasses him from a perch on the rail. Hodges comes out to see how all is going, and leaves again. At this point, the level of the writing takes a palpable leap upward:

"Well, I'll see you all later." Hodges walked toward the forward deck. The ship was pitching more than usual. The waves were becoming larger but overhead the sky was clearing and there was no storm in sight.

"Let's get this done," said Duval, "I'm getting cold."

"That's too bad. Maybe if you did some work you'd warm up."

"Come on," said Duval and he began to wrestle with the ventilator. It was six feet tall, as tall as Duval.

"That's no way to move it," said Bervick. He pushed the Chief away and he grasped the ventilator by the top. Slowly he worked it into place again. Duval watched him.

"See how simple it is," said Bervick.

Duval grunted and sat down on the rail again. Overhead a few stars began to shine very palely on the sea. Bervick hammered in the dark. Then, working too quickly, he hit his own hand. "Christ!" he said and dropped the hammer.

"Now what's wrong?" asked Duval irritably, shifting his position on the railing.

"Hit my hand," said Bervick, grasping it tightly with his good hand.

"Well, hurry up and get that thing nailed."

Anger flowed through Bervick in a hot stream.

"Damn it, if you're in a hurry, do it yourself." He picked up the hammer and threw it at Duval.

The hammer, aimed at Duval's stomach, curved upward and hit him in the neck. The Chief made a grab for the hammer and then the ship descended into a trough.

Duval swayed uncertainly on the railing. Then Duval fell overboard.

There was a shout and that was all. Bervick got to his feet and ran to the railing. He could see the Chief, struggling in the cold water. He was already over a hundred feet away. Bervick watched him, fascinated. He could not move.

His mind worked rapidly. He must find Evans and stop the engines. Then they would get a lifeboat and row out and pick the Chief up. Of course, after five, ten minutes in the water he would be dead.

Bervick did not move, though. He watched the dark object on the water as it slipped slowly away. The ship sank into another deep

trough and when they reached the crest of the next wave there was
no dark object on the water.

Then he was able to move again. He walked, without thinking, to
the forward deck. A wet wind chilled his face as he looked out to sea.
The snow clouds were still thinning. In places dim stars shone in the
sky.

The restraint, precision, and simplicity of the narrative has a
breathtaking effect: the reader feels as surprised, shocked, and
stunned as Bervick himself.

In the next scene, Bervick returns to the salon, where the innocent Hodges is building a house of cards on the table. All the
dialogue and action that had seemed so commonplace and dull
before, now shimmers beneath with an intensity of implication and
an overwhelming irony:

> "You and the Chief were really arguing," commented Hodges,
> putting a piece of the roof in place.
> "We're not serious."
> "You sounded serious to me. It's none of my business but I think
> maybe you sounded off a little too loud. He's one of your officers."
> "We didn't mean nothing. He talked out of line, too."
> "That's right. That's dangerous stuff to do, talk out of line. There
> can be a lot of trouble."
> "Sure, a lot of trouble. Sometimes guys kill each other up here.
> It's happened. This is a funny place. You get a little queer up here."
> "I suppose you're right." Hodges added a third story to his house.
> "Me and the Chief, we don't get along so well, but I ain't got any
> hard feelings against him, know what I mean?"
> "I think so. Started over a girl, didn't it?"
> "There're not many up here. The ones they've got there's a lot of
> competition for. We were just after the same one."
> "He got her?"
> "Yeah, he got her."
> Hodges began to build an annex on the left side of the house.
> Bervick hoped he would build one on the right side, too. It looked
> lopsided the way it was.
> "That's too bad," said Hodges.
> "I didn't like it so much, either."
> "I know how you feel."
> Bervick doubted that, but said nothing.

Hodges decided to build a fourth story. The house of cards collapsed promptly. "Damn," said Hodges and he did not rebuild.

Later that night, by himself in his cabin, Bervick reviews the events surrounding Duval's death and nearly succumbs to the temptations of selective memory and rationalized revisionism. But his essential decency and his guileless, straightforward nature, though much wounded by the fickle Olga and the cynical Duval, will not allow him a self-justifying reconstruction, and he remains troubled:

It was not his fault. He was sure of that. He had handed Duval the hammer. Well, he had thrown the hammer to him. He had not thrown it very hard, though. The Chief had lost his balance, that was all. Perhaps the hammer had hit him and thrown him off balance, but that was not likely. The ship had been hit by a wave and he was on the railing and fell off. Of course, the hammer might have been thrown much harder than he thought, but Duval had caught it all right. Well, perhaps he had not quite caught it; the hammer had hit him in the neck, but not hard enough to knock him overboard.

Then Duval was in the water and Bervick had tried to get help but it was too late. No, that was not right, he had not tried to get help: he had only stood there. But what could he have done? Fifteen minutes would have passed before they could have rescued him. Duval would have been frozen by then. Of course, he should have tried to pick him up. They couldn't lose time, though. Not in this weather. He had tried throwing Duval a line; no, that wasn't true at all. He had done nothing at all. . . .

Bervick slept uneasily. From time to time he would awaken with a start, but he could not remember his dreams. That was the trouble with dreams. The sensation could be recalled but the details were lost. There were so many dreams.

It is in terms of the reactions, or, more precisely, the absence of reactions to Duval's death that we can measure the extent to which human values have been flattened and distorted by the conditions under which these men have lived, worked, and interacted for so long. Most of the crew assume that Bervick was responsible for Duval's death, but they simply don't care. Bervick alone knows himself to be innocent, at least as far as intentions go; but when he compels himself to explain this to Evans, Evans only half-believes him: and in either case, it just doesn't matter.

Evans wondered absently if Bervick might not have had something to do with Duval's death. He examined the idea with interest. Bervick might have hit him on the head with a hammer and then he might have dropped him overboard. That was not at all unlikely. Evans smiled.

"What's so funny?"

"Nothing, nothing at all. I was just thinking."

"What about?"

"I was thinking what a funny thing it would be if you'd knocked the Chief on the head and tossed him overboard."

"Well, I didn't," said Bervick. His voice was even. "Don't know that I wouldn't have liked to."

"It doesn't make much difference one way or the other," said Evans, quite sure now that Bervick had killed Duval. "It doesn't make no difference at all."

Former Major, now Lieutenant Colonel Barkison has been appointed as Investigating Officer in the case. During the storm he had been frightened out of his wits; and afterward he had repeatedly praised Evans for what he had somewhat exaggeratedly perceived as coolheaded and decisive seamanship, promising to recommend him for a citation. But back on shore, his military ego and his new silver leaves, and perhaps the subconscious memory of his recent vulnerability and fear, demand that a proper distance be reestablished. He keeps the two men waiting in his outer office for fifteen minutes before telling them that he is going to file a report (yet another of his many important reports) concluding that Duval's death was a plain accident in the line of duty.

But in the process he cannot resist transferring the responsibility for the unfortunate trip onto Evans himself. Evans is far more aroused by this unjust criticism leveled by Barkison at his seaman's judgment than he is by Duval's death or what he believes to be Bervick's role in it. In consoling him for Barkison's unfair and highhanded treatment, Bervick seems to be evening the score between them: Evans has "supported" him, so he will "support" Evans.

"Well," said Bervick when they were outside the Adjutant's office, "there goes that medal of yours."

"I'd like to knock that little bastard's head in," said Evans with feeling. "Did you hear him say I showed bad judgment?"

"Well, he had to pass the buck; I mean, it would look bad if people heard he insisted on taking this trip in such bad weather. He just wants to cover himself."

"That man sure changed from what he was on the boat."

"He's just acting natural."

The cover of the latest (1989) paperback edition of *Williwaw* advertises it as "a story of men in war." That is only nominally true, unless we consider the assertion as a metaphor. Primo Levi relates in *The Reawakening* how, after being liberated from Auschwitz by the Red Army in 1945, he found himself in a refugee camp in Cracow, where he encountered a Greek veteran of the camps who scolded him for his failure to look for "good shoes" *before* food, "when war is waging":

> "But the war is over," I objected: and I thought it was over, as did many in those months of truce, in a much more universal sense than one dares to think today. "There is always war," replied Mordo Nahum memorably. . . . The Lager had happened to both of us; I had felt it as a monstrous upheaval, a loathsome anomaly in my history and in the history of the world; he, as a sad confirmation of things well known. "There is always war," man is wolf to man: an old story.

"'There is always war,' man is wolf to man: an old story." But surely there are conditions in which that savage relationship is tempered, softened, diffused: by the presence of family, home, wives, children, chosen work, neighborhoods, peace, personal freedom. All of these were absent in the lives of millions of American men during World War II, including the men in *Williwaw*. As the hero of Robert Lowry's *Casualty* observes, "The army brings out the worst in everybody."

Williwaw is a workmanlike novel by any standard, a candid, revealing, provocative, and psychologically realistic novel by the standards of American fiction published just after the Second World War, and a simply remarkable novel to have been written by a teenager. Perhaps I have given *Williwaw* a darker reading than the novel itself might insist on. Still, it seems to contain scarcely a trace of whatever redemptive experiences military service might conceivably provide. The occasional flickers of human connection, affection, and sympathetic understanding seem faint and far apart. Even the tenuous bonding of Bervick and Evans at the end of the novel seems informed mainly by their relief at having survived the storm, their mutual desire not to be bothered by Duval's death, and the chance they'll be sent to Seattle.

We needn't concern ourselves with the fate of pompous, self-satisfied fools like Barkison. But perhaps the others, those sad, separate, bored, resigned, hurt, and damaged younger men, might have fared better had they not been wrenched by the war into an environment almost entirely inhospitable to the cultivation of human and humane community, where their youth was put in hibernation and, when they came to reclaim it, it could not be reawakened. After all these years, *Williwaw* remains Gore Vidal's best attempt to tell part of what he himself calls their "great untold story."

4

The City and the Pillar *as*
Gay Fiction

CLAUDE J. SUMMERS

The decade following World War II saw both the beginnings of a new homosexual emancipation movement and the emergence of a new openly gay popular literature. In 1948 the first important American homophile group, the Mattachine Society, was proposed; the Kinsey report on *Sexual Behavior in the Human Male* startled the American public with its revelation that over one-third of the male population reported significant homosexual experience; and several important fictional accounts of homosexuality appeared, including Truman Capote's *Other Voices, Other Rooms*, Tennessee Williams' *One Arm and Other Stories*, and Gore Vidal's *The City and the Pillar*. By the end of this decade, homosexual themes and characters were, if not yet a staple of popular literature, at least no longer rare. In the literature of this period may be charted the transition of public opinion about homosexuality that E. M. Forster noted in 1960, the change from ignorance and terror to familiarity and contempt.[1] But countering a host of novels in which homosexuality is trivialized and sensationalized is a small but considerable body of popular literature that takes homosexuality seriously as a contemporary social issue and that seeks to interpret homosexuality in ways other than stereotypically. Prime among the novels that challenge the widespread Anglo-American contempt for homosexuality and homosexuals is Vidal's pioneering work, which is one of the first explicitly gay fictions to reach a large audience. Emphasizing the normality of gay people, *The City and the Pillar* traces the coming out process of a young man as ordinary and American as apple pie. Coming at the beginning of the postwar decade, the novel is an important and exemplary contribution to the emerging popular literature of homosexuality. Like many gay fictions that followed, it evokes central homosexual myths and reflects the social and sexual attitudes of its time even as it resists them.

In the Afterword to his 1965 revision of *The City and the Pillar*, Vidal explains the book's origin and his intention: "I wanted to take risks, to try something no American had done before. I decided to examine the homosexual underworld (which I knew less well than I pretended), and in the process show the 'naturalness' of homosexual relations, as well as making the point that there is of course no such thing as a homosexual."[2] Whatever Vidal's intent, the novel does not illustrate the latter point but rather its opposite, for despite the author's well-known belief in the natural bisexuality of the species and his frequent insistence that *homosexual* is an adjective rather than a noun (a position also held by Alfred Kinsey), the novel succeeds primarily as a bildungsroman tracing its protagonist's gradual acceptance of a homosexual identity. While the book certainly provides numerous examples of bisexual behavior and rejects the notion of homosexuality as a rigid classification, its denouement pivots on the inflexibility of sexual orientation, for the protagonist Jim Willard turns out to be exclusively homosexual and his idealized friend Bob Ford exclusively heterosexual (apart from his adolescent experimentation with Jim). Nor does the novel actually show the naturalness of homosexuality. Though it presents its gay hero as ordinary to the point of blandness, thereby challenging the stereotype of the homosexual as effeminate and exotic, and though it depicts gay lovemaking as altogether natural, the novel nevertheless rather contradictorily conceives of homosexuality as an abnormal state demanding psychological explanation. For all its reformist zeal, it is nevertheless clearly a document reflective of its era.

The City and the Pillar does, however, deftly accomplish what seems to have been one of Vidal's chief aims: it provides an unsensa-

tionalized portrait of the flourishing gay subcultures, first of Hollywood and New Orleans, then of New York, which is described as "a
new Sodom" where gay people "could be unnoticed by the enemy
and yet known to one another."[3] The novel thereby illustrates the
vast range and diversity of homosexuals and presents to a wide
audience the social dynamics, mores, and specialized language of a
hidden or at least masked society. It challenges some widely held
stereotypes and confirms others. Most refreshingly, while it recognizes the debilitating desperation that frequently characterizes the
subculture, unlike many works of its era it refrains from moralizing
and from casting the gay underworld as the villain of the piece. The
absence of a moralizing perspective not only distinguishes *The City
and the Pillar* from contemporaneous popular literature on the
subject, but it also facilitates the hard-edged irony that characterizes
the book's style.

By presenting the gay subculture through the eyes of its naive
hero, a native of small-town Virginia who must adjust to a new and
strange world, the novel becomes a kind of Baedeker of the 1940s
gay underground. In so doing, it captures well the coming out
experience as a time when a bewildering array of information is
mastered and the individual passes gradually through various stages
and levels of acceptance. Naturally athletic and apparently well-
adjusted, Jim Willard (whose profession as a tennis player may have
been suggested by the 1946 scandal involving tennis great William
"Big Bill" Tilden)[4] is at first an anomaly among the clique of gay
bellboys with whom he associates in Hollywood. They are shallow,
effeminate young men who all "desire to be wealthy and admired,
to move in narcissistic splendor through the lives of others, to live
forever grandly and not to die." But as he becomes more deeply
involved, Jim discovers a complex society that includes, in addition
to the stereotypical gay men and lesbians ("people so hunted that
they have, at last, become totally perverse as a defense"), a much
larger group of concealed homosexuals. As one character tells Jim,
there are "thousands like ourselves. Perfectly normal men and
women. . . ." Although the novel reflects its era in considering
homosexuality as a psychological problem, it also confirms what
Vidal wrote in his 1965 Afterword: "When legal and social pressures
against homosexuality are severe, homosexualists can become neu-

rotic, in much the same way that Jews and Negroes do in a hostile environment. Yet a man who enjoys sensual relations with his own sex is not, by definition, neurotic."

Central points of the novel are that repression distorts the expression of homosexuality and creates a subculture that itself contributes to that distortion. Were homosexuality accepted by the larger society, the subculture would not be necessary or at least would be less distorting. The novel is especially sensitive to the heavy costs in emotional stability exacted by the homosexual's necessity to disguise his sexuality. For example, several characters angrily protest the need to mask their sexual orientation. "There should be no need to hide, to submerge in a big city; everything should be open and declared," Paul Sullivan remarks, as he doubtfully considers the possibility of coming out publicly. "We live a short life and it's hard enough to find love in the world without the added hazard of continual pretense," he adds. Similarly, near the end of the book, when visiting his Virginia home for the first time in years, Jim Willard grows impatient of the heterosexual mask he must don for the visit and wonders "what would happen if he were to be honest and natural; if every man like himself were to be natural and honest." He concludes that "It would be the end of the submerged world and it would make a better beginning for others not yet born: to be born into a world where sex was natural and not fearsome, where men could love men naturally, the way they were meant to, as well as to love women naturally, the way they were meant to." But even as he contemplates the potential benefits of openness and a world liberated by truthfulness, Jim acknowledges that "it was a desperate thing to be an honest man in his world, and he had not the courage to be that yet." The novel defines freedom as not having to tell lies, but it also soberly recognizes that, for the gay man or lesbian in 1948 America, freedom is far from a reality.

A frequent subject of discussion in Vidal's gay subculture is the question of the origins of homosexuality, a subject also inevitably raised as part of the coming out process. Although the gay characters sometimes discuss in long, frequently stilted speeches the etiology of homosexuality, often attributing its prevalence in America to the baleful influence of women and mothers, and sometimes contrasting one form of homosexuality allegedly caused by the effeminizing of society with another supposedly more primitive and natural Teutonic form, the novel itself takes no stand on this issue. It merely repeats the various speculations of the day and in so doing locates itself as very much a product of late 1940s America. At one point, Sullivan, the novel's most articulate and best-educated character, attributes Jim's homosexuality to the fear of women, a popular psychological explanation of the period and one consonant with Jim's (and the novel's) horror of effeminacy. But this charge is disputed when Jim characteristically thinks of Bob Ford: "because of Bob everything Sullivan said was false; his homosexuality was not the result of negation, of hatred or fear of women; it came, rather, from a most affirmative love." Sullivan may speak for Vidal when he echoes Freud and professes to believe that homosexuality is a "normal stage in human development, sometimes arrested but not for that reason to be censured." He surely speaks for Vidal when he proclaims that "the real dignity is the dignity of a man realizing himself and functioning honestly according to his own nature." In the pre–gay liberation world of the 1940s, when homosexuals are too frightened to risk exposure, the only possibility of affirmation in the face of repression is to "Live with dignity . . . and try to learn to love one another."

Perhaps the most revolutionary gesture of *The City and the Pillar* is its suggestion that the homosexual experience itself is valuable, an insight that is extremely rare among the popular treatments of the subject in the postwar decade and that both hearkens back to the early emancipation movement at the turn of the century and looks forward to the "gay is good" philosophy of the 1970s. The experience of being gay in an unaccepting society may foster neurosis, but it may also lead to healthy introspection and valuable social criticism. Jim Willard acknowledges this at two points in the novel. When he is in military service and observes the enormous pressure for conformity all about him, he realizes that his life with homosexuals taught him an important lesson: "the importance of being one's self, to make as few compromises with one's real nature as possible." Later, on his return home for Christmas 1942, he becomes conscious of the limitations of the "safe secure people whose lives were running in a familiar pattern." He thinks, "There was no basis for understanding here. They had never been so emotionally severed

from society that they were forced to analyze and understand emotion." The point is the Forsterian one that the alienation suffered by
gay people affords them, at least potentially, important insights both
into themselves and into the society from which they stand apart, at
a slight angle to the universe. *The City and the Pillar* protests
against the injustices suffered by homosexuals, especially the repression that creates the need to disguise love; it exposes the mendacity
and ignorance of the larger society; and it discovers within the
homosexual experience the potential for heightened self-knowledge
and deepened social analysis.

Notwithstanding its undeniable importance as a pioneering ex-
ploration of a gay milieu and as a documentary that demystifies
homosexuality by showing its (relative) ordinariness and prevalence,
the novel has more than sociological interest. Although Anaïs Nin
complained that it was a "prosaic and literal book."[5] *The City and
the Pillar* is actually evocative and resonant. Its power resides in the
simplicity, subtlety, and apparent artlessness with which it connects
a contemporary gay odyssey with archetypal concerns. Indeed, the
book may be described accurately as a "mythic novel,"[6] and its
achievement as a gay fiction has less to do with its depiction of
homosexuality per se than with its incorporation and examination
of the myths of love, particularly those associated with homosexuality. These myths help shape the experience of Vidal's homosexual Everyman, and the novel itself becomes a reflection both of and
on those myths. The mythic dimension enriches the book's flat,
understated style, and imparts scope and significance to its account
of an unremarkable young man's journey toward self-knowledge.
Although it is severely flawed by its melodramatic ending (especially
in the original version), *The City and the Pillar* is an ambitious
attempt to trace realistically a homosexual's awakening in a particular time and place, while also locating this experience in the vast
expanses and repetitive patterns of myth.

The novel's title and bipartite structure rely on the central myth
of homosexuality in Judeao-Christian culture, the story of Sodom.
The curious tale of the destruction of the Cities of the Plain by fire
and brimstone, as recounted in Genesis 18 and 19, provides, of
course, the foundation for the religious and civil persecution of
homosexuality. In the biblical account, two angels are accosted by

the men of Sodom when they visit Lot. Even Lot's offer of his virginal daughters fails to dissuade the Sodomites in their desire for the angels. In consequence, the angels destroy not only Sodom but also Gommorah and all the plain, with everything growing there and everyone living there, save only Lot and his family. As Lot and his wife flee the burning cities, she lags behind and gazes backward toward the plain and is turned into a pillar of salt, presumably for disobeying the angels' warning not to look back. In Vidal's subversive interpretation of this perplexing and unedifying myth, the emphasis is not on the destruction of Sodom but on the pillar of salt. Even as the retributive plot may at first glance seem to confirm the dangers of homosexuality, the myth functions finally as a condemnation not of sodomy, but of the false romanticization of the past.

Vidal's bold reinterpretation of the Sodom myth provides the novel an important structural principle. The novel's plot is divided into a bifurcated flashback, framed by opening and closing chapters set in 1943. In "The City" portion of the book Jim completes a prolonged coming out process, while in "The Pillar of Salt" he regresses in an attempt to relive the past, especially his initiation experience, so that "the circle of his life would be completed." Jim is not destroyed by Sodom. In fact, the section of the book entitled "The City" charts a period of steady growth toward maturity. Jim's destruction results not from his acceptance of himself as a homosexual—his positive achievement in the novel—but from his fixation on the past, which finally turns him into a pillar of salt.

Vidal's seriously witty subversion of the Sodom myth is paradigmatic of his treatment of other myths in the book, both nationalistic and homoerotic. For example, he explodes that staple of American literature, the myth of innocence. In *The Apostate Angel*, Bernard F. Dick reads *The City and the Pillar* in light of Leslie Fiedler's *Love and Death in the American Novel* and concludes that Vidal's book demythologizes the American Wilderness novel, creating a homoerotic Eden that "ripens with purity and rots with experience." Dick is no doubt correct to perceive that in the idyllic scene of lovemaking by the river Vidal evokes the homoeroticism implicit in much classic American literature, including *Huckleberry Finn* and *The Last of the Mohicans*, but he is wrong to think that the novel's intent is merely to reveal "the awesome truth the myth concealed"[7] or to condemn experience. *The City and the Pillar* is more sophisticated than Dick's analysis recognizes. The book does expose American hypocrisy by making explicit the homoerotic source of an important romantic strain in American literature, usually expressed as an idealization of innocence and a fear of experience. But it is not so much interested in discovering this "awesome truth" as in depicting the dangerousness of such false idealization. What is condemned is not experience, but the fixation on innocence. The myth of Eden is revealed to be as dangerous as the myth of Sodom.

Moreover, the idyllic initiation scene that is to haunt Jim Willard throughout the novel evokes not merely the nationalistic myth of innocence but some crucial myths deeply embedded in the homosexual literary tradition. The pastoral setting, the bathing in the river, and the spontaneous sexual episode of the two boys constitute a tableau traditionally associated with homosexuality and may be traced to the *Idylls* of Theocritus. There is no more pervasive motif in gay literature than the homoerotic recognition scene involving an outdoor bathing episode. Its analogues include the eleventh section of Whitman's "Song of Myself," with its "Twenty-eight young men and all so friendly" dancing and laughing and bathing by the shore, numerous bathing scenes in late nineteenth-century literature and visual art, and the similar episodes in D. H. Lawrence's *The White Peacock* and *Women in Love* and Forster's *A Room with a View* and *Maurice*.[8] The fact that the lovemaking is preceded by playful wrestling is suggestive, as Roger Austen and Stephen Adams have pointed out, of the Hylas ritual in classical literature, as interpreted by Rictor Norton.[9] This ritual derives from an archetypal initiation ceremony that was eventually transformed into romantic homosexual love and underlies literature as different as Pindar's *Odes* and the wrestling scenes in *Women in Love* and *Maurice*. The irony of Vidal's use of this ritual which displaces violence with sex is made apparent in its reversal in the novel's grim conclusion, where a sexual overture ushers in violence.

But most significant of all is Vidal's allusion to the originary myth of homosexuality offered by Aristophanes in Plato's *Symposium*.[10] According to this myth, there were originally three genders: man, woman, and androgyne. These creatures were round, each having four feet, four hands, two faces, and two sets of genitals. In anger,

Zeus sliced each down the middle, thereby creating new beings. Men who love men are thus explained as slices of the original male, and they seek, like the other divided natures, completion by recovering their lost halves. This originary myth is clearly alluded to in Vidal's description of Jim's sexual initiation by the river: "their bodies came together and for Jim it was his first completion, his first discovery of a twin: the half he had been searching for." Throughout the novel, he is in quest of his lost half, in search of this sense of fulfillment, this assuasion of loneliness. Indeed, the words *complete, completely, completeness,* and *completion* recur over and over again in the novel, underlining the quest for wholeness as its central theme. As Jim comes to realize after he has experienced the novelty of gay life, what he really wants is "a companion, a brother . . . a mingling of his identity with an equal." Perhaps the most enduring of all gay fantasies, indeed all romantic desire, this quest for completeness through another is deeply rooted in homosexual myth and consciousness. But Vidal does not merely validate the archetypal search for a lost partner, he also indicates the dangers attendant upon such a quest, particularly its susceptibility to falsification.

Indeed, the hard edge of *The City and the Pillar* is the result of Vidal's exposure of the false idealization implicit in the very myth that motivates Jim and the other central characters, all of whom search for self-validation in a lost half that might make them whole. Even in the pastoral scene of sexual discovery, Vidal's wry irony is clear, at least in retrospect. The first clue comes in the different evaluations of the experience by Jim and Bob. While both participate with an equal awareness and both are "made complete" in the embrace, Jim's enthusiasm is pointedly not matched by Bob's. The older of the two assesses the experience as immature and unnatural. "That was awful kidstuff," Bob reflects, "I don't think it's right. . . . It's not natural." This assessment does not preclude his further participation in sex-play that weekend, but it contrasts with the enormous sense of release and self-discovery that characterizes Jim's response, and it foreshadows the devastating conclusion.

Most crucially, however, Vidal undercuts the idyllic scene, and signals its potential danger, by connecting it with dreams. For Jim, the experience of making love with Bob is one in which "half forgotten dreams began to come alive." After the lovemaking, he gains courage "now that he had performed a dream." In one sense, by linking Jim's sexual response to early childhood dreams that are made real in experience, Vidal validates the psychological insight of Aristophanes' myth of homosexuality by locating the desire for a lost partner deep in Jim's subconscious. The linkage certainly helps make credible the central premise of the novel, that Jim believes that in the encounter with Bob he has discovered something basic to his identity. And it helps explain the persistence of Jim's memory of the initiation scene, which for him is a recognition scene as well, one in which inchoate desires are literally made flesh. But dreams are deeply ambiguous. They may signify psychological truth, yet they are also illusory and can distort reality. This is exactly the double-edged way in which Vidal uses them in this scene (and throughout the novel). What begins as "a consummation in reality" becomes translated into a distorting dream that will haunt Jim's days and nights to come. By the end of the scene, Bob Ford becomes for Jim not a real person but "a conscious dream." In the circular shape of the novel's plot, Bob is a romantic "dream-lover" who will materialize in the harsh light of reality as a nightmarish demon.

Vidal's interest centers less on the contrasts of past and present, dream and reality. Thus, he appropriates for his own purposes another myth associated with gay men and women, the Freudian diagnosis of homosexuality as arrested development, an explanation that is explicitly evoked by Sullivan. But even as he provides in Jim's disturbed relationships with his bullying father and close-binding mother evidence for a psychological case history, Vidal subverts the Freudian myth by making it characteristic not of homosexuality per se but of American romanticism in general. Jim Willard, Ronald Shaw, and Paul Sullivan can be seen as cases of arrested development not because they are gay, but because they so idealize the past and so manufacture illusions that they are unable either to live fully in the present or to accept the imperfections of reality. These personal characteristics, interestingly enough, are also national characteristics, for as Vidal has frequently pointed out, the United States itself routinely falsifies and romanticizes its past. Thus Vidal's subversion of the American myth of innocence is intimately connected with his subversion of the Freudian myth. That he intends the arrested emotional development of his characters not to be read as merely a symptom of homosexuality is clear from the fact that Maria Verlaine suffers from the same affliction. She too harbors illusions about love and "would not accept incompleteness." Unfulfilled by heterosexual men, she falls in love with younger gay men, for with them "she enjoyed a greater illusion of completeness." All of the central characters are emotionally immature. Trapped by distorting dreams, haunted by their pasts, seeking the recovery of a lost wholeness, they live in a world of illusion.

Perhaps because they are so emotionally stunted, Vidal's characters are not very interesting. With the exception of Paul Sullivan, the minor characters are predictable and sketchily drawn. Ronald Shaw is a caricature of a movie star and Maria Verlaine an unconvincing portrait of a cosmopolitan "fag-hag." Only Jim Willard is affecting, and he commands sustained interest largely because he combines unexpected characteristics. Bland and ordinary, he nevertheless has an unusually well-developed interior life. Himself paralyzed by romantic illusions, he is surprisingly perceptive about the illusions of others. For all the novel's treatment of him as a case history, he nevertheless preserves an essential mystery. As Robert Kiernan comments, Jim Willard "is Everyman and yet he is *l'étranger*. . . .The net effect is paradoxical but appropriate, for it decrees that in the last analysis we cannot patronize Jim Willard, sympathize with him entirely, or even claim to understand him. Much more so than the typical character in fiction, Jim Willard simply *exists*, not as the subject of a statement, not as the illustration of a thesis, but simply as himself."[11] Appropriate for the protagonist of a coming out story, a genre whose narratives are always the same, yet always different, Jim Willard is at once a representative and a highly individualized figure.

The City and the Pillar in effect traces the successive stages through which Jim Willard passes in his coming to terms with himself as a homosexual, from his period of experimentation through his achievement of a gay identity. In this sense, the novel enacts a mythic quest for wholeness and self-acceptance. Thus, Jim may be regarded as a figure of mythic dimensions insofar as his coming out story recapitulates the experience of millions of other American homosexuals of his era. But his journey of self-discovery is highly individual, for it is conducted in the constant shadow of his romantic idealization of Bob Ford. The memory of a cabin and a brown river is a secret that grows inside Jim, interceding at crucial points to shape the contours of his life.

The effects of Jim's romanticization of Bob are apparent early in the novel as the young protagonist fumblingly gropes toward a grasp of his own identity. For example, when Anne, the girl he is fixed up with by his shipmate Collins, attempts to initiate a sexual encounter, he instinctively compares her with Bob. On this basis, he rejects her: "he thought of the cabin and the river and he knew it was not like this; it was not dirty like this; it was not unnatural like this. He didn't care now if he *was* different from other people." This embarrassing incident is an important step in Jim's growth toward self-knowledge. Even if he feels vaguely inadequate, he nevertheless recognizes that what might be natural for others is unnatural for him. When Collins labels him "queer" for his failure to respond to Anne, Jim must question himself and confront the puzzle of his differentness. But at this point in the book, his naive romanticism limits the answers that he finds.

The limiting tendencies of Jim's romanticism are also apparent when he compares himself to his peers in Hollywood. Jim is at first shocked to discover that the effeminate young men he works with not only had the same dreams he had "but practiced them fully when awake." This discovery leads him to "study himself in the mirror to see if there was any trace of the woman in his face or manner; he was pleased always that there was not." The popular association of homosexuality with effeminacy works to confuse Jim. Since he is not effeminate, then, he thinks, he must not be gay. Jim's disdain of effeminacy is shared by most of the characters in the novel; even the outrageous drag queens value conventional masculinity in others, if not themselves. This emphasis on masculinity anticipates the masculinization of American homosexuals widely noticed in the 1970s and often attributed to the pride inspired by the contemporary gay liberation movement, but which began much earlier and was probably at least partly influenced by the two world wars.

In a pattern familiar in the coming out process, Jim decides that he is unique. He believes his experience with Bob is utterly unlike that of his colleagues at the hotel, and he resists labeling it as homosexual. Yet he senses a connection between his dreams of Bob and the stories that the bellboys tell of their affairs with one another. He pretends that he associates with the bellboys only for "the pleasure of saying no" to their sexual advances. But for all his disclaimers of homosexual interest or of identification with the stereotypically gay young men, he nevertheless desires "to know more, to understand this twisted behavior, to understand himself." This desire for self-knowledge propels him to accept Ronald Shaw's sexual invitation.

Significantly, Jim is attracted to Shaw because he is masculine and he reminds him of Bob, "and that made it all right." Yet even as he finds himself responding sexually to Shaw, he compares the sensation to "a different night, a more important time." He does not find lovemaking with Shaw the "complete" experience it had been with Bob, but he achieves physical satisfaction and a kind of emotional contentment. Still, the relationship is shadowed by the inevitable comparison: "He was alive and aware that the last two years had been gray and without color; now he could only remember having lived on the peaks of sensation: Bob and now Shaw; the second not so good as the first but still exciting and almost satisfying."

The affair with Shaw is an important but preliminary stage in Jim's development, one that he must necessarily outgrow. In his unequal pairing with Shaw, Jim plays the dual role of the beloved and the somewhat detached student of gay life. At first he is impressed by Shaw's success and single-mindedness, "the glamour of his legend," and his kindness. As the object of Shaw's affection, Jim has only to accept, not to give. But he quite rightly comes to doubt whether Shaw is really capable of the love about which he so incessantly talks, and he understandably becomes impatient with the actor's self-pity. Moreover, Jim finally bridles under the restraints of the role in which he has allowed himself to be cast. He comes to yearn for a more active, less passive involvement, one in which he gives as well as receives.

For the mother-fixated Shaw, Jim is simply another in a long series of conquests. Shaw "chose the handsomest, most masculine boys he could find and he was never pleased with them: he resented it if they came to love him, came to disregard the legend, and he was hurt when they could not give him the warmth he wanted, the warmth his mother gave him as a child." Trapped in an emotional double-bind, Shaw constantly complains of "incomplete love," yet he is incapable of responding to a complete one. And at this point in his life, Jim is equally incapable of love. He does not pretend to be in love with Shaw: "'The idea of being in love with a man was still a ludicrous one; still seemed unnatural and rather hopeless: in every case except Bob's and that was different." He comes to realize that what he wants is not a father-figure, but a brother, an equal, ideally a twin. Jim recognizes the illusionary nature of Shaw's obsession with an ideal love, but he fails to see that his romanticization of Bob is itself also illusionary.

Jim's more nearly equal relationship with Sullivan represents an advance in maturity and self-knowledge, and another stage in his progress toward achieving a gay identity. Jim realizes that "now he wanted to possess as well as be possessed." Sullivan's smile reminds him of Bob, and he responds to the writer's masculinity and seriousness. Through Sullivan's agency, he comes to acknowledge his homosexuality. Ironically enough, Sullivan is attracted to Jim largely because he thinks him primarily heterosexual. Like Shaw and many other homosexuals of the day (and like Jim himself), Sullivan places a premium on heterosexuality, yet he also contradictorily yearns for "a complete and reciprocated love." Deeply wounded by a guilty Catholic boyhood, the writer clings to his painful past as tenaciously as Jim treasures his happy memory of Bob. Sullivan "could no longer give himself completely to anyone." As a kind of masochistic pleasure, he deliberately contrives to wreck his chances for happiness, as when he intentionally endangers his relationship with Jim by introducing him to Maria Verlaine.

Significantly, however, when Sullivan outlines several typical patterns of homosexual development, Jim secretly recognizes himself. Now he no longer thinks of himself as unique, but as "a man not unlike these others, varying only in degree from a basic pattern." Although he silently vows to "defeat this truth," he secretly acknowledges his kinship with the fraternity of men who love men. He desperately hopes that "should he ever have a woman, he would be normal," but as Vidal adds laconically, "There was not much to base this hope on." Moreover, whereas before he had cherished his presumed heterosexuality, now he is hurt to the quick when he learns that Sullivan considers him incapable of tenderness with another man. "He felt he knew what love was better than anyone who had ever lived," he thinks to himself and immediately relates his capacity for love to his memory of Bob: "He doubted if anyone had felt as desperate and as lonely as he when Bob had left. Yes, he was capable of love with Bob and, perhaps, with someone who could affect him in the same way, another brother." Unfortunately, however, his domination by the memory of the cabin and the river will preclude his full response to anyone in real life.

Jim's failure to respond sexually to Maria Verlaine finally confirms the secret knowledge of his gay identity. Their relationship is a kind of love affair, an attempt to find that elusive completeness sought by each. But more than a love affair, the relationship is also, and primarily, Jim's desperate attempt to defeat the truth of his homosexuality. Without sex, the affair is painfully incomplete for both of them. Repelled by Maria's softness, Jim realizes that "he would never be one with her or any woman." Still not wishing to be labeled, however, he is angered when she asks him, "Do you mind it very much, being different?" Yet when she defines love as "the thing that makes you dissolve, that makes you come together," he thinks of Bob and silently agrees: "He knew what it was." Finally, when Sullivan tells him that Maria "could rescue you from this world," Jim replies, "Why should I be rescued?" Here, for the first time in the novel, he accepts himself as a homosexual. He is no longer a tourist passing through the submerged world but one of its citizens.

Jim's acceptance of his homosexuality is verified by his increasingly frequent awareness of sexual attraction toward other men and by his pursuit of Ken Woodrow, the handsome corporal he lusts after in the army. In his successive relationships with Shaw, Sullivan, and Maria, Jim had been the beloved, the pursued, the object of their passion. Now, suddenly, the positions are reversed, and Jim assumes yet another role on his journey toward maturity, that of would-be lover and seducer. He is infatuated with Ken: "He was unable to think of anything else; he could not concentrate on his work, such as it was. He could only daydream and make himself miserable." He is inexperienced in the art of seduction, however, and although he manages to get the corporal into bed with him, his sexual overture is repulsed. Ironically, however, the unattractive Sergeant Kerwinski, whom Jim had spurned, apparently succeeds in his pursuit of Ken. The point is that Jim does not yet know how to play the game. He has arrived at a gay identity, but he still has much to learn, not only about gay courting rituals but also about himself.

As an inevitable part of the coming out process, Jim's acceptance prompts him to a period of intense introspection. During the lonely days he spends in the army, he probes his past, trying "to understand himself and the circumstances that made him the way he was." His self-examination is motivated not by doubt, but by curiosity and by a growing sense of solidarity with other homosexuals. "He was not displeased with himself; he had no feeling of sorrow or remorse for the sort of man he was and doubtless would remain. He was curious, however, to know more of himself and of others like himself." What bothers him is not the fact of his homosexuality, but the stigma attached to it. He reviews his early life, his friendship with Bob, which began when he was fifteen ("From that time on no one existed in the world except Bob"), his experiences aboard ship, and his liaison with Shaw. And though he recognizes that Sullivan and Maria had been important in his life, he knows that he was happiest with Bob. "The City" section of the novel, thus, ends with Jim having finally achieved a gay identity. Significantly, and forebodingly, however, at the end of the section, rather than looking forward to the future, he is gazing backward on the past.

The smaller, second part of the novel, "The Pillar of Salt," contrives to bring Jim in contact with those who had been important to him in the past—Shaw, Sullivan, Maria, his mother, and, finally, Bob. But there is a conspicuously stagnant quality to this section. Jim works hard, maintains nonromantic friendships with his former lovers, and has a lot of sex, mainly of the one-night-stand variety. Tellingly, however, he participates in no meaningful relationship. He discovers that it is easier "to have sex with other men than to have friends; he found it difficult to get to know people in New York though easy to have sex with them." Although he is introduced to the party circuit of wealthy queens and willowy young men with "sensitive girlish faces," he dislikes it intensely. He had hoped that by moving in this circle, he could accept this society and be happy in it, but he realizes that "he could not find what he wanted here;

there was an overripe, over-civilized aura about this society. Every-one deliberately tried to destroy the last vestiges of the masculine within himself, and this Jim found to be the worst perversion of all, the only perversion; because very often these people allowed the tyranny of their own society to geld them completely." Instead, he turns to the gay bars, "finding in them, at least, young men like himself who were still natural and not overly corrupt." Despite his sexual success, however, he remains vaguely unhappy. He realizes that "he would have to find Bob again before he could be contented and at ease."

In Jim's romantic imagination, he sees the reunion with Bob as the culmination of his long journey. He thinks that it will provide the security and completeness that he lacks. When he learns that Bob has married, Jim has a brief flash of conscious doubt. It occurs to him that "The dream he had been constructing for years might be false, a daydream with no reality in it." But he quickly dismisses the disturbing thought. "What had happened by the river had been too important, too large for either of them to forget," he insists. "Bob must *not* have changed and, therefore, he had not." He is even able to accommodate Bob's apparent heterosexuality into his fantasy. "It would make their affair more unusual for both of them, more bind-ing," he reflects. His privileging of heterosexuality here is typical of attitudes held by everyone in the novel, especially including the gay characters, but Jim's attempt to have Bob at once heterosexual and yet involved in a homosexual affair is an act of willful illusionism even more desperate than his earlier pretenses of his own heterosex-uality. This fantasy is worthy of Shaw or Sullivan, who similarly valued Jim's presumed heterosexuality, and indicates Jim's failure to grow beyond them. Even when he comes face to face with the newly domesticated Bob in Virginia, he convinces himself despite overwhelming evidence to the contrary that Bob had not changed. "He remembered many things," Jim reassures himself, "and he would not have forgotten that day by the river and its importance."

But for all Jim's rationalizations, he is nevertheless plagued by unconscious doubts. This is made clear in the nightmares he expe-riences when he becomes ill in the army. Then he dreams of "a menacing subtly distorted Bob, who would never come near him, who always retreated when he tried to touch him." In the nightmare, the river is not placid as it had been in reality and in memory, but "rushing over tall sharp rocks." Jim is in a boat crossing the river, "but the boat was always wrecked on the sharp rocks." In the disturbing dream, the journey is never completed. This nightmare is important not merely for its anticipation of the conclusion, but also as Vidal's counter to the conscious dream constructed by Jim. In its reflection of the subconscious, the unwilled nightmare is far more real than the lovingly evoked daydream. It expresses deeply repressed fears and doubts that Jim cannot consciously acknowledge. The truth of the nightmare is verified in the grim reality of the book's violent ending.

The original conclusion is unconvincing and melodramatic, and seriously mars the novel. Disregarding the overwhelming evidence of Bob's inflexible heterosexuality and, more important, the unmistakable signs that the experience by the river had had little meaning for Bob's life, Jim obeys his heart rather than his head, only to be rejected by his friend as "nothing but a damned queer!" The unconvincing scene culminates not only in the end of Jim's love but also in his murder of Bob in sheer fury. After the violence abates, Jim kisses his dead friend and then seeks forgetfulness in drink. In the novel's final pages, the consequences of the death of the dream are sketched: "It had ended at last: that part of his life which had belonged to Bob and to all men who might have been his brothers and his lovers the way Bob had been, once, years before." Jim initially thinks that his period of homosexuality is over: "He was changed; if he was not changed he could not live for he had destroyed the most important part of his life, Bob and the legend." But he hears the roar of a brown river and "he knew that he could not change, that no dream ever ended except in a larger one and there was no larger one." The problem with Vidal's original conclusion is not merely that it is melodramatic and unbelievable. It is also as falsely romantic as the modes of thought that the novel criticizes with such cool clarity. The original ending betrays the novel's carefully cultivated stance of detached irony.

The conclusion of the 1965 revision is altogether more satisfying. Here, when Jim makes a pass at the sleeping Bob, the latter initiates the violence. A menacing Bob, his fists ready, attacks Jim, and Jim, overwhelmed by an equal mixture of rage and desire, responds by overpowering and, finally, raping his dream lover. When the violence is over, Jim wonders "Was this all?" Disillusioned and rudely awakened to his own folly, he is forced to come to grips with the discrepancy between dream and reality. In the final pages he realizes that "The lover and brother was gone, replaced by a memory of bruised flesh, torn sheets, and violence." Most important of all, instead of belaboring the past, he looks to the future: "he would ship out again and travel in strange countries and meet new people." He determines to "Begin again." Not only is the revised conclusion less melodramatic, but its muted optimism is convincing and in harmony with the rest of the novel. In the revised version, the encounter with Bob, so unlike the reunion he dreamed of, is the final and crucial step in Jim's journey toward self-knowledge. It releases him to face the future free of the false romanticism that had chained him to the past. Jim now sees his life not as a circle to be closed, but as a line to be extended.

It is no accident that, in both versions, the violence is initiated by Bob's labeling of Jim a "queer," the same epithet that Collins had hurled at him when he was unable to perform sexually with a woman in Seattle and that Jim had suppressed in his mind as "what Collins had called him." Robert Kiernan severely criticizes Jim for this sensitivity, remarking that "the absence of a more profound response to his homosexuality makes him seem vacuous, half formed, and insubstantial."[12] But one of the distinctions of *The City and the Pillar* is its recognition of the profound effect of stigma on individuals. The difficulties in the coming out process have much less to do with acceptance of homosexual desire than with adjusting to the social stigma attached to homosexuality. Words and attitudes that may seem merely reflective of conventional prejudice, and therefore of little consequence, actually have the power to cut very deeply, perhaps especially those who romanticize their attachments. Rather than evidence of a childish or simplistic reaction to his homosexuality, Jim's sensitivity to the contempt concentrated in the word *queer* (so much more wounding in American than in British usage, perhaps because the word is used more commonly and benignly in England than in America), especially coming from someone he loves, is a poignant response to the psychic assaults gay people continue to face even after having accepted their homosexuality. This sensitivity may also be testimony to the continuing and perhaps ineradicable legacy of internalized homophobia borne by gay people who have matured in an antigay society.

The City and the Pillar is a significant contribution to the literature of homosexuality in the crucial postwar decade. Although marred by a melodramatic conclusion, the novel presents an accurate and unsensationalized portrait of the gay subculture of the 1940s, and provides the best account of the coming out experience of its time. The flat, nonmoralistic narrative of a young man's journey toward a gay identity is given mythic dimension even as it becomes the occasion for a trenchant critique of the false romanticism that traps its characters at various levels of arrested development. A remarkable achievement for a twenty-one-year-old author, *The City and the Pillar* is at once a penetrating study of self-deception and an unsentimental analysis of homosexual life in the 1940s.

Vidal's novel is especially distinguished for its social approach to the question of homosexuality. Although it is couched in the form of a "coming out" story, it is also a "problem novel" that recognizes the homosexual's dilemma as a socially significant issue. Placing the plight of its ordinary young protagonist within a broad context of American values, it both reflects and reflects on the sexual attitudes of its time. Driven by its thesis that homosexuality is a normal variation of human behavior, Vidal's flatly written, nonsensationalistic gay fiction is daring simply because it so calmly reveals a simple but profound truth about human sexuality and so unsentimentally depicts the struggle toward affirmation in a hypocritical and falsely romantic society. While exposing the mendacity and ignorance of the larger American society, *The City and the Pillar* suggests that the homosexual experience is valuable in its own right. Written before the virulent homophobic backlash of the 1950s, the novel somewhat underestimates the extent and ferocity of homophobia in American society and fails to probe very deeply its sources and causes. Thus, despite its melodramatic conclusion, the novel is essentially optimistic, sustained by a belief in its own power to help reshape social attitudes.

5

Gore Vidal: The Entertainer

BERNARD F. DICK

By 1950 Gore Vidal had acquired the reputation of being the most prolific of the postwar novelists. Within a five-year period he had published *Williwaw* (1946), *In a Yellow Wood* (1947), *The City and the Pillar* (1948), *The Season of Comfort* (1940), *A Search for the King* (1950), and *Dark Green, Bright Red* (1950)—a feat literary historians of the next century might ponder as they record the palmy days of Iris Murdoch, a similarly prodigious writer who contributed almost a novel a year to the Age of Aquarius.

Since Vidal was producing so rapidly, it was inevitable that his publisher E. P. Dutton would space the publication of his novels. Their decision was understandable; Vidal had completed *The City and the Pillar* before *In a Yellow Wood* was even in galleys, and had begun *A Search for the King* in November 1947, shortly after finishing *The Season of Comfort*. A novel a year was the publishers' desideratum; it was also the golden mean between familiarity that breeds contempt and oblivion that yields no royalties.

But the idea of bringing out *A Search for the King* and *Dark Green, Bright Red* within ten months of each other did not prove especially felicitous. Readers simply did not associate Vidal with the historical romance and the espionage tale, which were new genres for him. To most readers, he was the postwar wunderkind of *Willi-waw* who turned postwar profligate with *The City and the Pillar*; but another Thomas B. Costain or Eric Ambler he was not. "My two novels were entertainments," Vidal insists. "They were invented, totally made up. But nobody at the time wanted a skill-fully told story. It was the same with *Weekend*. Who cared about a quiet comedy?" Apparently only a few, for in 1968 it lasted a little more than two weeks on Broadway; and at mid-century only a few could accept a historical novel where the women were insignificant, and a tale of revolution where the men were idle dreamers.

When an author follows an autobiographical novel with a histor-ical romance, one is tempted to regard it as a divertissement or a respite from soul-baring. But Vidal never unknotted the cord of his life; in *The Season of Comfort* he only loosened some of the nodes. While *A Search for the King* was hardly a probing of the past, it was a return to the author's boyhood—to the attic library in Senator Gore's Rock Creek Park home where Vidal ruined his eyes reading the *Congressional Record* for his grandfather's edification and *The Book of Knowledge* for his own.

As a boy, Vidal was attracted to the story of Richard the Lion-Hearted and his troubadour Blondel; as a man he decided to write a novel about it. Although *A Search for the King* was an entertain-ment, it still manifested Jim Willard's quest for a world elsewhere in which devotion between men could have a sacramental character. This theme haunts the novel like some plaintive folk motif in Bartók where the race suffers with a musical purity the *Volksgeist* could never comprehend. Loss, love, the affection of an older man for a boy, and obligatory sex with females that mocks the undemanding camaraderie of males are all part of *A Search for the King*. Vidal merely transferred his earlier preoccupations to the twelfth century.

While *A Search for the King* will always be considered one of Vidal's minor efforts, one can respect the author's attempt to inject some art into the tired formula for historical fiction; and a formula is precisely what most contemporary novelists of this school employ. Take an era like the Middle Ages; define it in terms familiar to those who learned about the Crusades from Cecil B. DeMille and about Robin Hood from Errol Flynn. Select a speech pattern somewhere between the vernacular and the archaic; call it Twentieth-Century

Quaint. Have characters indulge in molten love-making à la Frank Yerby where a woman's conical breasts are always stabbing her lover's chest with their "firepoints." And by all means, stamp every page with the .watermark of living history by using (sparingly) key words like "hauberk," "bliaut," and "paynim." The reader need not know what they mean as long as they sound medieval.

Vidal's only concession to the formula is the dialogue, which attests to his familiarity with Universal's oeuvre, particularly films like *Arabian Nights* (1942) and *Ali Baba and the Forty Thieves* (1943). When the disguised Richard senses danger, he delivers his instructions like a stone-faced Jon Hall: "'Baudoin, William, Blondel and I will travel together. The rest of you must find your way back as best you can. Present yourselves to me in London when you arrive and I shall remember you. Now separate. In God's name.'"[1]

Most historical novelists never convince the educated reader they have researched their subject. Vidal does, and he offers more than a bookish allusion or a hint of documentation for the scholars who must justify their bedtime reading. Vidal knew that the lover in Troubadour poetry served the Lady the same way the vassal served his lord:

> For the Lady was many things. . . . The Lady was the comradeship of knights. The Lady was beauty. The Lady was the mother of God. So she stood as a symbol for many things, for all the passion and all the beauty in the world. (p. 51)

Vidal also knew how the Lady was addressed; she was called "*midons*," "my lord," not "my lady," in what Leslie Fiedler termed "the natural language of subordination." Furthermore, the author, who claimed descent from the troubadour Vidal, had read enough Courtly Love lyrics to realize that while these poems seemed pure of heart and imitative of the *Ave Maria*, they actually reflected the poet's hope of committing adultery with the lady of the manor.

By selecting twelfth-century Western Europe as a potential utopia for males in quest of pure comradeship, Vidal has again anticipated Leslie Fiedler's *Love and Death in the American Novel*. Fiedler began his inquiry into the origins of sentimental love with the Middle Ages, when the Lady, the White Goddess masquerading as the Virgin Mary, reduce her male devotees to whining melancholics. While the American wilderness novel with its unsuspecting homoerotics seemed eons removed from Courtly Love poetry with its manly knights, Fiedler saw a connection between them. Both stood in awe of the Great Mother; both merged into homosexuality:

> If on the one hand the code of courtly love blurs oddly into heresy . . . on the other, it even more strangely merges with homosexuality. Indeed, one senses from the start in the verse of courtly love a desire to mitigate by ritualized and elegant foreplay a final consummation felt as brutal, or else a desire to avoid entirely any degrading conjunction with female flesh. [2]

Although *A Search for the King* appeared a decade before *Love and Death in the American Novel*, Vidal came to the same conclusions in fiction that Fiedler reached in criticism. In fact, *A Search for the King* is a perfect illustration of Fiedler's thesis about Courtly Love. Naturally Richard's troubadour would seek a boy's devotion after years of prostrating himself before the Lady. Calling a woman "my lord" for too long can blur all sexual distinctions.

Behind the Courtly Love ballads, with their endearing conventions, was a theology of marriage which Vidal understood thoroughly. When Blondel encounters a monk, the conversation turns to marriage. Brother Antonio champions what C. S. Lewis in *The Allegory of Love* called "the 'sexology' of the medieval church": "'Procreation can be accomplished without lust. . . . It should be performed as a sacred duty rather than as a source of pleasure—the motive, unhappily, of most people'" (p. 170).

The monk's warped concept of sex has left its mark on the troubadour. If love between man and woman is merely flesh against flesh, Blondel wonders whether the whole Courtly Love tradition is not fraudulent. Perhaps the lyrics he sang were only "the debris of loving," meaningless formulae threaded into pearls of poetry. No doubt the twelfth-century poet faced a similar dilemma, wondering where genuine emotion began and metaphor ended.

Vidal also differed from other practitioners of historical fiction by his approach to Richard the Lion-Hearted, whom most novelists would have made the central character. But the King was merely another amorphous male in the tradition of John Martin–Robert Holton–Jim Willard–Bill Giraud. If not Richard, then his brother

John or his mother Eleanor would qualify. While they appear, their contribution is negligible. John is the villain of melodrama, and Eleanor is an aging matriarch. The novel is about Richard's troubadour, Blondel de Néel, and his need to possess in a male the perfection of love he ascribed to the female. It is as if one were to rewrite *Don Quixote*, making Sancho the hero and consigning the Don to a secondary role.

Blondel undergoes the usual trials of the faithful servant in search of his king. He soothes semiliterate Normans with a love poem at an inn, tangles with Hedwig of Tierstein, a *donna* who is hardly a lady, seduces a peasant girl, encounters a band of werewolves who are nothing more than thieves in wolves' clothing, and barely escapes a luncheon with a giant who cannibalizes boys. Finally Blondel meets his own adoring youth, Karl, and with this love comes a reversal of roles. It is Blondel who is the beloved, and Karl who is the lover. After years of vassalage, Blondel is now the object of veneration. He is *"midons."*

In his delicate handling of the bond between the boy and the troubadour, Vidal the classicist overcomes Vidal the medievalist. Blondel and Karl do not suggest Roland and Oliver as much as they do Achilles and Patroclus. Vidal obviously prefers the *Iliad* to the *Song of Roland*.

Karl was earmarked for destruction the moment he first approached Blondel and inquired breathlessly about the military life and the troubadour's vocation. Like Patroclus, Karl yearned for the *kudos* only battle could bring. The brief time Blondel spent with the boy recalls the halcyon days of Achilles and Patroclus—afternoons of silent camaraderie and evenings with the girls from the court. This was also Achilles' world, as Homer described it in the *Iliad*. The silence of the tent he shared with Patroclus was broken only by the songs they sang of heroes. At night, each slept with a woman by his side. The bisexual goal? If so, it was only realizable in the Heroic Age where gender and sex were not synonyms.

Patroclus demanded his *aristeia*, which led to his death at the hands of Hector. Karl also sought his moment of glory and was slain in battle. When Achilles learned of his friend's death, he began a threnody that reached the depths of the sea. But Blondel is a Homeric type, not a Homeric hero. There is no lamentation; Blondel is too shattered by the day's events to exhibit grief. As he cradles the boy in his arms, a spring rain falls, and with it comes the knowledge that his youth ended with Karl's death.

Again Vidal has argued that human relationships of any kind and any era are sadly ephemeral. Within the deceptively unphilosophical framework of the romance, he wrote his *envoi* to love; but he also reworked a boyhood story about a troubadour's search for a king into a poet's search for a union he could never find with the women he serenaded and laid.

Dark Green, Bright Red was also more than a "skillfully told story." The novel reflects Vidal's vision of Guatemala, where he lived, on and off, between 1947 and 1949. It was never a popular book, although a few laudatory adjectives were culled from the reviews to form a provocative blurb. However, it was one of the author's more successful attempts to amalgamate film and fiction; Vidal "shot" Latin America in a combination of vivid Technicolor and aquatint-pastel houses in a rose-white town, jungle foliage so green it made the sunlight emerald, leaves as translucent as stained-glass windows.

The plot recalls a host of movies without resembling any specific one. On August 30, 1949, a group of the most diversified revolutionaries imaginable gathered in Tenango to restore the fallen dictator, General Alvarez, to the presidency of the Republic. *Mirabile dictu*, one of John Wayne's minor epics, *Tycoon* (1947), was set in Tenango, a half-name (e.g., Chimaltenango, Huehuetenango, Quezaltenango) so phonetically sensuous it could convince any audience it was as real as Pago Pago or Bombay.

In the best tradition of the Hollywood scenario, Alvarez is described so generally he could be Juan José Arévalo or Akim Tamiroff; he is merely a composite of popular opinion. His nineteen-year-old presidency of the Republic came to an abrupt end when he was overthrown in a student-supported coup led by Ospina, a leftist professor advocating agrarian reform. The situation is promising; no clash is more exciting than one between a Catholic (Alvarez), who has revolution in his blood because the founder of his religion was a "right-on" radical, and a Bolshevik (Ospina) to whom revolution is an article of ideology rather than of faith.

But this is a soundstage revolution that can never accomplish its goal because no one takes it seriously. The participants are contract players, loan-outs, featured actors, each of whom plays his role as if he had entrusted his meager ability to a minor director who, in turn, diminished what little talent was already there. The protagonist, if one can use the term, is Peter Nelson, a court-martialed West Pointer turned soldier of fortune for no explicable reason. He is twenty-six, the mean age of the male in the early novels, vaguely defined and uninteresting. Nelson is John Martin in a cadre, Robert Holton trying to be *engagé* in Latin America, Bill Giraud drilling natives because the script calls for it. Peter's goal is hardly the social betterment of the working class; he "wanted money" and in this respect his values scarcely differ from Holton's.

Then there are the General's children, José and Elena. José is the stereotyped Latin jealously guarding his sister's virtue from the excitable Nelson who, one knows, will possess her before the novel ends. For a Catholic, Elena is not exactly the sacrificial type. She prefers the cultural life of New Orleans, where the family spent two comfortable years in exile, to the artistic cloaca of Tenango. Her *engagement* is so disarmingly vapid that one can accept her only as a parody of an ingenue. She defends her father with the flighty logic of an English major who discovered her social conscience in Ethnic Studies 101: "'Oh, but he wasn't a dictator! At least he wasn't like Hitler or Mussolini, not that kind at all. He was a very *special* kind of President. You see, since so few of the people read and write, people need somebody to look after them . . . somebody like Father.'"[3]

Every Latin American cadre should have an intellectual and a buffoon priest—the former for witty repartee, the latter for comic relief. The intellectual is Charles de Cluny, Noël Coward turned radical in middle age; de Cluny convinced himself he was a product of postwar disillusionment, renounced fiction, and became a speech writer for Alvarez. The priest is Father Miguel, an asthmatic with a blackhead-pitted nose who delivers panegyrics to Mother Church to justify his none-too-selfless role in the revolution. Let's not forget the Billie Burke type, Mrs. Eggleton, the wealthy American living in Tenango, gushing and scatterbrained. And at some point a living paradox should appear, to confirm the popular belief that revolutions are the last stronghold of heterogeneity. Enter an Oklahoma newspaperman whose burning ambition is to produce the definitive translation of Aristophanes' *The Birds*.

So much for the heroes. The villains are an enigmatic duo, Mr. Green and his nephew George, of the "Company." If one interprets the "Company" in the right way, the green-red symbolism becomes apparent: these were the colors of the original Ugly American, the United Fruit Company, which Pablo Neruda called "the dictatorship of the flies" in one of his poems. The Greens, who seemed to support the General's Catholic Socialist Party, were really in league with Ospina. Ospina gave Alvarez his brief gaudy hour because he knew the General would try to take the Republic by force and in so doing would expose himself as an anarchist. When the revolution collapses, the cast disperses, the flats are struck, and Peter Nelson leaves Tenango humming a popular song in another of Vidal's bluebird endings.

A revised *Dark Green, Bright Red*, of which Vidal is especially proud, came out a few months after the 1968 riots at Columbia and the Sorbonne. Measured against the revolutionary spirit of the late sixties, when the kids stepped into roles their elders were glad to relinquish and played out an unresolved scenario to its denouement of ennui, *Dark Green, Bright Red* is more of a parody of revolution than a novel of or about it. Its cynicism, which is not tempered in the revision, underscores Vidal's point that no one is selfless enough to make the revolution work. Even Alvarez, anti-Commie that he is, argues for keeping up with the times: "'The world is moving to the Left, my friends. I move with the world, just as the Republic must'" (p. 16).

Which side is anyone on? At times the novel seems to be more about a political convention than a takeover in a banana republic. Or perhaps there is no difference.

Dark Green, Bright Red is proof that Vidal "killed off" Hemingway and the telegraphic style. If the novel is a parody of revolution, then Peter Nelson of the wholesome name is a parody of the Hemingway hero. Exactly what the Ohio-born, ex-West Pointer is doing in Tenango is never explained. José Alvarez, an army buddy, invited him there, and having been court-martialed recently, Nelson accepted. Yet Nelson is totally uncommitted to the revolution or to anything. When he finally beds down with Elena, the pink and gold of the sky change to a sullen red as the two of them writhe with the frustration of novices aligning their bodies for intercourse. The unsatisfying attempt at sex is a metaphor for the revolution that was intended to unite men of varying backgrounds but only succeeded in separating them.

In the 1950 *Dark Green, Bright Red*, Vidal, who would later call himself a liberal Democrat, ridiculed political tags like "liberal" and "conservative"; in the 1968 revision, he darkened the so-called shades of meaning in "left" and "right" into shadows of confusion. When George Green tries to give Peter a clearer picture of General Alvarez's politics, he sounds like someone trying to explain the difference between William F. Buckley, Jr., and David Susskind:

> George looked suddenly fierce. "They want this whole place to go Commie, and it will if they keep meddling. They don't realize that these people are much better off with somebody like Alvarez . . . than with a half-baked intellectual like Ospina who isn't even a proper Commie; he just dislikes Rightwingers, which makes him what they call a liberal."
> "Confusing. So Alvarez is the Right—"
> "But has to pretend he's Left."
> "And Ospina's the Center—"
> "But is really Left, but pink not red."
> "Then who is the real Left?"
> "What they call intellectuals." (p. 62)

6

The Vidalian Manner: The Judgment of Paris, Two Sisters, Kalki

ROBERT F. KIERNAN

Gore Vidal is a difficult writer to categorize because he is a man of several voices. He has brooded over ancient empires in several novels, as though he were possessed by the spirit of Edward Gibbon, yet he has also written about the American *crise de virilité* and managed to sound a good deal like Hemingway. He has sent young Americans in search of Old Europe, as a dutiful son of Henry James, but he has also written novels about the American political system and acknowledged a debt to Henry Adams. In his essays he often seems like Lord Macaulay, magisterial and urbane, while in the Breckinridge novels he evokes Ronald Firbank, irrepressible and playful.

Nevertheless, there are aspects of Vidal's writing that are constant. Syntactically elegant sentences are a trademark, certainly, and understated structures and a coolness of tone are too. More than anything else, however, we have learned to expect amplitude from Vidal. We have learned to expect that his narratives will be enriched with gossip, incidental satire, self-mockery, and philosophical and historical asides, very much in the eighteenth-century mode of Laurence Sterne and other giants of the early English novel. Concomitantly, we have learned to expect antique literary forms from

Vidal, as if they were necessary to accommodate this old-world amplitude. Thus, his writings include historical fiction, moral essays, nonsense tales, mythography, and apocalyptic parables.

But Vidal is as much prankster as pundit, and his elegance, coolness, and learning derive a special piquancy from a wit always at the ready. "I am at heart a propagandist," he has written of himself, "a tremendous hater, a tiresome nag, complacently positive that there is no human problem which could not be solved if people would simply do as I advise."[1] There, in a sentence, is the Vidalian manner: the arrogance of the pundit solemnly and unabashedly put forth but undercut and put in amenable focus by the prankster's wit.

The Judgment of Paris (1952, revised 1965) is in several ways typical of Vidal's novels. Its central character is Philip Warren, a twenty-eight-year-old American just graduated from Harvard Law School, who dallies in Europe for a year with the intention of deciding at leisure what to do with the rest of his life. Three women dominate this *Wanderjahr*, and each suggests a different mode of life that Philip might pursue. He meets the first woman, Regina Durham, in Rome. She is a behind-the-scenes power in American politics, and she offers to create a major political career for Warren, not merely because she enjoys his bed but because she would enjoy managing his life. He meets the second woman, Sophia Oliver, in Egypt. An archaeologist, she advises Warren to undertake a dispassionate intellectual life, reasoning that ideas are more real and more lasting than the thinkers who conceive them. The third woman, Anna Morris, Warren follows to Paris after an encounter in Cairo. She is the wife of an American businessman, and she offers Warren occasional intimacies and love. At the end of the novel Warren rejects both Regina's public life and Sophia's intellectual life in favor of Anna's offerings, even though he knows that she will never leave her husband and that he may never see her again.

As the title of the novel suggests, its tripartite plot is based loosely on the incident in Greek mythology in which Hermes brings the goddesses Hera, Athena, and Aphrodite to Paris so that he may judge which is the most beautiful. Hera, the wife of Zeus, offers Paris kingship in return for his vote, and Athena, the goddess of war, offers him skill in battle (Vidal chooses to emphasize Athena's equally important role as the goddess of wisdom). It is of course Aphrodite, the goddess of love, whom Paris chooses, just as Philip finally chooses Anna's love.

It is entirely typical of Vidal that he treats this important aspect of his novel unimportantly and more or less ignores its ideational structure. Indeed, Warren chooses only superficially among the power, knowledge, and love that his three women dangle before him, for Regina's life of power and Sophia's life of knowledge hold no allure for him, and he has no illusion that the world would be well lost for Anna's will-o'-the-wisp love. What Warren really chooses—almost consciously—is to step out of himself for the first time in his life and to connect vitally with another human being. Having a considerable fear of death, a marked distaste for physical contact, and some reluctance even to be understood, he senses accurately that he holds his selfhood too tightly and that his future should involve more than the self-aggrandizement that Regina and Sophia would foster. As he turns to Anna in the last paragraph of the novel, it is significant that a mirror dissolves mystically before his eyes, "dispelling its ungrieved ghosts like smoke upon the night," and that he passes beyond that narcissistic mirror into a "promise at the present's furthest edge."

At the climax of his *Wanderjahr*, then, Warren chooses between two kinds of psychic orientation, not among the more obvious choices arrayed in the mythic analogue. Since the myth coincides with Warren's psyche so imperfectly, one even wonders whether Vidal means to disparage the modernist belief that mythology provides a gloss for every psychological state. I think it more likely that Vidal is simply not very interested in his plot, especially since Warren's decision to relax his hold on selfhood has little dramatic substance and is scarcely more successful than the myth in holding the novel together. Vidal typically understates his plots, in fact, as if plotting were alien to his auctorial sensibility. When he does not under*state* the plots, he is apt to under*mine* them, parodying the need for plot.

Vidal understates his main characters, too. Philip Warren is a rather dim young man, not exactly naïve but amenable to the point of vacuity. Regina Durham is a decently rounded character, but Sophia Oliver never engages the reader's interest, and Anna Morris is hardly characterized at all. On the basis of such understatement, the critic John W. Aldridge has likened *The Judgment of Paris* and the novels that precede it to badly balanced darts thrown at a moving target. "They have never been entirely successful because they have never known precisely where they were supposed to go," Aldridge wrote in 1952, voicing an opinion of Vidal's novels still current today. "Too many of them appear to have been written not out of a deep urge in Vidal to get something said, but out of a disturbing suspicion that, having missed the target the first time, he had better throw another dart."[2]

The metaphor is shrewd, but I find Aldridge unduly puristic in censuring the early novels simply because Vidal has no overriding passion to vent, no overriding vision to impart. A less solemn notion of the writer's obligation would suggest that Vidal treats his typical story line rather like a clothesline, hanging on the story line whatever turns up in his literary hamper. There is an abundance of both minor plots and minor characters in *The Judgment of Paris*, certainly, none of which has much to do with the novel's larger plot and all of which hang rather shapelessly on the line—but each is in itself a marvelous bit of color, an objet trouvé, as it were.

In the first section of the novel, Warren becomes entangled with the homosexual dilettantes Clyde Norman and Lord Ayre Glenellen and their mad plot to restore the Italian monarchy. Acting as Glenellen's reluctant courier, Warren tries to deliver a message to the eccentric Signor Guisardo, who affects animal masks as a disguise. Warren makes an appointment to deliver his message in the ruins of a mountain chapel at midnight, but Guiscardo fails to keep this Gothic assignation, and an animal mask abandoned in the ruins is the only clue that some mysterious fate has befallen him. The message entrusted to Warren is melodramatically cryptic: it is the single Greek word *asebia*, which connotes a failure to worship the gods. Glenellen subsequently denies having sent the message, of course, and in a dazzling turnabout abandons his campaign to restore the house of Savoy and becomes, illogically, a communist. He surfaces again in the third section of the novel as part of a ludicrous transvestite cult that revolves around an androgyne known alternately as Augusta and Augustus.

The flip-flop inconsequence of all this is not without point. The string of incidents is both a parody of spy fiction and a camp trivialization of homosexualist interests, and it is ultimately an attack on the literary mystique of plot, inasmuch as the Norman-Glenellen axis of events succeeds as a kind of plot despite its alogical seriality.

Each of the two later sections of the novel has a string of events that similarly defies the mystique of plot. The Egypt section introduces a man named Briggs Willys who is afflicted with taedium vitae but cannot manage to organize a suicide despite several sincere attempts. He therefore engages Mrs. Fay Peabody, a doyenne of detective fiction, to dispatch his very considerable flesh. Regarding the assignment as a challenge to her plotting ability (she is Agatha Christie, thinly disguised), Mrs. Peabody sets in motion a series of harebrained murder schemes that evoke the airier flights of the locked-room detection novel. All of them, of course, fail dismally. The Paris section of the novel deals not only with the cult of the androgyne, in which Glenellen's plotting instinct finds an outlet in a pseudoreligious vesting ritual, but also with the plots of a stupendously vulgar hostess named Zoe Helotius to crash the royal house of Windsor. Mrs. Helotius is as mad in her own way as Mrs. Peabody, Lord Glenellen, and Signor Guiscardo, and such highly colored characters throw Warren's bland sanity into nice relief, just as their madcap plots flatter the understatement of the novel's main plot.

Indeed, this understatement of the main plot allows Vidal to expend a wealth of invention on minor characters without creating an aesthetic imbalance. The octogenarian Duchesse de Lyon et Grenoble, who grandly mishears everything that is said to her; a Russian spy who pretends to be an Indian princess and speaks of herself in the third person under the impression that she is using the royal plural; a field marshal who tears apart prize roses, pace Dickens: all are bits of color in the novel's bright motley. Vidal's understated plot also allows him to adorn the novel with a wealth of interesting asides, such as Warren's speculation that energetic mediocrity is politically more useful in a republican society than brilliance, wit, or passion, and Mr. Norman's speculation that Europe's old-world manners would have expired long since had it not been for the unexpected applause of the Western cousins.

Even more important, perhaps, the understatement of the basic story line allows relatively free rein to Vidal's wit. He has a great deal of fun with homosexuality and spoofs the reputation as homosexual novelist that *The City and the Pillar* had earned him. His joke is that Philip Warren is relentlessly *hetero*sexual, although homosexuals dominate the circles he moves in. Vidal even sends Warren to a male brothel, where Glenellen purchases a handsome youth for him and leaves him to his pleasure, very much to Warren's embarrassment and Vidal's arch amusement:

> It would be startling to report that the stalwart Philip succumbed to pagan vice, that the habits of his maturity were in an instant undone by this classic figure which, against his will, he found himself admiring. But we must remain true to the fact of Philip's character and report, truthfully, that nothing happened.

Vidal's fine impudence vis-à-vis the conventional aesthetics of the novel is particularly evident in his revival of three characters from earlier novels—Robert Holton from *In a Yellow Wood*, Jim Willard from *The City and the Pillar*, and Charles de Cluny from *Dark Green, Bright Red*—all of whom play insignificant roles in *The Judgement of Paris*. It is Vidal's tongue-in-cheek conceit, I suspect, that he is writing something on the order of a Faulknerian saga, a massive roman-fleuve, perhaps. But these resuscitated characters are so many red herrings to send us off in search of the grand design of a life's work that has no grand design but is rather a series of colorful moments, pleasantly and wittily arranged—rags of narrative, perhaps, but sequined rags that flash nicely on the clothesline. In short, Vidal's talent is for the small scene, not the large design, and for the sketch that tends toward caricature rather than the full-dress portrait. *The Judgment of Paris* is the first of Vidal's novels to showcase this orientation of his narrative gifts, and it must be accounted the first of his mature works.[3]

Two Sisters (1970) is also typical in several ways of Vidal's oeuvre but at a higher level of art than *The Judgment of Paris*. Subtitled "A

Novel in the Form of a Memoir" on its jacket and subtitled teasingly "A Memoir in the Form of a Novel" on its title page, the story is related by an autobiographical V. who dallies with a former mistress named Marietta Donegal in Rome in 1968. After they discuss the critics' reaction to *Myra Breckinridge* V.'s most recent novel, the former lovers reminisce about Paris in the 1940s and about a pair of extraordinarily beautiful twins, Eric and Erika Van Damm, who were among their acquaintances at the time. Marietta has in her possession a film script which the recently deceased Eric had written in 1948, and V. reads it at her request, together with Eric's journal, to judge whether it is worth the $100,000 Marietta hopes to command for it. *Two Sisters* consequently takes the form of nested stories. At its center is the complete text of Eric's screenplay, entitled "Two Sisters of Ephesus"; enveloping the screenplay is the text of Eric's 1948 journal, which is addressed to Erika; and enclosing both is V.'s narrative, which not only frames Eric's manuscripts but regularly interrupts them so that V. can interject a query, a differing recollection, or an anecdote.

Eric's screenplay is set in the fourth century B.C. and deals with the sibling rivalry of Helena, a widow of the Great King of Persia, and Artemisa, the widow of a demoted Carian satrap. The various attempts of the two sisters each to outshine the other reach a climax when Artemisa announces her imminent marriage to Achoris, the richest man in the world. Helena is indignant because she had been planning to marry Achoris herself, and to upstage her sister she therefore commits suicide. But Eric shifts the focus of the screenplay at this point to the sisters' half brother, Herostratus, who has been conspiring to free Ephesus from Persian domination. When Herostratus realizes that his sisters' rivalry has led to the betrayal of his conspiracy, he avenges himself by setting fire to the Temple of Diana during Artemisa's nuptials, thereby outstripping the sisters' bid for notoriety with a more egregious bid of his own. "So remember me, that I do not die," he intones solemnly to future generations at the end of the film script. "Forget the two sisters of Ephesus for what are they but simply witnesses to Herostratus? who burned the temple of Diana which was the wonder of the earth."

Eric's journal deals with situations as exotic as those in the film script. He talks in veiled terms about a standoff with V., who would like to share Eric's bed but has to settle for Erika's, and he talks in terms even more veiled about his incestuous relationship with Erika, with whom he has fathered a child. In a lighter vein, he talks about his dealings with a libidinous Hollywood mogul named Morris Murray, who wants to turn "Two Sisters of Ephesus" into a bubble-bath classic.

But the immediate impact of *Two Sisters* derives not so much from its miscellaneous exotica as from the reader's sense that the novel is a roman à clef. V. is of course Vidal himself, and the novel is replete with autobiographical allusions to the novels Vidal has written, to his more established opinions, and to his family and friends. Many of these allusions have the charm of self-parody. Eric notes in his journal, for instance, that "V. is as sharp about the motives of others as he is evasive about his own," and V. is several times brought up short by Eric's low opinion of Vidal's novels. V. even serves up the Bouvier sisters, Jacqueline Onassis and Lee Radziwill, with whom Vidal shares a stepfather. In an allusion to Nina Auchincloss Steers, to whom the novel is dedicated, he says:

> As if being my sister was not sufficient burden she is also stepsister to the two most successful adventuresses of our time. For someone with a virtuous (in the ancient sense) disposition, to be associated with that never-ending soap opera is a curious punishment. She is also the heroine of a droll revision of the Cinderella story: the two wicked stepsisters move in and take over Cinderella's house; then one marries Prince Charming and the other marries a second Prince Charming, leaving Cinderella to settle down to a quiet life with a good citizen.

The sisters Bouvier, however, receive much less attention on the roman à clef level of the novel than the diarist Anaïs Nin, one of Vidal's early friends in the literary establishment and the model for Marietta Donegal. Marietta talks at length about releasing the inhibitions and about "flowing" as a mode of life, very much in Nin's vague manner, and all the confidences Marietta seeks out are so much raw material for her public diary, just as such confidences were for Nin. "To be candid with Marietta means to be fixed for all times in the distorting aspic of her prose," V. observes wryly, and Vidal takes his revenge for Nin's disclosure of some of his confidences[4] by suggesting that Marietta's fame is based on a lifetime of kiss and tell:

> At eighty she will still be making love and writing about it in that long autobiography which begins with our century and will, I am certain, last well into the next for, like it or not, we live in *her* age—was she not the mistress of D. H. Lawrence (two volumes hardly described the three—or was it four?—times she bedded that ensorcelled genius) as well as the beloved inspiration—and brutal seducer—of so many other writers, painters, sculptors and even one President, though whether it was sunrise or sunset at Campobello has never been entirely clear (out of admiration for Eleanor Roosevelt she has yet to give us the entire story).

Other celebrities are alluded to under their real names in anecdotes that one presumes are sketched, from life. "Of all the power-lovers I have known Eleanor Roosevelt was the most divided and so the most interesting," V. comments, and he goes on to tell of a dinner party celebrating the fall of Carmine de Sapio at which Mrs. Roosevelt revealed a surprising vengefulness. An anecdote Vidal tells about the "beat" novelist Jack Kerouac set the gossip columns humming. "I have usually found that whenever I read about an occasion where I was present, the report (except once) never tallies with my own," he says as a prelude to elaborating that anecdote—an occasion described by Kerouac in *The Subterraneans* (1958) and perfectly recalled, V. says, "until the crucial moment when Jack and I went to bed together at the Chelsea Hotel." An especially bewitching anecdote commemorates Vidal's visit to André Gide in 1948; another commemorates a still-extant brothel Marcel Proust set up for an Algerian boy friend.

Because it is host to a wealth of such anecdotes and allusions, *Two Sisters*, like *The Judgment of Paris*, is vintage Vidal. But because the novel's plot, typically, is almost swamped by such asides, one must wonder whether Vidal is at heart an essayist, as many of his critics theorize. It is undeniable, I suppose, that one of the greatest pleasures of Vidal's fiction is the fine essayistic excursus. One enjoys the asides on Eleanor Roosevelt and on the brothels of Paris, for instance, quite independently of the novels that embody them; the urbane rendering of the asides is a complete and sufficient pleasure. If the pleasure of such moments were all that *Two Sisters* offered, one would have to agree that Vidal mistakes his genre.

But the novel's plot is not quite swamped by asides, and *Two Sisters* is somewhat more than an anthology of fine essayistic excursus, as it is somewhat more than a roman à clef. The novel makes a firm appeal to the aesthetic sense inasmuch as the screenplay, Eric's journal, and V.'s commentary echo each other to such a degree that the three narratives seem to replicate a single story line. Herostratus' relationship to Helena echoes Eric's relationship to Erika, for instance, and Vidal's evident affection for his half sister strikes a resonant chord on the auctorial level. The Bouvier rivalry echoes significantly with the Helena-Artemisa rivalry, especially when we recall that Artemisa marries the richest man in the world after a resonant widowhood; and Herostratus has even aspired to be a playwright, like Eric and like Vidal. A motif of fiery death is of especial importance in unifying the three levels of the narrative. Just as Herostratus' setting fire to Diana's temple is tantamount to committing suicide, so Eric apparently commits suicide by plunging into a burning building, as if his fictional surrogate had enacted his fate before him. There is even a passage in which V. dreams of his father, cremated the winter before, and sees bright flames where his eyes should have been. "Ultimate fate of watery creatures in a fiery universe," he murmurs in epitaph, and in the last paragraph of the novel he reflects on Eric's death in a way that suggests that these fiery correspondences are the novel's central point:

> So at the end, fire. What else? For the three of us and all the others, too, when time stops and the fiery beast falls upon itself to begin again as dust-filled wind, without memory or you, Herostratus.

In light of such correspondences, we must conclude that the story of Herostratus and his sisters is the transposed story of Eric and Erika and that the story of V. and Marietta is the transposed story of Vidal and his stepsisters. The correspondences are loose, but no looser than the roman à clef correspondences, and the looseness of these large correspondences seems to be a contrived effect, suggesting what the mirroring subtitles of the novel hint: that any novel—*Two Sisters* in particular—is virtually a hall of mirrors, with a lonely auctorial self flashing agitated signals down the corridors of memory and imagination. Whether the author is created by his own imagination, or the other way around, is his unresolved problem. That the characters are only his projections of himself is a disturbing possibility. A terrible sense of metaphysical loss is the burden of the auctorial condition, Vidal seems to say, for the agitated flashing of reflections—memoir to novel and novel to memoir, each tending to transmute into the other—involves an irredeemable loss of everything that is private and personal. Indeed, the novel has its most telling moments in passages that eulogize losses tantamount to the loss of self—the suicide of Eric, the death of Vidal's father, the end of youth:

> Death, summer, youth—this triad contrives to haunt me every day of my life for it was in summer that my generation left school for war, and several dozen that one knew (but strictly speaking did not love, except perhaps for one) were killed, and so never lived to know what I have known—the Beatles, black power, the Administration of Richard Nixon—all this has taken place in a trivial after-time and has nothing to do with anything that really mattered, with summer and someone hardly remembered, a youth—not Eric—so abruptly translated from vivid, well-loved (if briefly) flesh to a few scraps of bone and cartilage scattered among the volcanic rocks of Iwo Jima. So much was cruelly lost and one still mourns the past, particularly in darkened movie houses, weeping at bad films, or getting drunk alone while watching the Late Show on television as our summer's war is again refought and one sees sometimes what seems to be a familiar face in the battle scenes—is it Jimmy? But the image is promptly replaced and one will never know whether it was he or only a member of the Screen Actors Guild, now grown old, too. [5]

The ultimate subject of *Two Sisters* is dividedness. Just as V. longs fruitlessly for union with Eric, his auctorial alter ego, so Eric longs for union with Erika, his feminine alter ego, and with Herostratus, his activist alter ego, and so on, ad infinitum; all modes of such longing reflect the cravings of Plato's animus for a wholeness dimly recalled. Dividedness seems to subsume almost every aspect of *Two Sisters* and of Vidal's entire oeuvre. The struggle of Vidal's essayistic moments against his narrative forms is perhaps its ultimate foregrounding, but dividedness subsumes as well the yearning of his characters to overcome their inevitable estrangement from one another, the aspiration of his adults to touch again the dead hand of childhood, the instinctive attraction of his dispassionate observers to his men of power, and the clash in his own manner between the prankster and the pundit.

It must be remembered, however, that this dialectic is itself only one half of Vidal's art. The civilized high jinks, the mordant roman à clef, and the anecdotal billets-doux remain a vital part of *Two Sisters*, *The Judgment of Paris*, and the great body of Vidal's fiction. Half grimace, half high spirits, the wry smile is Vidal's most telling expression.

The mix of ingredients in *Kalki* (1978) is also typical of Vidal's fiction, although the novel is somewhat less successful than *Two Sisters* or even *The Judgment of Paris*. The narrator of this dooms-day odyssey is Teddy Ottinger, a plainspoken, bisexual aviatrix, a feminist who can boast of cauterized tubes, alimony payments to her ex-husband, and a best-selling autobiography, *Beyond Mother-hood*. Because she is behind in her alimony payments, Teddy agrees at her agent's behest to fly to India and interview James J. Kelly, a Vietnam veteran who has styled himself "Kalki" and claims to be the last avatar of the Hindu god Vishnu. Ever vulnerable to physical beauty, Teddy is quickly smitten by the golden blondness of both Kalki and his wife Lakshmi, the former Doris Pannicker. Vaguely in love with the two of them, she is persuaded to sign on as Kalki's personal pilot and to become part of a cadre that includes Geraldine O'Connor, an MIT biochemist, and Giles Lowell, a medical doctor also known as R. S. Ashok, Ph.D. Kalki declares that the five of them are Perfect Masters and will preside over the end of the world when Siva the Destroyer, one of Vishnu's manifestations, brings human life to an end. He even sets a precise date for doomsday— April 3.

Teddy is more difficult to seduce intellectually than aesthetically, however, and she retains deep misgivings about Kalki and his cult, not only because of her atheism but because of persistent rumors that the cult camouflages a major drug operation. The cult is indeed supported by drug sales, but Kalki sincerely believes that he is Vishnu, and he fully intends to terminate human life. After a major publicity campaign, including the elaborately staged murder of a

Kalki look-alike, Kalki performs Siva's Dance of Eternity on April 3; when he is finished, everyone in the world is dead except for the five Perfect Masters. Teddy later discovers that she was the agent of death. On Kalki's orders, she had spread a lethal bacteria throughout the world via her airplane without knowing what she was doing. Like the other Perfect Masters, she survives the virus because she had been inoculated against its effects.

The five survivors organize their subsequent lives first in New York, then in Paris, and finally in Washington, where Kalki and Lakshmi take up residence in the White House. Gradually, Teddy realizes the fullness of Kalki's mad plot. Because Giles, Geraldine, and she are all sterile, Kalki and Lakshmi will be the parents of a new human race, and Kalki will thus play Vishnu the Creator as well as Siva the Destroyer. But Giles, the villain of the novel, has another scenario in mind. He carefully neglects to inform Kalki and Lakshmi that their blood types are incompatible, and after their first child is stillborn, he further neglects the steps necessary to ensure the safety of future births. Not really sterile at all, he plans to replace Kalki in Lakshmi's bed and himself father the new race. Kalki kills him as soon as he realizes the situation, however, thereby ending all hopes for the continuation of the species. The four survivors live out their life spans quietly, with Teddy working on the written record that is the novel. Kalki is the last to die, as he tells us in a postscript to Teddy's text. In a last gesture of divine magnanimity, he bequeaths Earth to the monkeys.

As this synopsis suggests, *Kalki* is a very modish novel. Laboratory-controlled genetics, ecological disaster, jet-set travel, entropy, Eastern religions, birth control, bisexuality, violence, drugs, feminist tracts, Walter Cronkite presiding benignly over the mix—*Kalki* has them all. As an aviatrix with no fear of flying, Teddy seems to be reconstituted from Erica Jong's popular novel *Fear of Flying* (1973), and the Kalki cult suggests in many ways the followers of the Korean evangelist Sun Myung Moon who were so much in evidence during the 1970s.

This modishness tends to create satiric effects even when it is merely true to life. Teddy's mother-in-law is rather proud of the possibility that she has cancer, for instance, regarding the "Big C" as a status symbol outranking even the "Big O" in the alphabetics of the decade. Hollywood's most successful pitchwoman has a gallbladder-shaped pool with imitation gallstones on the bottom—a play on kidney-shaped pools, circa 1940, in the overdone style of 1970s wit. A technical director of the television show *60 Minutes* assures Teddy that he is giving Kalki's doomsday announcement major attention, "maybe ten, ten and a half, maybe even eleven minutes, you know, an in-depth study." Government agencies are satirized more cavalierly though not untowardly. Both the Drug Enforcement Administration and its watchdog committee in the Senate have as their goal the increased sale of drugs all over the world, we are assured, since without such enterprise they would not be funded. CIA agents misrepresent themselves so consistently that Teddy is willing to believe that Giles is *not* with the CIA only when he says that he *is*. An IRS accountant explains, somewhat madly, "We at the IRS never assume that anyone is innocent until he is proven guilty."

Because this preposterous farrago is essentially the 1970s scene, hardly exaggerated at all, Vidal seems to be following the principle laid down by some black humorists that contemporary realities are so innately absurd that to write comic fantasy one need only straightforwardly report things as they are. Certainly Vidal has never done less to enhance his satire than in this novel. The stylized syntax that focuses a satiric point, the commentary that elaborates the point, lending it emphasis, grace, and dispassion, all the rhetorical tricks that make Vidal's usual satire a deadly but elegant cocktail are eschewed in *Kalki* in favor of mere exposure—murder by suicide, as it were. It is a valid technique, of course, especially for a humorist in a black mood, for it suggests that things as they are merit neither wit nor stylization. It is ultimately a nihilistic kind of satire, perhaps the most difficult kind to achieve successfully.

Teddy Ottinger is an appropriate vehicle for such satire, for she is determinedly unsentimental and carefully unfeeling, as bland a consciousness as a nihilist could wish. Meeting her ex-husband after a long interval, she says,

> I must have felt *something* for him once, I thought, staring through the martini's first comforting haze at my ex-husband's pale double chin.
> Tears came to my eyes. There were tears in his eyes, too. Love?

Tenderness? Regret? No. It was the red-alert smog, creeping up the Santa Monica canyon from the Pacific Freeway.

On being told that she has killed four billion people, Teddy's only reaction is to look in a mirror and check that her face is suitably blank, although she confesses later to a modest depression. It is perhaps not surprising that she considers herself "in heat" rather than "in love" when she thinks of Kalki, but it is surprising that for all her vaunted love of flying, she never once conveys the ecstasy of flight. Vidal quashes all vibrancy in Teddy because if she were more vital, she would be less likely to think the Earth well rid of her kind. But as it is, Teddy and Geraldine sit in New York City's Bryant Park shortly before The End and watch a "parade of monsters" that Teddy happily consigns to oblivion:

> Drunk, drugged, mad, they staggered past us, talking to themselves. I thought it very apt that on a building opposite us was one of the KALKI, THE END billboards. I could not imagine any of these people wanting to go on.

In fact, Teddy's assent to Kalki's genocide is implicit in a number of her remarks: "But then [if I were God] I would not have gone to the trouble of inventing the human race"; "I did not believe that Kalki would switch off the human race . . . as desirable a happening as that might be." Like Vidal, she sees no point to a world in which matrons pride themselves on their cancer operations and derelicts await the apocalypse on park benches. Nothing is really worth saving, she believes, and the novel goes beyond the usual limits of doomsday fiction, therefore, by saving nothing, not even Teddy.

A nihilistic point of view is never far from the surface of Vidal's art, but nowhere else in the oeuvre is it expressed by such an understated technique. And if *Kalki* is less successful than the other novels of Vidal's maturity, the reason is simply that its low intensity is inconsistent with Vidal's gifts, which run to high style and flashing wit. Too many of *Kalki's* modish allusions waste a satiric potential. The Katmandu ashram is wired with muzak, but Teddy's only response is to observe that the tapes are out of date. The enervating blandness of the muzak receives no verbal attention, nor does its inappropriateness in a Hindu monastery, although Vidal surely intends these points to score satirically. Similarly, when the five survivors meet to plan the education of the next generation, they agree immediately to reject the new math but plan no further. Fair enough, perhaps, but is it really enough? As one longs to have Vidal elaborate on the vapidness of the muzak, so one longs for him to strike sparks from the new-math debacle and to devise a total education that would savage contemporary schooling.

One always has the impression that the text of *Kalki* is straining to escape its straightforward manner. In particular, Vidal is unable to resist adding touches to Teddy's character that are ultimately functionless yet suggest that she might have been more interesting had her nihilistic straitjacket allowed it. Teddy is a great fan of Antoine de Saint-Exupéry's aviation literature, for instance, and she agrees with his interesting notion that the natural aviator is a fascist, determined to be outside, above, and beyond the human race. Does she then secretly long for Kalki's apocalypse because it places her in this superior position? Is her expressed distaste both for the apocalypse and for continued existence hypocritical? Teddy is also a devotee of the aviatrix Amelia Earhart, which on the face of things is natural enough, but she also dreams that Earhart is her mother. Her real mother, an embittered, jealous woman, committed suicide the day Teddy won a prestigious aviation trophy, and so Earhart is clearly her mother's surrogate. Thus, when we are told that Teddy started sleeping with older women after her mother's death, we assume that she was both reaching out to her dead mother and searching for Earhart.

Complicating this strand of meaning still further, Vidal tends to merge with Teddy, for he too was estranged from his mother, and his father was one of Earhart's friends. Is Vidal foregrounding himself, then, and admitting to a wish fantasy that Earhart were *his* mother? Conceivably, but as soon as one admits such provocative strands of meaning in the text of *Kalki*, things fall apart. One demands a connection that does not exist between Teddy's search for a mother and her involvement with Kalki. One demands a more elaborate connection between Teddy's fly-girl fascism and the coolness with which she faces The End. One demands a connection, more autobiographically explicable, between Vidal and his fiction.

The novel's style has something of the same problem. Teddy is acutely aware of the clichés with which her prose is burdened and apologizes for them ad nauseam, as if the deterioration of language alone justified man's extermination. Yet her narrative has moments of stylistic gold. About the end of the human race, for instance, Teddy says with eloquent simplicity, "You cannot mourn everyone. Only someone." And in a rare moment of wit she remarks, "I was able to read the odd page by Joan Didion, the even page by Renata Adler," efficiently making the point that she can read neither.

This failure of *Kalki* to abide by its chosen ineloquence suggests once again that Vidal's genius is for the quick effect, not the sustained technique, for the clothesline, not the story line. Typically, the larger techniques of *Kalki* fall prey to Vidal's impulses of the moment, and so we have those sudden elaborations of character and golden phrases that are marvelous in themselves but discountenance the ploys of the larger fiction. Perhaps this is why Vidal's first-person narratives are generally more successful than his third-person narratives and why the imaginary journal, requiring so little in the way of plot, has proven his most successful narrative form, *Kalki* excepted. In short, Vidal's particular gifts demand an open narrative form that will host many narrative postures. Think of the joke about the chameleon suffering a nervous breakdown on the bolt of plaid cloth. Because he is a sort of chameleon, Vidal is equally at odds with intricate patterns.

7

A *Note* on *Vidal's* Messiah

ALAN CHEUSE

Americans don't have ideas, they experience them . . . No ideas
but in things . . . He had a mind so fine no idea could penetrate
it . . . Such is the unconventional wisdom of our century, expressed by some of our finest writers, about the relationship of ideas
to the American work of art. Given this context the only labor more
difficult than composing an authentic American novel of ideas
might be that of recognizing it when it comes along.

Gore Vidal's *Messiah*, his sixth novel and a pivotal work within
the canon of his production, had no such luck. After its hardcover
publication in 1954, it soon appeared in paperback under the Ballantine imprint, which specialized in science fiction books. Better
read than dead, you might say, but this format undoubtedly skewed
the possible additional audience for a novel that deserved a wider
group of appreciators than mere teenagers lost in thought about
weird civilizations and life on other planets. Lucky for me that I was
one of them or I would not have read the novel for the first time so
early in life. It's easy to see, of course, why the book went into the
science fiction pigeonhole. It is an extremely deft and convincing
novel about a future America given over to a cult of death led by
John Cave, a self-styled visionary from California with a mesmeric

television presence. The book generates ideas about our culture and civilization, its idiocies and possibilities, with as much ease and certainty as its creator Vidal, in one of his own frequent appearances before the television cameras.

From his long-time hiding place in provincial Egypt, the narrator, who calls himself Eugene Luther, tells the story of John Cave's rise to power and the subsequent global impact of his new religion: Cave preaches the nugatory nature of death and makes it seem to millions and millions of Americans who live in fear of it as appealing as a family picnic. Until the time that Luther begins his story, Egypt and much of the rest of the Muslim world had been free of the influence of the proselytizers for Cavesway, as the religion was dubbed by the marketing expert Paul Himmel, who has taken the former California mortician with visions (Cave) and turned him into a charismatic leader of worldwide proportions. We soon learn that Luther's own role in the early days of the Cave organization included the composition of the group's "bible," a compilation of speeches and sermons under the heading of "Cavesword" and attributed to the leader (who seems almost completely inarticulate away from his pulpit or the TV cameras).

Luther, like many of Vidal's early protagonists, is a smart and sensitive young man adrift in a society of the beautiful and the rich. His desire for companionship, not necessarily sexual but connected in some way to sensual longing, leads him to an attractive woman named Iris; it is through her that he first comes into contact with John Cave and Paul Himmel, the public relations man who seeks to make the odd, visionary undertaker into a big business. It turns out that a lot of other Americans, most of them not anywhere as intelligent and talented as Eugene Luther, feel the same sense of longing for spiritual fulfillment of one kind or another. The Cave movement catches fire and soon develops into a national mass movement. In an attempt to complete his memoirs while in hiding, Luther conjures up the struggle between the Caveites and the American religious establishment, particularly the Catholic Church; he writes as well about Cave's own strangely stunted private life, and the attempt by Himmel and his flunkies to arrange the martyrdom of their leader so that they can gain full control of the movement. Luther challenges them, with the help of Iris, but too late to save

Cave's life, and later flees to Egypt, far away, he hopes, from the long arm of the Cave movement.

Explained solely in this way, the novel might appear to be a satire on contemporary American religion. Certainly the names Vidal uses for some of his central characters ("Luther," "Himmel") might suggest that this was his main purpose. However, Vidal's reach extends to include American advertising and public relations as well as television and its impact on the manners and mores of a country in which, as Luther puts it, a nonconformist could no longer "escape disaster if he unwisely showed a strange face to the multitude." Even so, the novel does not appear to be strictly satirical of such customs as in Vidal's later *Duluth*, a much more savage and ultimately darker takeoff on American life than *Messiah*.

In this book Vidal seems more interested in portraying ideas than in attacking them, or so we may surmise from Luther's meditative account of the events leading up to the advent of Cave and the Cavites. Self-analysis and therapy held sway in the days prior to the rise of Cave, our narrator informs us. He then goes on to add that

> men of letters lugubriously described their own deviations (usually political or sexual, seldom aesthetic), while painters worked devotedly at depicting unique inner worlds which were not accessible to others except in a state of purest empathy hardly to be achieved without a little fakery in a selfish world. It was, finally, the accepted criterion that art's single function was the fullest expression of a private vision.

Vidal's own aesthetic, as expressed in this novel, points in the opposite direction, away from the inner world and into the light of the public arena. The frame of the book establishes at the beginning a distance in time as well as geography, and Luther's backward glance assumes the possibility of coherent historical analysis both of the personal and the relation of the personal to the life of the culture. Luther is at the start an individual who seems to be a twentieth-century version of the romantic hero, a figure such as we find playing a major role in the novels that precede *Messiah* (*Williwaw, The City and the Pillar, Bright Green, Dark Red*, etc.). In the novels that follow, this figure, if he appears at all, is changed into a different sort of hero as the romantic impulse takes a back seat to the role of historical figures and the impact of ideas in history.

Messiah is, in fact, the book in which Vidal first seems to turn away from conventional narrative romanticism and shine his light on broader matters, whether they be the continuation of his investigation into theological mania (as in *Kalki*, which with *Messiah* stands as the second part of a de facto diptych on the religious impulse in the modern world) or the Washington sequence, in which he attempts to turn his nonconventional view of American history into an entertaining series of novels that persuade as they amuse. In almost all the books that follow *Messiah*, politics, history, and philosophy play a part equal to individual desire, and narrower motifs (such as critiques of American manners) Vidal treats in the satirical mode.

All of these streams flow out of *Messiah*, an authentic American novel of ideas using the genre of science fiction to achieve its ends. It may be a private joke on the part of the author that Eugene Luther is writing a life of the emperor Julian when he becomes sidetracked by the need to compose his memoir of his days in the cult of John Cave. Still it does announce to the reader one of the major projects the author had on his mind while creating the novel at hand, a project that would reveal Vidal as a novelist of much greater pretensions and achievement than any of his previous fiction might suggest. Rather than seeing *Messiah* as a science fiction novel that seems a diversion from Vidal's main course toward mastery of his vision, we might do better to recognize it as the gateway from whose vantage point one can view the faint outlines of the larger work to come.

8

The Fiction of History in Gore Vidal's Messiah

HEATHER NEILSON

> It is the perquisite of power to invent its own past.
> —*Julian*, p. 349

Messiah and *Julian* exemplify the problem of how the works of a prolific novelist should be "mapped." Vidal himself tends to divide his novels into two categories, the "inventions" and the "meditations upon history." They can also be readily divided into two groups according to merely chronological criteria. Vidal's first eight novels were published between 1946 and 1954, *Messiah* being the eighth. Despite the success of *The City and the Pillar*, the author turned, for financial reasons, to writing for film and television. In 1964, *Julian* was published.[1] Following on his successful return to novel-writing, Vidal in 1965 produced revised versions of those of his early works that he "wanted to save"[2]—*Williwaw, The City and the Pillar, The Judgment of Paris*, and *Messiah*. This revisiting and reassessing by the author of his early stage at this point can be read as his signaling of its closure, as he commences on his "mature" career. In an alternative reading, the whole oeuvre has been described as a series of pairs, John Leonard having remarked on Vidal's apparent tendency to "twin" his novels.[3] Leonard saw *Julian* and *Creation* as belonging together, as historical fictions set in premodern times, and *Messiah* and *Kalki* as reflecting each other insofar as they each portray the rise of a destructive mortal god. All four of these novels are presented as written testaments, enforced and made ironic by hindsight as a discursive principle. However, there would seem to be as much reason for "twinning" *Messiah* and *Julian*, in both of which Vidal treats the history of the Christian religion from the perspective of non-Christian philosophical standpoints.

Notwithstanding Vidal's objections to the reading of a "unifying theme" into a writer's oeuvre,[4] such a reading is also an option. If there can be said to be a common thread running through Vidal's fiction, it is the idea that fiction can portray the past more "truly" than historiography. Whether the ostensible subject of the novel is the creation of a religion, the history of the United States, or (as in *Myra Breckinridge, Myron,* and *Duluth*) the formation of "artistic" genres themselves, this premise provides the novel's polemical impetus. In Vidal's conception of historiography, testament, as mediation, necessarily becomes distortion: the word of religion similarly mutates with the passing of time, and there is a degeneracy among those who witness it.

Both *Messiah* and *Julian* portray the triumph of one religion over its adversaries, a triumph rued in both instances by the elderly narrators. *Julian* consists of the ostensible private memoirs of the eponymous emperor, framed and interrupted by the comments of the philosophers Libanius of Antioch and Priscus of Athens. In *Messiah* two stories are related mosaiclike as, piece by piece, the octogenarian Eugene Luther, exiled under the pseudonym Richard Hudson, records the events of the last days of his life and the historical crisis that happened forty or fifty years earlier. The narrative of the "present" unfolds as a detective story with a Borgesian twist. Luther's waiting for the end is disrupted by the arrival of the first American he has encountered in twenty years, and that of the man's colleague shortly afterward. Luther fears that his identity has been discovered and that either man may have been sent as his assassin. Eventually the second visitor will confess that he had suspected the old man of being the original "Lutherist," but had subsequently learned that no such being had ever existed. His name having been expunged from history, and from those texts he had written, Luther commits a final useless act of defiance, the reconstruction of the "true" origins of the Cavite religion in the 1950s.

Messiah calls attention to itself as in part an anticipation of

Julian. Since Eugene Luther Vidal is the real name of Gore Vidal,[5] the name of the protagonist of the earlier novel immediately signals a ludic and complicating autobiographical aspect. Prior to his involvement in the rise of the messiah John Cave, the novel's Eugene Luther had been working on a biography of the apostate emperor Julian, only to relinquish the project as impossible.

> The human attractive part of Julian was undone for me by those bleak errors in deed and in judgment which depressed me even though they derived most logically from the man and his time: that fatal wedding which finally walls off figures of earlier ages from the present, keeping them strange despite the most intense and imaginative re-creation. (pp. 45–46)

As Robert F. Kiernan has suggested, in *Messiah*, "Eugene Luther's discovery that Julian was too remote to be evoked successfully ceased to be Vidal's artistic problem and became his artistic theme."[6] Also, in *Messiah* the failure of the historical Julian to crush the new and, in his terms, deadly religion of Christianity comes to function as an analogy for his would-be biographer's ineffectual attempt to thwart the worldwide death-cult whose emergence he had, to a large extent, contributed to. The narrator's acknowledged inability to fathom the emperor sufficiently to represent him fully in writing serves to reinforce the doubts Luther himself introduces as to his auctorial capacity to portray accurately John Cave's career and his own.

Although Vidal has firmly dissociated himself from the tradition of Hawthorne and Melville, his preoccupations in *Messiah* and *Julian* are essentially the same as those of the "romancer" Hawthorne: the past and its authority, and the role of Christianity in his culture.[7] Insofar as *Messiah* and *Kalki* manifest Vidal's apocalyptic vision, he is in line with the mainstream of American letters in which the millennial theme has always played a major part.[8] It seems appropriate that the work of Hawthorne for which Vidal has the most respect is *The Blithedale Romance*,[9] the depiction of a mock-millennium in a failed utopia told, as is *Messiah*, by a skeptical yet naive participant.

As William Shurr's *Rappacini's Children* seeks to demonstrate, the now canonical authors were writing in a milieu that was strongly Calvinist, influenced by "one of the few forms of Christianity in which this last assertion could be made, that the probabilities are in favor of Satan in his war with Christ for domination of the world."[10]

And Norman O. Brown has argued that the rise of Satan was con-comitant with the emergence of Protestantism itself: "In Luther this experience of omnipresent and uncontrollable evil generates the theological novelty that this world, in all its outward manifestations, is ruled not by God, but by the Devil."[11]

By the fortuitous factor of his given names, Vidal is able to add an overtly allegorical dimension to the protagonist of *Messiah* by em-ploying such a reading of Martin Luther as paradoxical summoner and sustainer of his enemy. Eugene Luther's potential assassin tells him that the term "Lutherist," meaning one who willfully refused to know the truth, had been derived from the name of the earlier Luther, archetypal protester against the corruption of a religion. Eugene Luther, now (in the novel) a man without historical exis-tence, has ironically served to preserve the identity of his greater precursor, evidence of whose life might otherwise have been erased by Cavite Incorporated, along with all other evidence of Christianity.

To Hawthorne and his contemporaries, engaging in their fictions with the Calvinist premises of original sin and predestination, the Calvinist God was a potentially malignant presence, whose crea-tures could never know if they had been found worthy of grace. Where the sense of sin is greatest, so is the sense of death. Not differentiating between the various branches of Christianity, Vidal has called it "a death-cult in spades,"[12] abhorring what he sees as its emphasis on the hope of a future existence at the expense of the quality of life. Where Vidal exceeds Hawthorne in his subversive reading of America's major religion is in his equation of the powers of darkness with Christianity itself. The contention of *Julian* is that the passing of the pagan gods was the passing of the light. Libanius at one point describes Christianity as a religion that had initially tried to allay man's fear of death, but that had evolved into a "death-cult" because of "their curious hopelessness about this life, and the undue emphasis they put on the next" (pp. 331–32).[13] In *Messiah*, the first principle of Cavesword is that death is good, and its main injunction to its followers is that suicide is righteous. In Vidal's terms, Cavesword is the logical culmination of Christian tenets and what he perceives to be the murderous instincts of the religion's absolutism.[14] John Cave is a mortician's assistant with little educa-tion but possessed of an extraordinary capacity to mesmerize an audience—a capacity later enhanced by television, which enables him to promulgate globally his own idea:

> It was, finally, the manner which created the response, not the words themselves, though the words were interesting enough, especially when heard for the first time . . . for he had been born a remarkable actor, an instinctive rhetorician. (*Messiah*, p. 59)

With "a pair of initials calculated to amaze the innocent" (p. 31), Cave is figuratively aligned with Jesus Christ and also with John the Baptist, according to Eugene Luther's final realization that Cave was "meant" to be merely the preparer of the "way." However, he is also an antitype of John Calvin, in Vidal's reading of Calvinism as the ally of Thanatos, which is Eugene Luther's nemesis as Satan was that of Martin Luther.

Messiah depicts the period of the 1950s, in which it was composed, as an age of anxiety and superstition, of supernatural phenomena, ripe for a new object of worship. The era is compared specifically first to the time of hysteria in Britain when Titus Oates fabricated a Papist plot against the life of Charles II (p. 13). The text, though, is more concerned with drawing parallels with the time of Jesus' mission, and with the fourth century A.D., Christianity's crucial formative period.[15] As the narrator argues in *Julian*, because none of the pagan cults exhibited a strong missionary drive or aimed to exclude other cults, their tolerance for coexistence accounted in part for their defeat by Christianity. In Vidal's satirical analogy, mid-twentieth-century Christianity, democratized and weakened by its long reign, is at a loss at first to realize the extent and danger of the authoritarianism of Cavite Incorporated:

> "Some people been telling me you can't be a good Catholic and go for this guy. But why not? I say. You still got Virginmerry and now you got him, too, for right now." (p. 123)

Just as the early church had appropriated pagan myths and festivals, and Christian scholars would continue to read "anticipations" of Christianity in pagan legend and philosophy, so the Cavites would redesignate Christmas Day as "Cavesday" and Easter Day as "Irisday" (after Iris Mortimer, who had become the controller of the religion after the death of the messiah). As the Athanasian and Arian Christians of the fourth century bitterly contested over the

doctrine of the homoousian and the homoiousian, the third generation of the followers of Cave would fall into dispute as to the nature
of the relationship between the "Liberator" and Iris. In the belief of
one sect, they were man and wife, and in another brother and sister.
In the Irisian sect, Iris is revered as the symbolic mother of the
faithful. The Irisians infer from Cavesword the prospect of a sort of
afterlife, reinterpreting death, which Cave had alleged to be a state
of nothingness, as a return to an interuterine existence.

> "Anyway, some of the younger fellows, the bright ones like Jessup,
> have got attached to Iris, not that we don't all love her equally. It's
> just that they've got in the habit of talking about death being the
> womb again, all that kind of stuff without any real basis in Cave."
> "It runs all though Cave's work, Bill. It's implicit in all that he
> said." Jessup was amiable but I sensed a hardness in his tone. It had
> come to this, I thought. (p. 184)

The Vatican's dogmatizing of the Assumption of the Virgin Mary in
1950 has a correlative in *Messiah* in the special interpretation, for
the case of Iris, of the doctrine pertaining to Cavesway (suicide). Iris
had died of pneumonia but, having undoubtedly intended to take
Cavesway she had, it is decreed, taken Cavesway in spirit and therefore in fact. As if to place in relief the parodic representations of
Christianity, there is a surprisingly respectful depiction of a Christian leader in the minor but sympathetic character of the Episcopa-
lian Bishop Winston, spokesman for his religion in its dying days:
"he filled his historic function with wit and dignity, and we admired
him tremendously" (p. 171). In Bishop Winston's name, *Messiah*
also pays tribute to George Orwell's *1984* and invokes it as a generic
precursor. [16]

It has been assumed in certain critiques of *Messiah* that Eugene
Luther's role as evangelist for Cavesword, analogous to that of the
four Gospel writers, corresponds most closely to Luke's. [17] However,
Luther's primary task in Cavite Incorporated is that of providing an
intellectual sanction for Cavesword by delineating a respectable
ancestry in earlier philosophical systems. He is thus arguably closer
to John, whose narrative is the most self-consciously typological of
the four records of Jesus' activities. Theodore Ziolkowski has described *Messiah* as a "fifth gospel," situating it in a subgenre of what
he terms "fictional transfigurations of Jesus."[18] Common to all these

fictional transfigurations is a Christlike central figure—a man innocent of sin and yet subject to temptations, and whose beliefs bring
him into conflict with the laws of his society. His sufferings are
partly willed so that he does not become merely pathetic. John Cave
fits the type of the redeemer as naïf, a being apparently devoid of
physical desires.

Ziolkowski defines the "fifth gospel" according to the detachment
of nonbelief through which the material of the New Testament is
approached, as the work makes use of the events of Jesus' life as
depicted in the Gospels and the Acts of the Apostles. The crux of
Messiah's demythologizing intent is the distinction it urges between
the "facts" of the messiah's life and the kerygmatic metamorphoses
of those facts, insinuating that the same distinction should be recognized in considering the story of Christ. The most darkly comic
instance of this is the historiographical transformation of Cave's
brief internment for hit-and-run driving into The Time of Persecution, with consequent discovery of The Prison Dialogues (purported
conversations between Cave and Iris Mortimer).

> Reflections behind bars are always penned in guiltless blood. The
> reasons for incarceration soon become historically unimportant as
> time embosses them with an antique sheen. The fact that we speak of
> Plato's "Prison Dialogues" or of certain of St. Paul's letters as the
> "Prison Epistles" indicates that we are all mythopoetic at heart.[19]

Plato is a pervasive presence in Messiah. Sometimes the allusions
appear just to exemplify the narrator's tendency to pedantic pon-
derousness, as when he compares his "Dialogues" with Cave to
those of Socrates and Alcibiades, only to disclaim the comparison
immediately (p. 164).[20] However, as Bernard F. Dick has noted,
Cavesword is in part an attempt to apply some of the theories of
Plato's Republic to the modern world.[21] In Socrates' hypothetical
ideal state, the arts, the religions, and the occupations of the citizens, as well as their choices of spouse, would be strictly controlled. Vidal has interpreted the Republic as dystopian, describing
it as "a blueprint for any dictatorship."[22] Nonetheless, in a section
that draws heavily on that portion of the Republic which deals with
the projected abolition of the family for the Guardians, the elite
class, Eugene Luther recalls his composing, in dyspeptic irritability,

the Cavite text that will result in the end of marriage and the transference of the rearing of children from parents to the state.[23]

> "I'm quite sure you have abolished marriage."
> "As a matter of fact, yes, this morning."
> "And now you don't know what to do about the children."
> "Precisely. I . . ."
> "Perfectly simple." Clarissa was brisk. (p. 158)

The passage as a whole is a curious eruption in the text, since the effects of Luther's undermining of the family and his fellow-director Clarissa Lessing's endorsement of controlled breeding are not referred to again. While having declared himself to be for strict governmental control in the public sector and total freedom in the private,[24] Vidal was for a time deeply concerned with global overpopulation. In one of his more controversial statements on propagation (in 1969), Vidal advocated planned breeding, the communal upbringing of children, and "an intelligent program of eugenics."[25] Eugene Luther's desire is to remove restraints upon personal freedom of action, to diminish the sense of sin culturally associated with sexual activity, just as, in his initial wishful interpretation, Cavesword dispelled the inhibiting superstitions surrounding the subject of death. Through his liberal intentions, he provides the tools for an irreversibly totalitarian regime. The author is perhaps, by implication, indicating both himself and his character as theorists whose philosophizing and predisposition to legislate sometimes distract them from the human context.

Much of the novel's syncretic burden of multiple allegory centers upon the five founding directors of Cavite Incorporated, characters who at times appear to be self-consciously allegorical in their functions. (By the time the group is sanctified in history as The Original Five, a feckless minor screenwriter, Edward Hastings, has been substituted for Eugene Luther, and Luther's writings attributed to him.) Paul Himmell, Cave's brash and unscrupulous publicity manager, is a patent parody of the Apostle Paul as arch-distorter of The Word. Depicted stereotypically as the unlikable advertising man, he (together with the characters Stockarin and Clarissa) is an application of Vidal's maxim that monomania is the secret of comedic invention.[26] Although Stockarin fires the gun that kills Cave, it is effectively Paul who murders him, with the ambition of establishing once and for all the Cavite kingdom, as the death of Jesus ensured the perpetuation of the legend of Christ. Stockarin, Paul's Jungian analyst, who eagerly seizes upon Cave as a "racial folk father figure," represents in farce Vidal's delineation of psychoanalysis as the alternative twentieth-century religion. In the Cavite religion, the confessional and pastoral counseling are constituted in therapy, in which indoctrination and catharsis are simultaneously effected.

Clarissa Lessing is a middle-aged woman whose wealth and desire for diversion provide the initial impetus for the rise of Cave. Her most bizarre trait is the conviction that she is twenty-two hundred years old. This foible enables Vidal, through Clarissa's "memories" of historical figures, sporadically to contextualize the story of *Messiah*.

> Her accounts of various meetings with Libanius in Antioch were brilliant, all told most literally, as though she had no faculty for invention, which perhaps, terrifying thought, she truly lacked. (pp. 29–30)

At the same time, one of the novel's underlying themes, the spuriousness of the reliability generally attributed to the "eyewitness," is reinforced. Clarissa's garrulousness and frivolousness belie her soundness as a seer. It is she who warns Eugene Luther against Iris, perceiving that the disciples had quickly taken control of the master, and she who prophesies a future of enforced conformity as the legacy of Cave. Her astuteness and prescience make her ultimately reprehensible in her abnegation of moral responsibility.

Eugene Luther and Iris Mortimer, "a flawed Mercury and a dark queen of heaven" (p. 52), are the most complexly developed characters in *Messiah*. Eugene Luther falls in love with Iris; however, not only does he have a mysterious sexual affliction, but Iris is entirely devoted to the untouchable Cave. Vidal manages to keep the triangle from its potential for absurdity. Iris is the pagan goddess whose sign, the rainbow, heralds her coming to earth to effect some change in human affairs. Iris Mortimer, as her name connotes, is a goddess connected with death. However, she is initially a figure of Eros, who undergoes a transition to become a figure of Thanatos, acting out, as it were, the proposition of Plato's *Phaedo* that, wherever there is a pair of opposites, they are generated from each other in a cycle of perpetual recurrence.[27] In what at first appears to be paradoxical, it is only for the duration of the life of Cave, the preacher of death, by whom she is mesmerized, that Iris is an agent of the life-force.

> "I give myself and what I take is life, the knowledge that there is another creature in the world whose wonder, to me at least, is all satisfying by merely being." (p. 129)

Having ousted Paul Himmell after the murder of Cave, Iris is elected as the messiah's heir, the Guardian of Cavesword, during the first Cavite Council. The fundamental question faced by this synod is the emphasis to be given to Cavesway. The four other members of the Executive Committee are divided as to whether facilities in the Cavite Centers should be expanded so that every Cavite could take Cavesway as soon as he or she felt their usefulness to be over. Eugene Luther opposes the expansion, and Iris ends the deadlock by endorsing Cavesway. Cave's last words were "Gene was right," as, in the end, he does an about-face, wanting to halt the flow of suicides he has inspired and to break the spell of death. Iris' choice is thus a definitive betrayal. She takes advantage of an attempt on her life to denounce Luther and assume total control of the enterprise but, feeling compassion for her erstwhile ally, she secretly facilitates his escape to Egypt. On the metaphorical level, Eros and Thanatos have generated each other in the shifting stances of Iris and Cave, and the Cavite religion becomes bipolar as the cult of the Mother grows to vie with the worship of the patriarch.

The readiness of the reader of *Messiah* to suspend disbelief depends finally upon the plausibility of the protagonist, Eugene Luther—or rather, of the two Eugene Luthers, the narrator and his reconstructed earlier self. The development of the one serves to reconstitute the portrait of the other, the physical depiction of both being one example of this. Vidal always depicts in intimate detail the symptoms and frustrations of the aging process of his elderly characters, such as Burden Day, Charlie Schuyler, Libanius, and Cyrus Spitama. In *Messiah* the unstated contrast between the coldly composed young Eugene Luther's succinct acknowledgment of his body and the old man's wry detailing of his deterioration gives a certain poignancy and immediacy to the protagonist. The success or failure of Eugene Luther as a character hinges on whether a balance or an incongruity is achieved in his representation as a dispassionate relativist and the eagerness with which he discovers and embraces his "one true conviction," that "life is all while death is only the irrelevant shadow at the end, the counterpart to that instant before the seed lives" (p. 102).

> He has lived through some of the most crucial events of history. He has read all the books, listened to all the psychiatrists, and been thoroughly purged of dogma and prejudice. The experience has left him with the virtue of an open mind. But it has taught him one thing which it is sheer suicide for a writer to learn too well—that all things are relative and that there are at least twenty sides to every question. [28]

This evaluation of Gore Vidal, early in his career, reads as an astute, if inadvertent, assessment of the existentialist Eugene Luther, who finds that his admirable sense of the inconsequentiality of human affairs and his restraint from easy judgments are not, just in themselves, moral excellences. These characteristics lead Eugene Luther at crucial moments to passive credulity. He stands indicted by his failure to act after Cave's murder, in contrast to Iris' immediate seizure of responsibility. His justification of his decision not to expose Paul but to work quietly toward his eventual demise, so that the work of the previous few years should not be put at risk, is not entirely convincing. It is a reneging that will ensure the final identification of Cavesword with the cult of death.

The essential circumstance in which the various elements of the Eugene Luther character mesh is his epiphanic apprehension, recorded at the conclusion of his narrative.

> I was he whom the world awaited. I was that figure, that messiah whose work might have been the world's delight and liberation. But the villain death once more undid me, and to *him* belongs the moment's triumph. (p. 221)

In his symbolic aspect, Luther, the afflicted hypothetical messiah, is likened by sheer contiguity to the dismembered god Osiris, from whose statue in the garden of his Egyptian hotel he draws constant comfort. He is also a reverberation of the Fisher-King, whose diseased world participates in his sterility.

When asked about the meaning of Eugene Luther's mysterious impotence, Vidal accounted for it with the suspect ingenuousness of the overinterviewed.

> I thought it would be highly disturbing—Eugene Luther has so much to do, and there's so much going on—to give him a sex life. And I thought, wouldn't it be interesting to have a young male character in an American novel, set in the year 1950, who has absolutely no sex life at all.[29]

Ray Lewis White has suggested that *Messiah* is a fictionalized account of Vidal's defeat of his own personal death wish.[30] Given that later, in *Kalki*, Vidal would effect the genocide of the entire human race, his defeat of a death wish (had there been such a death wish) that *Messiah* was meant to exorcise is inconclusive. There is at least as much ground for suggesting that Vidal employed Eugene Luther as a means of cryptically—and hyperbolically—commenting on his own political aspirations.

At the end of the early essay "The Twelve Caesars," Vidal warned that the sociopolitical climate in the United States was such that "we have been made . . . vulnerable to the first messiah who offers the young and bored some splendid prospect, some Caesarian certainty."[31] Vidal's admonition recalls Lincoln's in the Springfield address, where he spoke against the tyrant who might arise and destroy what his predecessors had done, a speech Vidal has read as Lincoln's warning against himself.[32] Of the self-reflexive naming of Eugene Luther, Vidal has said,

> I was having some fun with the idea of myself as somebody who wanted to be a politician, but had taken a path that made it quite impossible to have a conventional political career, and I was quite aware of that.[33]

Anaïs Nin realized that Vidal may have sabotaged his chances in politics with the publication of *The City and the Pillar*, written when he was twenty.[34] Vidal had ostensibly intended, through this novel, to shatter the conception, which he construed as part of American folklore, that homosexuality is a form of disease. While firmly maintaining the privacy of his personal life, Vidal has not concealed his bisexuality and has, throughout his career, been a vociferous advocate of the right of individuals to freedom in sexual matters. The affliction of Eugene Luther, the messiah who should have been but could not be, is perhaps a metaphorical expression of the fact that Vidal could not at that time have become America's messiah (the President) because anything other than consistent heterosexuality was perceived as an affliction in the United States.

Interpreting the character Eugene Luther without his allegorical trappings, the reader can accept Luther's epiphany as a vision of truth, or take it to be the mad megalomania of an aged man in exile (*homo incurvatus in se*). In either case it is a culmination that is highly ironic. In the former reading, Luther can be seen to have missed his destiny by attempting to maintain his philosophical integrity, constituted in both his close attention to details and (as he believed) his lack of either ambition or the true spark of the divine. In the latter reading, the vision interpreted as a symptom of insanity, the irony consists in the contrast between Luther's apparently eminent stability to this point and what seems to be a retreat into a solipsism that casts its own light on what has preceded. In any case, Luther's own narrative betrays him as being deluded in the conception he has of himself as unburdened by the religious needs of the rest of the race. It is he who first mentally likens Iris to a gentle mother, at Cave's veritable Last Supper with his five directors, where Luther himself unwittingly plays the Judas who precipitates Cave's death by chancing to expose Paul's designs: "I realized whom it was she resembled, the obscure nagging memory which had disturbed me all through dinner. She was like my mother, a woman long dead" (p. 192).

Likewise, it is also Luther's iconic vision that translates a portrait of Cave, dappled with sunlight behind Iris's desk, into a Byzantine mosaic (p. 214). Whether the remembered metonymic observation (Cave as mosaic implying Cave as deity) is actually the young Eugene Luther's or the retrospective coloration of the old narrator is undecidable. The historian and his former self as subject become blurred, and the device of the two Luthers, with its shifting perspectives, remains a teasing and perplexing problem for the reader. In the *Phaedo*, Socrates describes the concern of the philosopher as "this and nothing else . . . the release and separation of soul from body." Following Plato, in *Julian* Libanius asks Priscus, "is not all philosophy but preparation for a serene dying?" (p. 13). In the end, Luther stands as a failed philosopher, one whose heed to the Delphic injunction to know oneself is insufficient. Yet, in *Messiah*'s final irony, it is Eugene Luther's incompleteness that brings him near the status of tragic hero. In his relinquishment of philosophy, he at least achieves quixotic grandeur in his futile commitment to rage, until the last, against the historiographical "perquisite of power" and against death.

9

Vidal as Playwright: In Gentlest Heresy

RAY LEWIS WHITE

Gore Vidal confesses readily that he is not at heart a playwright. He is

> a novelist turned temporary adventurer. . . . The reasons for my conversion to piracy are to me poignant, and to students of our society perhaps significant. If I may recall in nostalgic terms the near past, I did, as a novelist, enjoy a bright notoriety after the Second World War. Those were the happy years when a new era in our letters was everywhere proclaimed; we would have, it was thought, a literature to celebrate the new American empire; our writers would reflect our glory and complement the beautiful hardness of our currency. But something went wrong.[1]

The "error" was the refusal of the public to buy enough of his books to give him a decent living, for "by the 1950's I and my once golden peers were plunged into that dim cellar of literature characterized as 'serious' where, like the priests of a shattered establishment, we were left to tend our prose privately, so many exiles, growing mushrooms in the dark."[2] Turning to the theater for money, Vidal found that the New York City audience was, to say the least, a discouraging one:

It is middle-aged expense-account audience, suffering from the bourgeois *malaise* so well diagnosed by Sartre when he remarked that the
middle class will endure any sort of shock or discouraging statement
about the human conditions as long as the author makes it perfectly
clear that no change is possible. For change is the enemy, reminding
the audience not only of revolution and the loss of money, but finally
(and most secretly) of death. For a social meliorist like myself, the
Broadway audience present a tricky problem: how to get them to
recognize certain flaws in our society (and possible reforms) without
openly antagonizing them. (*Three Plays*, p. ix)

Vidal has not taken to the theater any illusions about the extent of
his dramatic talents. As a playwright, he is "a sport, whose only
serious interest is the subversion of a society that bores and appalls
me."[3] With no interest in the future of any play, Vidal cares less
about the well-made play than about the well-unsettled audience:
"what I have done, and what interests me, is to clown, to be funny,
bizarre—and I enjoy comedic invention, both high and low, there is
almost nothing so satisfying as making an audience laugh while
removing their insides."[4] Audiences have enjoyed two of Vidal's
plays—*Visit to a Small Planet* and *The Best Man*. But they have
been dubious about one of his dramas, *On the March to the Sea*,
and actually hostile to another, *Romulus*.

Vidal's first full-length drama, Visit to a Small Planet,[5] is the
most humorous of his four published plays. The first version of *Visit
to a Small Planet* was presented as a one-hour television drama on
May 8, 1955. The success of this version encouraged Vidal to
develop the brief television script for commercial production in
New York City, where, in 1957, the play enjoyed a long season, one
followed by success in Europe and by adaption into a film.

Vidal accepts the criticism that *Visit* is more an entertainment or
vaudeville than a regular drama: "the comedic approach to the
theme tended to dictate the form. Having no real commitment to
the theatre, no profound convictions about the well-made or the ill-
made play, I tend to write as an audience, an easily bored audience.
I wrote the sort of piece I should like to go to a theatre to see: one in

which people say and do things that make me laugh. And though monsters lurk beneath the surface, their presence is sensed rather than dramatically revealed."[6]

The action of *Visit to a Small Planet* takes place between one summer evening and the next in the home of Roger Spelding, outside Manassas, Virginia. Spelding is "a confident middle-aged man with a receding hairline and an odd double manner: when he is being a television commentator, he is warm, folksy, his accent faintly southern; when he is himself, the accent is more national, the tone more acerb and sophisticated" (*Three Plays*, p. 9). As the play opens, Spelding is talking with General Tom Powers, "an adept politician of the services, devoted to his own advancement, which has not been as rapid as he'd anticipated. He ascribes all set-backs to treachery in high places" (ibid.). Powers complains volubly over having been taken away from "the new Laundry Project—something really exciting" to handle an alleged Unidentified Flying Object seen over the Virginia countryside for the past twelve hours. When Powers insists that the object is really there, Spelding's first worry is that he has just taped a news analysis for television in which he has told "Mother and Father America that there 'jest ain't no sech animal.'"

Reba Spelding, "a vague grey woman, beneath whose gentleness glints the iron will of the faddist," welcomes her husband's old friend, although her main concern at the moment is whether her daughter Ellen—to the consternation of the Speldings—is sleeping with Conrad, a young neighboring farmer who is more interested in agriculture than in money making. Conrad is "an ordinary-looking youth, more earnest than serious," and Ellen is "a splendid girl of nineteen, iron-willed but appealing." Their main concern is daring to check bravely into motels; at the last one Conrad signed the register as "Mr. and Mrs. Ulysses Simpson Grant *and wife.*" As they are planning to carry a suitcase filled with telephone books to a motel that night, and as Reba Spelding is locating a pamphlet on birth-control for her daughter, the flying saucer lands in the family's rose garden.

The occupant of the vehicle is Kreton, "a visitor from outer space . . . a pleasant-looking man with side whiskers . . . dressed in the fashion of 1860." Kreton, who came to earth to view the

Battle of Bull Run at Manassas in 1861, is mistakenly a century late. He is on a pleasure trip, "a visit to your small planet. I've been studying you for ages. In fact, one might say you're a hobby of mine . . . especially this period of your development" (ibid., p. 24). Reba pragmatically invites Kreton to stay for dinner, and General Powers takes over the house to question the alien and to fill out the necessary forms (in quadruplicate) for the Pentagon.

General Powers, anxious to guard the security of his country, considers Kreton "a spy sent here by an alien race to study us, preparatory to invasion": "We'll fight them with everything we've got. We'll fight them with the hydrogen bomb, with poison gas, with broken beer-bottles if necessary; we'll fight them on the beaches; we'll fight them in the alley" (ibid., p. 28). Kreton, able to hear people's thoughts, delights in the general's "vibrations." The authorities, however, are not soothed by the visitor's insistence that he has come alone and that "no one would ever dream of visiting *you!* Except me. But then, of course, I'm a hobbyist. I love to gad about" (ibid., p. 29). The government becomes especially upset at Kreton's announcement that he loves earthmen so deeply that he is taking control of the planet, of his "dear *wicked* children," and that "tomorrow will be a wonderful day for all of us."

Act II opens the next morning with Kreton and the family cat telepathically discussing dogs, mice, and the delights of being feline. Vidal originally opened this act with a conversation between Kreton and the Secretary-General of the United Nations, but the subject—war—disturbed the audiences: "At each performance the audience, which had been charmed by the precedent fooling, grew deathly cold as the debate began: this was not what they had anticipated (a fault, I own, of the dramaturgy), and their confidence in the play was never entirely regained. . . . The substitute was engaging; the play moved amiably; no one was shocked."[7]

Knowing Ellen's passion for Conrad, Kreton regrets having upset their plans: "You had planned to devote all of last night to wild abandon, you and Conrad and the four telephone books. How glorious you must be! Tangled in one another's arms, looking up telephone numbers. . . . I suppose that's what you *were* planning to do with those books. So bizarre, the whole thing" (*Three Plays*, p. 41). Unable to understand their objections to his urgent request to watch them at play, he raves over "these primitive taboos. You revel in public slaughter: you pay to watch two men hit one another repeatedly, yet you make love secretly, guiltily and with remorse . . . too delicious!" (ibid., p. 42). On Kreton's world, there is no passion at all; people have become "intergalactic bores." To escape this boredom, Kreton has visited earth, where he enjoys "absolutely wallowing in the twentieth century."

But the twentieth century—at least in the United States—decides that Kreton would be the perfect weapon in possible international warfare. Unfortunately, war is Kreton's mania, he has begun maneuvering Russia and the United States into such mutual suspicion that nuclear warfare is imminent: "I simply dote on people. . . . Why? Because of their primitive addiction to violence, because they seethe with emotions which I find bracing and intoxicating. For countless ages I have studied them and now I'm here to experience them firsthand, to wallow shamelessly in their steaming emotions . . . and to have fun, fun, fun! . . . How? . . . Well, I do believe I have started a war. At least, I hope so. After all, that's what I came down here to see! I mean, it's the one thing they do really well" (ibid., p. 52).

Dressed as a Confederate general, Kreton is prepared to enjoy the disaster. He tries to arouse war fever in Conrad, who prefers sex and agriculture to war, by singing the patriotic songs guaranteed to motivate savages to bloodthirst. When this motivation fails, he cleverly gets Conrad, a sensible pacifist, to fight a soldier attracted to Ellen; for even Conrad is primitive when he is properly stimulated: "Savages, blood-thirsty savages. That's why you're my hobby. That's why I've returned to the Dark Ages of an insignificant planet in a minor system circling a small and rather chilly sun to enjoy myself, to see you at your most typical" (ibid., p. 73).

In Act III, Vidal averts nuclear warfare with a deus ex machina ending for his play. Ellen, having been taught some slightly advanced mental tricks by Kreton, telepathically calls for aid to prevent the war; and another visitor arrives—Delton 4. He stops the war by "bending" time back to earth's pre-Kreton hours, explaining that Kreton "is a rarity among us. He is morally retarded, and, like a child, he regards this world as his plaything." (ibid., p. 78). Kreton goes into space to return to his "nursery"; and the play closes—time bent back—as the first lines of Act I are repeated.

This stage play is an improvement over the earlier television script of Visit. The love antics of Ellen and Conrad, the delightful loquaciousness (rather than dire threats) of Kreton, and the visitor-cat interview are fortunate additions. However, Vidal admits to having tailored his script to protect the investments made in his play; it was obviously better to produce a play that would be popularly successful and mildly satirical than one that would be mildly successful and bitterly satirical: "I was obliged to protect an eighty-thousand-dollar investment and I confess freely that I obscured meanings, softened blows, humbly turned wrath aside, emerging, as we all wanted, with a successful play which represents me very little. It is not that what was fashioned is bad or corrupt. I rather fancy the farce we ended up with, and I think it has a good deal of wear in it. But the play that might have been, though hardly earth-shaking, was far more interesting and true. I played the game stolidly according to rules I abhor."[8]

In the guise of this science-fiction fable, Vidal manages to entertain the reader or the audience with vaudeville tricks—mind-reading, weird sounds, teleportation—and to satirize some of the ridiculous aspects of American society in the 1950s: nationalism, patriotism, sexual hypocrisy, the military mind, nuclear warfare, and birth control. A painfully funny play, Visit to a Small Planet reflects Vidal's interest in immediate world problems and his conviction that only direct action can give man even a slight chance of surviving self-destruction: "My view of reality is not sanguine and the play for all its blitheness turns toward a cold night."[9]

Vidal's second full-length drama, The Best Man,[10] opened in New York City in March 1960 and became even more successful than his earlier Visit to a Small Planet. The year 1960 was a fortunate time to present a play about politics because Vidal was then a candidate for Congress and because the United States was to hold a presidential election in November 1960. The Best Man concerns the national conventions held by the American political parties to select candidates for the presidency. It is strange that the inspiration for this political satire came to him from his consideration of the narrative method of Henry James: "I wonder if, really, I am taken with James's way. Is he too neat? Too artificial? Too classical? Too much devoted to balance? Item: *The Tragic Muse*. Each of four characters begins at the farthest extremity of an X; they cross; each ends in an opposite position. One wonders, does a living pulse beat? Or is it only a metronome?"[11]

Deciding that he did not like the sterile neatness of James' plot, Vidal imagined how a modern writer might use the method:

> It was all a trick, an easy parlour-game. As if one were, in contemporary terms, to take—just for example—a man of exemplary private life, yet monstrous public life, and contrast him to a man of "immoral" private life and exemplary public life. That was just the sort of thing James would do. How he would enjoy mechanically turning the screw upon each character. For the sake of argument, make the two men politicians, perhaps fighting one another for the Presidency. Then demonstrate how, in our confused age, morality means, simply, sex found out. To most Americans, cheating, character-assassination, hypocrisy, self-seeking are taken as the way things are, not pleasant perhaps but: son you've got to look after number one because there's a lot of competition and . . . I had the characters for *The Best Man* (*Three Plays*, p. 155).

With the characters established. Vidal decided to set his play at the nominating convention held in Philadelphia by an unnamed American political party. The scenes alternate between action in the hotel suite of candidate William Russell and in that of his opponent, Joe Cantwell. As the play opens, Russell is the favored contender at the convention. Russell, "a strong youthful-looking man of fifty" and formerly a Secretary of State, is aided in his campaign by his manager, Dick Jenson, "in his late forties: intense, devoted, apprehensive by nature," and by his wife, Alice, "in her early forties . . . a handsome, slender, grey-haired lady of the Old Establishment, not quite as diffident and shy as she appears."

Russell is a caricature of the very clever, rather pompous intellectual who, knowing his own great wit, enjoys using it to the confusion of less clever men. Asked how many delegates he has "sewed up," Russell replies: "When it comes to delegates, we neither sow nor do we reap" (*Three Plays*, p. 160). He refuses to speculate on a "dark horse" candidate, saying: "I'm sorry, but I'm not about to build up a dark horse when I'm doing my best to look like the light horse" (ibid.,

p. 161). Russell subjects even newspaper reporters to a statement of his political creed: "life is not a popularity contest; neither is politics. The important thing for any government is educating the people about issues, *not* following the ups and downs of popular opinion. . . . If the people want the wrong thing, if the people don't understand an issue, if they've been misled by the press . . .—by *some* of the press—then I think a President should ignore their opinion and try to convince them that his way is the right way" (ibid., p. 161). He alludes to Oliver Cromwell, William Shakespeare, and Bertrand Russell and then ends the interview with the old cliché— source of the title of the play—"may the best man win!"

Russell promises his worried aide that he will resist impulses to refer to Charles Darwin and all ancient Romans, but he admits to being unable to pass a mirror without regarding his reflection and to studying the future in multiples of three. However, his more serious concerns are whether American women will vote for a man not only intelligent but also promiscuous and whether everybody will learn of his unhappy marriage to Alice. The women's vote is supposed to be represented by Mrs. Sue-Ellen Gamadge, who not only dislikes wit ("eggheads") and all first ladies since Grace Coolidge but who warns Russell that his opponent plans to use "smear tactics" in the campaign.

Alice Russell is helping her husband in the campaign by pretending that their marriage is conventionally happy. Her motives are unclear even to herself: "I want to be First Lady. Or perhaps I look forward to seeing you occasionally. . . . Don't look alarmed! Only in line of duty. You know, an unexpected meeting in the East Room, an ambiguous encounter in the Lincoln Bedroom" (ibid., p. 171). Sadly aware of her husband's promiscuity, Alice worries that the public will learn of Russell's past nervous breakdown—obviously the "smear" the opponent will use.

Joe Cantwell, the opponent, "is in his forties. His manner is warm, plausible. Though under great tension, he suggests ease. He has a tendency not to listen when preoccupied" (ibid., p. 181). For public support, Cantwell relies on his senatorial investigations of organized crime, on his clean image, and on his pose as the average American, equal to his countrymen but in no way superior to them. His marriage to Mabel Cantwell, "a blond, pretty woman of forty," is a happy one in the mindless American way of mediocrity, except that in private Joe and Mabel revert to their usual baby talk; they play Papa and Momma Bear. Cantwell tailors his statements to parallel the opinions of the majority of voters, he needs the support of ex-President Hockstader, and he plans to ruin his opponent by revealing Russell's psychiatric record.

Cantwell threatens to publicize Russell's nervous breakdown because, as Vidal says, "The *Zeitgeist* is full now of the buzz of psychoanalysis; everyone's mind is cluttered with at least a few misunderstood clinical phrases and conceptions. If William Russell had once had a nervous breakdown, and Senator Cantwell were to get his hands on Russell's case history and threaten to reveal the contents to the delegates at the convention, it was unlikely Russell could survive politically. A presidential candidate can have many faults, but even a hint of mental instability is disqualifying."[12] Hockstader, who has really planned to back Cantwell as nominee, changes his mind at the threat, telling Cantwell: "It's not that I mind your bein' a bastard, don't get me wrong there. . . . It's your bein' such a stupid bastard I object to" (ibid., p. 193).

Russell, suspecting Cantwell's tactics, is planning a public statement from his doctor; but his manager has found a method of countering Cantwell's threats. Vidal explains the countermeasures thus:

> What could be brought up about Senator Cantwell? I wanted something ambiguous: it might or it might not be true but, true or not, Russell must resent having to reveal it, even to save himself. This was limiting. If Cantwell had stolen money, got a girl pregnant, run away in battle, taken dope, been a Communist or a member of the Ku Klux Klan, Russell might be reluctant to bring the matter up, but he would certainly not hesitate to save himself, especially if he were convinced the charges were true. Homosexuality was about the only thing left. It was a charge which, true or not, Russell would detest exploiting. (*Three Plays*, p. 156)

The evidence for Cantwell's supposed degeneracy rests on statements volunteered by Sheldon Marcus, his fellow officer during World War II when they had served in the Aleutian Islands. Cantwell rather plausibly denies the charges as vengeance for not having promoted Marcus and explains his role as having been an official spy on a circle of homosexual soldiers. Hockstader personally does not care "if Joe Cantwell enjoys deflowering sheep by the light of a full moon," but he forces Russell to confront Cantwell with the charges. But Cantwell, knowing his opponent's distaste for the whole matter, bluffs successfully and releases Russell's psychiatric profile to the delegates.

The issues established, Vidal brings *The Best Man* quickly to a close. Russell withholds his charges; Cantwell makes his charges public; and Hockstader dies, saying "to hell with both of you." When neither candidate can get a majority of votes from the delegates, Russell ends his own chances and prevents Cantwell's nomination by giving his support to a political unknown, "a man without a face": "Don't underestimate him. Men without faces tend to get elected President, and power or responsibility or honour fill in the features, usually pretty well" (ibid., p. 238). A safe man nominated, evil having canceled out good, Vidal commits a distasteful dramatic impropriety by letting Russell and his wife decide to try for a reconciliation; Russell is, "of course, happy: the best man won!"

The Best Man seems to be the author's comment on some aspects of American politics: "the best man" may be neither the ruthless opportunist nor the gentle intellectual but rather a man of no public renown—a compromise candidate. Of course, the play operates on hyperbole and simplification. It assumes that the two secrets would have been kept hidden in an otherwise open society, that the candidates themselves would do the dirty work, and that the nominee would become President in spite of opposition by the other political party. To all attempts to allegorize his drama, Vidal replies: "Contrary to rumor, I was not writing about Adlai Stevenson, Richard Nixon and Harry Truman. There were elements of these men in each of the characters, but no more. At a crucial moment in our history I wanted to present to an audience of voters a small essay in Presidential temperament."

The Best Man is probably his most topical play and, therefore, quite easily dated in its appeal and comprehensibility. The success of the performances in 1960 was due not only to the impending presidential election but to Vidal's changing the script to suit the audience, as he had done earlier with the script of *Visit to a Small Planet*:

In the play's first version, I allowed the opportunist Senator Cantwell to win. The good man was too weak, the bad one too tough. The play was black and I was willing to fight to keep it so (and enjoy almost certain popular failure) if I had been entirely convinced that a man as bad as Senator Cantwell could get elected. After much thought I changed my mind. Cantwell could not prevail—at least nowadays—because in its idiot way our system, though it usually keeps us from having the very best man as President, does protect us from the very worst. That is two cheers for democracy. (*Rocking the Boat*, p. 299)

On the March to the Sea (in *Three Plays*, pp. 87–150) is another expansion of a television script into a full-length drama. According to Vidal, "the play began as an hour drama produced on television in 1956. I called it *Honor*[14] and in that form it was, generally, successful. The story was very American: a businessman named Hinks imbues his sons with a lofty rhetorical notion of honor and duty which does ennoble them; yet when he himself is put to the test, he fails, but in his failure discovers that he has never in his heart believed his own cant."[15] The play based on this script has never been performed in New York City, although it was acted in Bonn, Germany, in 1961, and in summer stock at Hyde Park, New York, in 1960. *On the March to the Sea* has been reworked by Gore Vidal several times; but as published in *Three Plays*, it remains the least successful of his four dramas.

On the March to the Sea, set in Waynesville, Georgia, in 1863–64, is a drama of the American Civil War. John Hinks, the protagonist, is "a powerfully built man in his late forties, rough of speech, vigorous in manner; he limps stiffly; one leg is false but he uses no stick" (*Three Plays*, p. 90). The limp dates from an accident in Hinks' youth, when he was a homeless orphan befriended by Mr. Grayson, in whose mill Hinks was injured. Having envied Grayson and other members of the aristocratic gentry of the antebellum South, Hinks has worked hard enough to achieve wealth comparable to theirs; and he has adopted their code of honor. As the play opens, Hinks is celebrating his achievement of equality with the landed gentry; he has just finished building a great plantation home on his own extensive estate.

This first party in the new house is Hinks' opportunity to entertain his son Grayson, home on leave from the battles in the Northern states of the Confederacy. Grayson pretends to share the ideals of the South, but he has survived enough battles to know that "honor" is hollow on a battlefield and that the South has in reality never had a chance to win the war. Grayson's main concern is that his younger brother, Aaron, a student at the university, will not enter the army. Grayson realizes that the South will need men like Aaron to rebuild civilization after the war is lost.

Aaron himself wishes to avoid entering the service; he is a sensible boy, silently peaceful and mainly interested in marrying Amelia Blair, daughter of aristocratic neighbors. Before Aaron can announce his plan to marry the pregnant Amelia, Hinks forces him to accept "with honor" a commission in the Confederate Army. The sons are to fight together to defend the South and their father's new mansion: "these things come down on us like storms in summer and who is right and who is wrong is maybe impossible to judge. But what matters is what you *do*, whether it is to offer your life like Grayson here, or me goin' broke sellin' grain below cost to my state. It is what you *do* that makes you what you are, not what you say, not even what you think. It is what you do in the world. The thing you *have* to do because something tells you inside: that is honour" (ibid., p. 103).

Seven months later, the Northern Army is near Hinks' new home. He has volunteered to lead his neighbors in burning all their homes to prevent the Yankees from using or looting them—the "honorable thing to do." There has been no news of either of his sons, but defeat has not lessened Hinks' business sense: he generously pays the worthless Confederate money to his friends in exchange for land sold in their despair. But, when Union soldiers requisition his house for quarters, Hinks is constitutionally unable to burn his own home. The businessman in him defeats the pretension to gentility and honor.

Hinks is contrasted to Colonel Thayer, leader of the Union troops. A contractor and architect in peacetime, Thayer describes himself as "just an ordinary innocent killer of men." He does *his* duty as a soldier, although he hates himself for so easily being a barbarian and destroying life and property: "in all conscience, don't tempt me to

hurt you. . . . Because I want so much to be cruel. Do you hear that?
Do you know what it is to revel in destruction? To delight in the pain
of others? Oh, it is ravishing to be cruel and I confess it! If only
you knew how gladly I would burn this house and you and the
whole earth if I could get it in my hands! Do you hear that? I am
drunk with cruelty and I hate it even as I love it and I beg you . . .
please . . . help me and save yourself . . . help me and save me,
too!" (ibid., p. 120). Aware of the business sense in Hinks, Thayer
preserves the house to quarter his officers before they "march to
the sea."

A week later, the officers are planning to give themselves a party
in Hinks' home to celebrate leaving to join in the siege of Atlanta.
The townspeople hate Hinks for not burning his house and for
seeming to cooperate with the Yankees. Amelia Blair, now obviously pregnant, appears just in time to learn from a letter inter-
cepted by Thayer that Grayson is missing in action and that Aaron is
dead. She and Mrs. Hinks realize that Aaron has been sacrificed to
his father's inconsistent sense of duty and honor.

While the officers enjoy their party upstairs, Grayson surrep-
titiously visits his parents. He berates his father's selfishness and false
sense of duty—the cause of Aaron's particularly horrible death (he
lay wounded and unattended between the lines for two days, unable
even to kill himself). When Hinks tries to keep Grayson from leaving to rejoin the Confederate Army, Grayson insists on doing his
duty, for Hinks' sons have taken seriously their father's cant about
"honor." They have become what he wanted, while he has revealed
his hypocrisy in wanting what they have become. As Grayson
leaves, disgusted with his father, Hinks set fire to his fine home—to
the admiration of Colonel Thayer!

There are several rather obvious flaws in On the March to the Sea.
Each of the characters except Thayer is a stereotype from the romantic American versions of the Civil War: Grayson, the chivalric son
and bravely defeatist soldier; Amelia, the aristocratic but strong girl;
Mrs. Hinks, the simple-minded wife in silent subservience to her
husband; and Hinks, who is no more than one of William Faulkner's
Snopeses achieving some self-awareness. Aaron, the only intelligent
Southerner in the play, could have been given more significance as a
pacifist in wartime instead of being shuffled off the stage, an easy

victim of his father's pride. And Thayer's function as a sympathetic foil to Hinks is confused when the Northerner is given the role of philosophic sadist and commentator on the effect of war on otherwise "decent men."

Finally, there is doubt over the meaning that Vidal assigns to Hinks' final act. Burning the house is not an acceptable "offering" for having encouraged one's sons to die uselessly; it resembles too closely the "happy ending" school of drama. Arthur Miller's *Death of a Salesman* (1948), a play remarkably similar to *On the March to the Sea*, demonstrates the quality missing in Vidal's denouement— irony. Willy Loman's suicide is both noble and useless, but Hinks' new self-knowledge seems to insist on his nobility—in a play that (in the character of Thayer and in the words of Grayson) explodes the whole myth of nobility and "honor." According to Vidal, "Hinks is the self-made man, the opportunist, the brigand founder of a dynasty, an embodiment of the life force . . . or a traitor, depending on one's own point of view, and that is where my failure began."[16]

However, resolving, the uncertainty over Hinks' character would not necessarily improve this play. Because the cast of characters is stock and the theme is trite, *On the March to the Sea* should wisely be left in print but not put upon the stage.

Vidal first wrote in 1959 of the work of Friedrich Dürrenmatt, the Swiss dramatist and novelist, who happened to attract his attention just when he had decided that "Love" as the universal panacea operative in every American play had become reprehensible to him: "But, now, like an avalanche in far-off mountains, comes Friedrich Dürrenmatt, a Swiss detective story writer with a genius for the theater, to give us a new theme, or rather to remind us of an ancient one: justice. And he has arraigned with wit our Loving time before that austere tribunal."[17] The two writers met, and Vidal arranged to adapt Dürrenmatt's *Romulus der Grosse* for presentation in New York City, although the play had failed in Germany, France, and England.

Thinking that he could make *Romulus der Grosse* interesting enough to succeed in the United States, Vidal justified the practice of adapting another man's play by invoking the names of such adapters as William Shakespeare, André Gide, Albert Camus, Tennessee Williams, Thornton Wilder, and Arthur Miller. He then decided that Dürrenmatt's play "was undramatic"[18] because the theme was stated too early and then merely repeated for four scenes and because the characters were classical rather than Shakespearean. One other change, and the adaptation was done—Vidal added many topical jokes:

> True comedy uses everything. It is sharp; it is topical; it does not worry about its own dignity; it merely mocks the false dignity of others. Aristophanes did not write to be great in eternity. He wrote to influence the life of his day. He used every kind of joke he could think of, and many of them concerned people sitting in his own audience, references often unfathomable to us now. But Aristophanes endures because of his engagement in the vulgar life of his own time. *Romulus* in its way is equally a speaking picture of some of our day's follies and foibles. (*Romulus*, p. xiv)

Romulus takes place from March 15 to March 16, A.D. 476. The last emperor of the Roman Empire, named for the legendary founder of Rome, is a quiet chicken farmer who stays at his Tivoli villa and does not worry about the state of the empire, rapidly being conquered by the armies of Ottaker the Goth. Romulus is the negligent husband of the Empress Julia, who married him because, being the daughter of a slave, she needed a patrician husband in order to become empress. They have a daughter, Rea—formally engaged to Aemillian, for years a captive of the Goths—who usually conducts herself as though she were acting in one of the classical tragedies which she studies. There are courtiers who consider themselves the last preservers of world order and bureaucrats who know that good governing is done on paper. Not far away the Goths battle the last Roman army—and win.

Romulus knows that he is ruling in the last days of the Roman Empire. A former professor of history, he should know how to govern well; but his policy has been one of nongovernment. Romulus has judged the past and decided that the guilt of Rome's history must be expiated in its present:

> *I* did not betray Rome. Rome betrayed herself. Long ago. Rome knew truth, but chose power. Rome knew humaneness, but chose tyranny. Rome debased herself, as well as those she governed. . . .

This throne is set upon a mountain of empty grinning skulls, streams of blood gush upon the steps to this high place where Caesar sits, where *I* sit, presiding over those cataracts of blood which are the source of power. . . . Rome is old and weak and staggering, but her debt is not yet paid, nor her crimes forgotten. But the hour of judgment is near. The old tree is dying. The ax is ready. The Goths have come. We who have bled others must now ourselves be bled. You have asked for justice. I shall give it! I sentence Rome to death! (*Romulus*, p. 61)

The emperor ignores entreaties to "save the state" from "the international menace of Gothic-ism." He feeds the chickens, named for former emperors and for Ottaker (the most productive hen of all). When Julia and the bureaucrats try to move the government to Sicily, all are drowned; the Byzantine emperor pleads for asylum; and Otto Rupf offers to save the empire.

Rupf, dressed suggestively like a modern international business-man, is a manufacturer of pants, the new garment worn by the Goths and, therefore, the style of the future. He thought first of buying the empire, but its precarious financial state dissuaded him. In exchange for marriage to Rea, Rupf will now *pay* the Goths to withdraw from the empire instead of conquering it. Romulus, who rejects the offer, encourages Rea and Aemillian, escaped from a Gothic prison, to marry and be happy—in other words, to forget a dying empire and to accentuate the human. They, too, drown.

Romulus is almost assassinated (by everyone in Tivoli) before he can carry out his plan of dissolving a moribund empire, but he survives to meet Ottaker, fearsome ruler of the Goths. Ottaker, to Romulus' surprise, is himself a chicken farmer—and a warlord be-cause his subjects, dressed as modern German soldiers, force him to lead them in battle. Ottaker wishes to prevent the future militarism of the Germans; Romulus wishes to expiate the sins of Rome's militaristic past. Knowing that they must both fail, the two rulers agree to survive in peace: to "act as if all the accounts in the world were finally balanced, as though spirit had finally triumphed over matter" (ibid., p. 78).

This little intellectual comedy could not possibly have flattered audiences accustomed to serious discussions of world war and world peace and to idealized faith in their political leaders. Surely, one should not joke about patriotism, militarism, and the "patterns of world history"! And New York audiences did rebel at the ironic idea of justice. Vidal recalls, "I used to listen to the odd laughter at *Romulus*. It would begin after a line the audience thought funny; then it would die in the throat and there would be a half gasp . . . what *are* they saying? Can it be that we are not loved in this house, but judged? I put the case more strongly than the play warrants. Romulus was more good-humored than not."[19]

The humor in *Romulus* may be gentle and good, but behind it is Vidal's knowledge (apparently shared by Dürrenmatt) that "I and my race are nothing in eternity. . . . I know we shall not endure. The present is all time."

10

Vidal's Satiric Voices

WILLIAM H. PRITCHARD

Over the years since Gore Vidal published his first novel, *Willi-waw*—the unvoiced narrative of a toneless narrator—his work both in fiction and criticism has become increasingly bristling in its tone and subtle in the effects it orchestrates. Literary theorists who like to subvert the notion of a speaking voice in the literary text, by proving there's no such thing, would have difficulty dealing in such a manner with a typical passage in, say, "Pink Triangle and Yellow Star," Vidal's 1981 piece in the *Nation* on homosexuals and some of their critics. The essay's most memorable section considers the assumptions and statements made about gays by Midge Decter in her *Commentary* article, "The Boys on the Beach"—except that Vidal does not commonly speak of "gays." He finds that so-called politically correct term "a ridiculous word to use as a common identification for Frederick the Great, Franklin Pangborn and Eleanor Roosevelt." Vidal prefers to call it "same-sex sex" and to characterize its practitioners with traditionally abusive and contemptuous words like "faggots," "queers," and "fairies." Or, more clinically, he employs his own favorite coinage—"homosexualist."

Decter is one of a group of New York Jewish writers who, Vidal claims, engage in "fag-baiting" (in an earlier essay, "Sex Is Politics," he referred to "a Catskill hotel called the Hilton Kramer," alluding to another icon of the neoconservative crowd associated with commentary). She is introduced in "Pink Triangle . . ." with a parenthetical allusion: "Mrs. Norman Podhoretz, also known as Midge Decter (like Martha Ivers, *whisper* her name)." Whether one is generally sympathetic or not to Decter's politics, the allusion to Martha Ivers is diverting since *The Strange Love of Martha Ivers* is a 1946 Barbara Stanwyck movie about a woman on the make. Advance publicity for the film made use of the terse command "Whisper her name," and those of us (like Vidal) whose adolescence or young adulthood took place during the 1940s will catch the fond remembrance even as it warns us to beware of Decter.

Having previewed the excitements to come, Vidal paraphrases some of her observations on the behavior of "pansies" (his term, of course, not hers) at a Fire Island resort called the Pines. Decter observed that, over the years, "the boys on the beach" had become more militant and also (Vidal interpolates) less well-groomed: "What indeed has happened to the homosexual community I used to know—they who only a few short years ago ["as opposed to those manly 370-day years," Vidal again interpolates] were characterized by nothing so much as a sweet, vain, pouting, girlish attention to the youth and beauty of their bodies?" Instead of answering her irrelevant question, Vidal pounces on one of Decter's footnotes in order to create what is probably the single most outrageously funny sentence he has ever written:

> "There were also homosexual women at the Pines [Decter writes] but they were or seemed to be, far fewer in number. Nor, except for a marked tendency to hang out in the company of large and ferocious dogs, were they instantly recognizable as the men were." Well, if I were a dyke and a pair of Podhoretzes came waddling toward me on the beach, copies of Leviticus and Freud in hand, I'd get in touch with the nearest Alsatian dealer pronto.

The style accommodates, in a fairly short sentence, "dyke" and "Leviticus" and "Alsatian dealer," even as the alliterative "pair of Podhoretzes" are made to waddle along the Fire Island beach. The sentence begins with a relaxed but ominous "Well," and ends, in a masterstroke, with "pronto," a word nobody ever uses in conversation or in writing, and which has therefore a distinct, archaic charm.

In the words of a now-dead expression, the whole passage is Too Much; like the earlier reference to Martha Ivers, it almost goes too far. Vidal's scathing contempt for Decter's tone and ideology, nevertheless, feels freer, funnier, and more exhilarating coming forth in a beach-fantasy like the above. Having let himself go this far, a more prudent combatant would have desisted; instead Vidal is spurred to further inventive invective, as if to prove he can top the one he'd just thought up (as indeed he can). So he chooses another of Decter's musings, this one concerning a supposedly relative lack of body hair on homosexuals as compared to their heterosexual counterparts: "We were never able to determine just why there should be so definite a connection between what is nowadays called their sexual preference ["previously known to right-thinking Jews as an abomination against Jehovah," intrudes Vidal] and their smooth feminine skin. Was it a matter of hormones?" Vidal suggests that, because of her "essential modesty and lack of experience," Decter has been privileged to see few gentile males without their clothes on:

> If she had, she would have discovered that gentile men tend to be less hairy than Jews except, of course, when they are not. Because the Jews killed our Lord, they are forever marked with hair on their shoulders—something that no gentile man has on *his* shoulders except for John Travolta and a handful of other Italian-Americans from the Englewood, New Jersey, area.

The great strokes here are not only that trick first sentence, with its profferred formulation comparing relatively hairless gentiles to hairy Jews (which then takes it all back with the minimally stated but absolute reservation—"except, of course, when they are not"), but also, later, the marvelous entrance of John Travolta onto the scene, bringing along with him a spurious demographic swipe at the Englewood, New Jersey, area.

Hugh Kenner once said about Eliot's "young man carbuncular" in the third book of *The Waste Land*, "If he existed, and if he read these words, how must he have marvelled at the alchemical power of language over his inflamed skin!" One imagines, just for a moment, that when Midge Decter read (if she ever did) Vidal's retort to her, she might have marveled or even laughed aloud at what her biased observations of certain homosexual lifestyles had been turned into. The mocking tone of Vidal's extravagantly gleeful correctives is such as to move any argument he has with someone like Decter to another level—an aesthetic level, I'd call it (though Decter herself may have found other words for it). At any rate, for all Vidal's witty ability to deflate someone's oversized ego or to squelch the wrong-headed opinions of an antagonist, his approach invariably has something "positive" about it. In this connection, one wonders if the vituperative critic John Simon was able to derive any instruction from the following sketch of himself in Vidal's essay, "Literary Gangsters":

> A Yugoslav with a proud if somewhat incoherent Serbian style (or is it Croatian?—in any case, English is his third language), Mr. Simon has for twenty years slashed his way through literature, theater, cinema. Clanking chains and snapping whips, giggling and hissing, he has ricocheted from one journal to another, and though no place holds him for long, the flow of venom has proved inexhaustible. There is nothing he cannot find to hate. Yet in his way, Mr. Simon is pure; a compulsive rogue criminal, more sadistic Gilles de Rais than neighborhood thug.

(A footnote adds: "Mr. Simon has since instructed us that English is his fifth language.") Vidal knew that with John Simon he had on his hands no mere neighborhood thug—that Simon's critical steamroller deserved nothing commonplace in the way of abuse. Thus are brought in the metaphorical chains and the whips, the giggling and hissing suitable to an uncommon "literary gangster."

In 1959, when Norman Mailer had his say about some contemporary American novelists ("Evaluations—Quick and Expansive Comments on the Talent in the Room," in *Advertisements for Myself*), he wrote two interesting paragraphs about Vidal praising his "good formal mind" and the "brave and cultivated wit" of his essays. Mailer opined that Vidal's "considerable body of work" showed as yet no novel that was "more successful than not." But he asserted that Vidal had "the first requirement of an interesting writer—one cannot predict his direction." Although, as often, the essay (and book) was couched in terms of typical Mailerish self-promotion, this was also a prescient statement about Vidal. To measure the distance between *Williwaw* and *Lincoln*, or between *The City and the Pillar* and *Duluth*, is to realize that "development"—the critic's usual term for artistic maturation or change—is scarcely the word to describe such scope and diversity in a novelist's work. I don't propose to explore the subject beyond noting that (in Mailer's phrase) Vidal's "cultivated wit" played almost no part in the early novels, whether their scene was contemporary or historical. But by the late sixties, with the publication of *Myra Breckinridge*, and such essays as "The Holy Family" and "Doc Reuben," he was fully launched on a satiric style that came to full expression in *Myron, Duluth*, and in essays like "Pink Triangle . . ." (noted above).

Or, say, rather, satiric *styles*. To simplify matters perhaps unduly, the "Pink Triangle" style is very much a voiced one, and the voice is marked by its commanding insolence toward the fools and knaves it opposes. I don't know if Mailer's prose work in the 1960s was of any specific use to Vidal in loosening up his own style and broadening the range of his targets, but *Advertisements for Myself, The Presidential Papers*, and *Cannibals and Christians* must at least have had the force of example. In fact, when Vidal made his infamous coupling of Mailer with Charles Manson (in "Women's Liberation meets Miller-Mailer-Manson-Man"), which led to the famous confrontation between the two on *The Dick Cavett Show*, Vidal himself was being rather Mailerish in his aggressive, free-swinging ripostes. And though Mailer has typically been louder and, sometimes, cruder in striking blows against politicians or writers he doesn't admire, he and Vidal do share a savvy wit and a genius for constructing bizarre creative fantasies.

In the 1970s, as Mailer occupied himself scarcely at all with evaluating the talent of his younger American contemporaries, Vidal grew bolder and (from one angle at least) more conservative in his pronouncements on what sort of fictional thing would or would not do. His special scorn was reserved for practitioners of what he called "fiction's R and D [Research and Development]." These novelists were themselves teachers, and if they were not exactly "scholar-squirrels" or "the hacks of academe" (Vidal's affectionate names for members of the profession), they wrote "teachers' novels." Often in Vidal's opinion, they didn't write well: John Barth's *Giles Goat-Boy* "is a very bad prose-work"; Donald Barthelme's *The Dead Father* "is written in a kind of numbing baby talk" which "of course" Barthelme means to be ironic and that he also knows is "not very interesting to read"; Pynchon's *Crying of Lot 49* is notable for its cute names, bad grammar, and homophobia, while *Gravity's Rainbow* is "the perfect teachers' novel." That these novelists and their professorial explicators deserve one another is the clear implication of Vidal's treatment. It may well have been that as his own fiction grew more unexperimental—as he began to write longish historical works that unfolded through a relatively conventional narrative texture, and through sentences not designed (like Barth's or Barthelme's) to "self-destruction"—his contempt for "teachers' novels" sharpened and intensified.

Yet between 1968 and 1983 he published four comic novels whose sentences, if they don't exactly self-destruct, cannot be read with a straight face. Compared to the vigorous insolence and mischief of the "Pink Triangle" satire on Decter, the style of these novels is fastidiously bogus. All of them are written in purposely "dumb" voices, and their construction must have furnished their author with considerable pleasure. These books are filled with movie lore, and in *Myron*, Myra Breckinridge finds herself inside the filming of a 1948 film, *Siren of Babylon*, starring Maria Montez. When, with "spitfire intensity," Maria utters the following question ("You who have debauched thousands and listened to evil councillors, now will you listen to the voice of the One True God?") to Louis Calhern's King Nebuchadnezzar, Myra can barely contain herself for the thrill of it all:

> Every time Maria says this line I shiver and want to pee and am covered with gooseflesh. Her air to Puerto Rican majesty combined with a Santo Domingan accent result in a performance which is, voice-wise, superior to that of Loretta Young as Berengaria in *The Crusaders* (1935) when Loretta said so movingly to her husband Richard the Lion-Hearted, "Richard, you gotta save Christianity," and equal to that of Lana Turner's portrayal of a priestess of Ba'al who is stoned to death in *The Prodigal* (1955); a performance which

was, very simply, the high point of 1940's movie acting in a 1950's film.

"Voice-wise" this passage is delightful in its "authoritative" pronouncements about Puerto Rican majesty and Santo Domingan accents, and in the precise distinctions and comparisons made between three immortal (Camp-wise) films and actresses. (Who else but Myra—or Vidal—could state that Lana Turner's work in *The Prodigal* was "very simply" the high point of 1940's movie acting in a 1950's film—an extremely refined discrimination that could just possibly be true.)

As noted, one occasionally reaches for the term *camp* to label this sort of thing—but Vidal's effects often elude the term and sometimes even have an almost poignant ring to them. In *Myron* there is a mention of an all-but-forgotten 1940's leading man, Lon Mc-Callister, who, though we are told he lives on in Malibu, "is of course no longer the boy who broke your heart in *Stage Door Canteen*, playing Romeo to Katharine Cornell's gracious Juliet nor can he ever again go home, except on the Late Show, to Indiana." It is as if some central part of the writer's own heart has gone into salvaging poor Lon. The most useful and shortest definition of Camp I've encountered says that it takes opposite attitudes ("Of course it's dreadful, but it's *wonderfully* dreadful") toward whatever subcultural artifact (say, Maria Montez's acting) is up for inspection. But Myra isn't camping it up, she simply adores Maria Montez; while Vidal thinks Maria is so awful that she's wonderful. Camp is boring when the "positive" element in it—the "wonderfully" component—lacks conviction or sufficient inventiveness. Flushed with enthusiasm, the voice of Myra Breckinridge can produce ultimate questions like the following, provoked by (in reference to great film moments) "those strips of celluloid which still endure":

> Could the actual Christ have possessed a fraction of the radiance and mystery of H. B. Warner in the first *King of Kings* or revealed, even on the cross, so much as a shadow of the moonstruck Nemi-agony of Jeffrey Hunter in the second *King of Kings*, that astonishing creation of Nicholas Ray?

Surely a rhetorical question, but both *Myra Breckinridge* and *Myron* (especially the latter) have enough of such reflections to ensure their endurance as minor classics. Indeed, the movie-camp trivia seems to me funnier and more rereadable than the sex-change business in both novels.

A related but somewhat different bogus style is found in *Kalki* and especially *Duluth*, and it has affinities with Terry Southern's procedures in *The Magic Christian* and *Candy*. Southern, his books out of print and his name unknown to younger readers (none of my students, canvassed recently, had even heard of him) was, along with Lenny Bruce, the most remarkable darkish comedian of the sixties. In Mailer's words, he represented, as does Vidal, "The aristocratic impulse turned upon itself," and he produced in *The Magic Christian* what Mailer rightly called "a classic of Camp." Vidal's *Duluth* has similar classic ambitions, though it fails to achieve them because it's rather too long a book (Southern's novel, by contrast, is wickedly short). But sentences like the following, pretending to describe the "barrios" of Duluth, packed with illegal aliens ("overheated wetbacks") and women "folding their tortillas with practiced fingers," sound exactly the right note of inspired bogusness, as a white alien policewoman invades the aliens' turf:

> Obsidian black inscrutable eyes in age-old Mayan or Aztec faces immediately recognize Lieutenant Darlene Ecks, Homicide, whose recipiency of the Civic Achievement Medal has not gone unremarked in the Spanish press. As Darlene, a dazed smile on her moist lips, pauses at a colorful outdoor market where chiles and peppers and black beans are bought and sold by women in the colorful black dresses of their original homeland, Pablo and two accomplices materialize just back of the chickpea stall.

Such riveting thriller-writing (note the artful repetition of "colorful" and the ominous rising action behind the chickpea stall) is the staple of narrative news in *Duluth*. If *Gravity's Rainbow* is a perfect "teachers' novel" since it gives teacher plenty to do (every paragraph with its own built-in knot to unravel), Vidal's *Duluth* is full of cheesy thirdhand imaginings ("a dazed smile on her moist lips") which don't tempt anyone to interpretive academic strategies.

But neither did the progenitor and masterpiece of all modern comedies, Evelyn Waugh's *Decline and Fall*. In that classic, the Welsh schoolmaster, Dr. Fagan, remarks to Paul Pennyfeather, the novel's hapless hero, that "We schoolmasters must temper discretion with deceit." True enough about schoolmasters, it is also true about satirists like Waugh and a latter-day practitioner such as Gore Vidal. It was in Waugh's second novel, *Vile Bodies*, where the word *bogus* made its appearance in relation to a Bright Young Thing named Archie Schwert ("the most *bogus* man" says Agatha Runcible, spiritedly). But Waugh was already an expert in constructing bogus sentences that discreetly and deceitfully pretended to be observing life—to register the look and feel of a world "out there"—when in fact they were merely opportunities for striking off humorous (sometimes cruelly humorous) juxtapositions. At the end of Lottie Crump's party in *Vile Bodies*, "Judge Skimp was sleeping, his fine white hair in an ash-tray," and the sentence which notes that "fact" pretends to responsibility toward the way things are, even as it scores nicely off the judge. Like Waugh, Vidal decided that it was not for him to explore the mysteries of the human heart; decided that he didn't want to know all, and thus have to forgive all. Instead he became, in his comic novels and prose, a considerable satirist the essence of which activity (as Wyndham Lewis pointed out most clearly) is to be unfair.

To conclude this brief sampling of Vidal's satiric voices, it may be helpful to remember Eliot's remarks about the nature of Ben Jonson's comedy—that it is "only incidentally satire, because it is only incidentally a criticism upon the actual world." Eliot found the source of Jonson's art not to lie "in any precise emotional attitude or precise intellectual criticism of the actual world," and claimed that it was "creative" rather than "critical" in its character. Yet it is probably no coincidence that Jonson was also a fine critic, and surely no coincidence that the journalist-reporter Vidal, who provided us with so many engaging and incisive criticisms of America in the 1960s and beyond, should also figure as a first-rate creative satirist.

11

Living Appropriately: Vidal and the Essay

SAMUEL F. PICKERING

"Even good authors," Montaigne wrote "are wrong to insist on fashioning a consistent and solid fabric out of us. They choose one general characteristic, and go and arrange and interpret all a man's actions to fit their picture; and if they cannot twist them enough, they go and set them down to dissimulation." Imagined worlds are complex and inconsistent, sometimes as inconsistent as lives. As a result interpretation distorts. Much as biography presses life into a form, so interpretation forces writing into patterns, snipping off the loose strands of variety and discovering cause amid inconsistency. Particularly susceptible to distortion is the essay. Ours, in fact, may be the age of the essay. Having blown across the country from Washington and Hollywood, the cult of personality has infected the university, and literary critics now see themselves as creators not commentators. Implicit in the cult of personality is the celebration of self and the denial of community and responsibility, even the responsibility to write clearly. Consequently chic critics celebrate autobiography and the personal essay, forms in which voice is some-times more important than idea. Behind voice, of course, lurks a writer, the soft malleable stuff of interpretation.

In truth I don't like discussing Vidal's essays. Not only will what-

ever I write be reductive, but Vidal like Alexander Pope has fashioned a *Dunciad* and I don't look forward to finding myself consign-
ed to a rancorous footnote amid chaos and the dark. What I much
prefer is quoting Vidal, without attribution, for Vidal has attacked
so many of the dolts and serfs of Upper Humbug that he is not quite
respectable. His very name raises the learned eyebrow and provokes
the long look. On several occasions recently I have used his phrase
"stern tolerance" to criticize polemical do-gooders. Unlike these
aggressive goose-steppers whose moral vision brooks no dissent,
Vidal knows that life and books are various and complex, and he
champions thoughtful tolerance, one not based upon hard law or
harder sentiment but upon reason. He knows that man is not rational, yet he advocates, not preaches, reason. Most of the positions
he supports are common-sensical. On sexual matters, one of his
favorite subjects, he argues that an individual's private life should be
left to his own conscience. "The human race is divided into male
and female," he writes; "Many human beings enjoy sexual relations
with their own sex; many don't; many respond to both. The plu-
rality is the fact of our nature and not worth fretting about." He is
absolutely right. The government has no business pulling people
out of closets and living rooms and regulating intimate doings in
dens and tree houses. Who does what to whom and how, so long as
the folks are, as the phrase puts it, "consenting adults" is the stuff of
private pleasure and maybe public gossip, not law. Of course the rub
comes when the abstraction turns concrete, when the tolerance
proposed for society affects our lives. To put it more simply, what is
fine for the general population (that great heap of drug dealers,
snake handlers and chiropractors, Republicans and Democrats)
won't do for my family. For them I want heterosexual lives, crawling
with babies, bumptious and breast-fed. I want their days to be
boring and safe. I don't want them ever to write a book, and I'm not
sure that they ought to read. Behind my feeling, not thought (for
such is not thought) may lie the source of discomfit with Vidal. He
is right, but if his rightness were ever to take effect, lives would be
radically changed, probably for the better. But for a while we'd be
damned uncomfortable, something I, at least, want to avoid.

Still, my humors, like those described by Montaigne, "shift with
the shifts in the weather," and I find Vidal's descriptions of sexual

doings entertaining. Particularly memorable is his account of taking the Glorious Bird, Tennessee Williams, to meet the Kennedys. Vidal and Williams visited the Kennedys in Palm Beach and for a time did some target shooting on the patio. "While Jackie flitted about," Vidal writes, "taking Polaroid shots of us, the Bird banged away at the target; and proved to be a better shot than our host. At one point, while Jack was shooting, the Bird muttered in my ear, 'Get that ass!' I said, 'Bird, you can't cruise our next president.' The Bird chuckled ominously: 'They'll never elect those two. They are much too attractive for the American people.' Later, I told Jack the Bird had commented favorably on his ass. He beamed. 'Now, that's *very* exciting,' he said."

Anecdotes are the staple of Vidal's essays. Generally the anecdotes are literary or political. Although Vidal's essays have increasingly become more personal (in *At Home*, for example, he writes about his father in "On Flying"), his stories are usually not familial. In contrast to essayists who ransack their children's conversation for the telling phrase, Vidal rummages through history, citing Suetonious or Lincoln much as I would quote my Francis or Edward. Mind you, for most readers, Suetonious, Plutarch, and Herodotus sound like the names of pizza restaurants and reek more of pepperoni and the St. Pauli girl than they do of history. By citing my children I try to broaden my readership and touch feelings. For Vidal such doings are romantic pishposh, smacking of the sappiness of Wordworth's infant philosopher. Instead of feelings Vidal aims for that higher thing, the mind. When he does touch a feeling, it is usually anger, most particularly when he details the doings of successful poltroons: "public servants" who mouth high platitudes while groping the felonious low ground. Vidal casts a wide net and along with mud and shards pulls in assorted fishy characters: psychologists, sexologists, "Christers," university professors, every sort of quack except those, it sometimes seems, adept at biting heads off live chickens. Like most of us Vidal enjoys quacks. Not only do they make good copy but often in their absurdity, there is a strain of fervent honesty. In the bang of General William Booth's big drum there was little of the tinkling cymbal and the sounding brass. Only when quacks become manipulatively self-serving do they become evil. When Vidal gets his pen into a quack, the prose runs colorful, though on occasion he can go a little to far, or so my friend Josh tells me. "At two points, Dr. Reuben is at odds with Moses," Vidal writes of the now-forgotten author of *Everything You Always Wanted to Know About Sex But Were Afraid to Ask.* "He thinks Onan was quite a guy, and his lonely practice particularly useful in toning up those of our senior citizens whose wheelchairs will not accommodate two people; and he has a positively Updikean enthusiasm for cunnilingus. Dr. Reuben would like everyone to indulge in this chivalrous practice—except women, of course. Lesbianism is 'immature.' He is also sufficiently American to believe that more of everything is best. At times he sounds not unlike the late Bruce Barton extolling God as a super-salesman. 'Success in the outside world breeds success in the inside world of sex,' sermonizes Dr. Reuben. 'Conversely, the more potent a man becomes in the bedroom, the more potent he is in business.' Is God a super-salesman? You bet!—and get this—*God eats it too!"*

Poseurs and Machiavellian self-promoters, not quacks, are Vidal's real villains, writers like Hemingway and then Faulkner with his "High Confederate" style. Especially irritating to Vidal are the "hacks of academe," in Vidal's view people who not only write poorly but reduce complexity to simplicity. Even worse, they pontificate, in the process elevating criticism and themselves above literature. Instead of breaking minds and pencils by writing poetry and novels, the hacks write books about books, a comparatively low occupation done in the high seriousness mode.

Vidal's criticism of hacks makes me uncomfortable, in part because I am one myself and in part because the target is too slow and has an easy history of lending itself to the comic. Most of my hack friends are nice, well-meaning, even bright people. They live ordinary lives, terrified of cancer and worried about their children. They nurse ailing mates and care for aging parents. They teach, and occasionally they write books, to be sure books about books and books which sometimes pontificate. To some extent our environment shapes us, and to be treated as Delphic by students is probably not good for a man and certainly not good for criticism. Also, contemporary critics, despite their hankerings for things French, are the evangelical, not stylistic, descendants of Matthew Arnold. After Arnold generations of academics have confused literature and religion, seeing literature as, in the words of that once prominent but now forgotten critic, John Churton Collins, "the revelation of the eternal, the unchanging, and the typical which underlines the unsubstantial and ever-dissolving empire of matter and time." To see literary texts as sanctified and as shapers of the moral conscience elevates teachers of English to the pulpit, giving them a sense of mission and importance. Although critics often resemble "Christers" in their fervor and certainty, literature isn't religion, and education itself, despite all the slick packaging, is not going to cure the ills of society. Indeed instead of attacking those lower acolytes who occasionally torch books in the *New York Times* Vidal might accomplish more if he battered at the supports of the educational temple itself. Although they appear raised on fieldstone, the supports usually rest on flimsy platitude. I don't want the temple to tumble about my head, but a little modesty might improve education and criticism, or so I want to think.

Like Fielding, Vidal thinks affectation the source of the ridiculous and then, in Vidal's case, the source of presumption and even danger. Often Vidal advocates modesty, not so much for the individual writer though, as for the imperial nation. Writers have to be tough to survive outrageous criticism, the ad hominem attacks that result when created worlds are reduced to sociology and polemic. "What matters," Vidal writes, "is not the world's judgment of oneself but one's own judgment of the world." Since the acquisition of the Philippines in 1898, our nation, Vidal argues, has swollen immodest. Instead of reforming our society and seeing our country simply as one country among many, we have become victims of our own propaganda. Mouthing platitudes about duty and responsibility, we meddle in faraway affairs, our ignorance often bringing blood not enlightenment. Particularly galling to Vidal is our nation's unthinking support of Israel. "We have supported Israel for forty years," he writes; "No other minority in the history of the United States has ever extorted so much Treasury money for its Holy Land as the Israeli lobby, and it has done this by making a common cause with the National Security State. Each supports the other. I would have us cease to pay for either." He is, of course, sensible, but nothing Vidal writes will influence government. Nationalism is a booming industry, in Europe, the Soviet Union, and the Middle

East. Israeli nationalists are particularly effective ones, realizing that money is controlled by politicians, not writers. To them Vidal is just a nuisance, a stinging gnat to be swatted at occasionally by *Commentary* or the *New Republic* and then ignored. Still to criticize Israel or any of the "holies" of foreign policy or American life takes courage. To be always out of step with one's neighbors, even if those neighbors are below stairs, drains energy. How much easier it is to be a cheerleader, leading the crowd through an enthusiastic "sis-boom-bomb."

Platitudes, whether of thought or policy, have an underside, and Vidal delights in flipping them over and making the conventional classes squirm. Turning platitudes over is not difficult, however. The problem, alas, is that under any platitude swarm other platitudes, eager to wrinkle into the sunlight and swell fat and greasy. On the most mundane level educational psychologists, for example, lecture parents of young children on the necessity of being firm. "Once you tell a child *no*, you must," the pundits preach, "stick to your word so the child will respect you and learn that there are absolutes in life." Like so many things educational and psychological the statement is plausible but half-baked. My children never accept *no*, and are almost always successful in pestering me into, if not *yes*, at least an affirmative "damnit to hell, all right, just leave me alone." For a while I worried about being soft. What lesson, I wondered, was I teaching the children. But then suddenly I flipped the psychologist's advice on its back and realized that my children were learning that all-American virtue persistence. When the going gets tough, as football coaches say in moments of eloquence, the tough get going, and my children will dig their cleats in and, throwing forearms and knees around, and biting first this and that, will be unmovable. When other children hoist the white flag, my children will refuse to give up, shouting "nuts" to defeat, and the Hessians will hang on to victory and the academy awards.

Of course when Vidal flays what he sees as an unpleasant truth of American life, he offends the conventional classes. To win a political election, so the accepted wisdom has it, one must avoid offense, and it is not surprising despite his garnering large numbers of votes that Vidal has not been a successful politician. Recently, my friend Josh thought about running for our town council. To start his campaign off, he said, "with a bang," he wrote to the local newspaper criticizing the state's plan to place a minimum security prison in the town. Although I warned him against writing, Josh was headstrong, insisting that "it was time someone told the truth." The prison, he wrote, was a human toxic-waste dump, and as town officials had the right to know what pollutants were being dumped in the landfill so they should have the right to know what vile waste was being stored in the prison. The prisoners were not there, he wrote, for taking candy from babies. They were hard cases, villains, who had plea-bargained the brutality out of their crimes, rapists who appeared to have reformed, only because there were no women to attack in the prison. If the bureaucrats who ran the prison system refused to make their files available to the public, claiming legal precedent and the prisoners' right to privacy, town officials should swarm over the jail. Armed with bushels of state codes, they could find so many violations they could demand closure, all the time taking the high ground saying they were only concerned with the prisoners' welfare and their rights to effective rehabilitation. The letter itself was effective, starting Josh's campaign with an explosion, so great a one that he is no longer running for office. Preferring to believe the old lie that bad people often become good, readers were upset by Josh's letter. Even I found myself saying, behind Josh's back, that I thought him elitist and lacking compassion for those less privileged than himself.

For Vidal many of society's cherished beliefs are superstition. Under the guise of promoting cultural diversity and understanding, universities now require courses in toleration. Certainly no sensitive academic, who values his pension, can oppose tolerance, even when the tolerance applies to the intolerable. At the University of Connecticut the Department of Student Affairs recently published a pamphlet listing the signs of "Harassment, Discrimination and Intolerance." The signs ranged broadly including "Making inconsiderate jokes," "Stereotyping the experiences, background, and skills of individuals," "Imitating stereotypes in speech or mannerisms," and "Treating people differently solely because they are in some way different from the majority." If a person experienced or "witnessed" signs of such intolerance, he was, the Department of Student Affairs instructed, to inform the "Discrimination and Intolerance Response

Network," or the DIRN, as my friend Josh calls it. As might be expected Josh has written a letter to the university administration, calling the policy "the ipso-facto do-wa-diddy end of free speech." Like me Josh is a literary hack, and in his letter he concentrated on the policy's effects upon the English department. Because they used stereotypes or told jokes, he wrote, Shakespeare, Swift, Dickens, George Eliot, Charlotte Brontë, Richard Wright, and the Hebrew prophets could no longer be taught. Moreover, he declared, the Age of Ethnic Pride was finished. Because they presupposed some general or stereotypical experience, courses could no longer be offered in French, Italian, or Irish literature. "The gals teaching Women's Studies," he said, "would have to shut up the sewing bag and put away the hat pins, for the assumption that women, simply because they were women, shared a general experience was a particularly invidious form of harassment." Librarians, he noted, would have to slice dialect out of all books in the "Learning Resource Center." He knew right-thinking university officials would open classes and dormitories to the lost souls in the local prison, for, he declared, ax-murderers and dope fiends must, according to the policy, be treated just like Methodists. Not only that, he said he was urging the English Department to fire a woman who wrote a study of female humor, in the process telling inconsiderate jokes about men. "Of course," he told me, "you must be fired because you are a stereotype and speak in an egregiously cartoonish dialect." While fulminating against the Department of Student Affairs, Josh remembered my use of the phrase "stern tolerance." When he learned I borrowed the phrase from Vidal, he insisted upon quoting him. He did this, I must add, against my advice. I warned him Vidal's pronouncements upon genital matters undermined his authority with conventional liberal thinkers. "He could sleep with a duckbill platypus for all I care," Josh said; "Vidal is on target and I am quoting him." "A profound tolerance is in the land," Vidal stated and Josh quoted, "a tolerance so profound that it is not unlike terror. One dare not raise one's voice against any religion, idea, or even delinquency if it is explicable by a therapist."

Vidal believes people ought to accept responsibility for their actions and should be responsible enough to expose superstition and sloppy thinking. Consequently he criticizes not only the cults of love and psychology but also devotees of religion, generally not latitudinarians civilized beyond faith and fervor, but dervishes, energetic primitives, committed to bettering your life and mine. In a letter to Thomas Jefferson, John Adams wrote, "Twenty times, in the course of my late reading, have I been on the point of breaking out. 'This would be the best of all possible worlds, if there was no religion in it.'" "Religion is an endless and complicated matter," Vidal comments, "and no one in his right mind can help agreeing with John Adams." On matters religious many students have told me they are praying for me, and so to protect myself from importunate good will, I have hedged my statements about religion. Nevertheless, I suspect Vidal is right. The profession of religion, though, not faith, is part of the air of this country. Almost like oxygen religion is breathed in and becomes a person, practically without his knowing it.

On several occasions, indeed with ardor throughout his career as an essayist, Vidal notes that the principal characteristic of the middle class is hypocrisy. I don't think he has examined the middle class closely enough. More analysis would reveal, I suspect, as high a percentage of unadulterated scoundrels in the middle as in the upper class, perhaps even a higher percentage. Besides no class holds a monopoly on any of the virtues: prudence, fortitude, temperance, justice, or hypocrisy. In contrast to the hypocrisy of the middle class, Vidal notes that he finds the candor of the aristocracy refreshing, albeit sometimes frightening. Although "means" or an "old" family may free one from social platitude, Vidal seems simply to be recycling the saw which states that what appears as bad taste or lamentable ignorance in other classes becomes charming eccentricity in the wealthy. For my money, and there isn't much of it, the aristocracy seems as bedeviled by platitude as the middle class, though, I should add, I'm not certain who are the aristocrats in this country, a sure sign, I suppose, that I'm not one. That aside, however, cash, old or new, does not free one from platitude. In our society, foundation and university have replaced the church as object of adoration and conveyor of pardons. To atone for ancestral sins, the descendants of those nineteenth-century entrepreneurs whom Teddy Roosevelt once described as " malefactors of great wealth" ceaselessly donate vast sums to universities or establish foundations to support sweetness and light. In being transferred to university endowments, profits of old sin miraculously become the means of virtue and free heirs to become tediously eccentric, even aristocratic.

Often freed from labor and the necessity of currying the favor of others, aristocrats are able to indulge themselves with artifacts and gossip, this last the appealing bric-a-brac of a social world from which ideas have been banished as at best meaningless and at worse vulgar. Like collections of knickknacks gossip can be enthralling. In accounts of misdoing is story, told not to bamboozle one into proper behavior but merely to delight. Vidal is a splendid gossip. The small tales he tells are wondrously entertaining, and his essays tingle with bright mischief. Because of his enjoyment of gossip, he occasionally reviews chatty books, letting their authors babble appealingly. Hollywood came Nancy Reagan's way, he writes, "in the form of Benny Thau, a vice-president of MGM. Nancy had a 'blind date' with him. In 1949 Thau was a great power at the greatest studio. He got Nancy a screen test, and a contract. By now Nancy was, as Mr. Leamer [author of *Make-Believe: The Story of Nancy and Ronald Reagan*] puts it, 'dating Benny Thau. Barbara, the pretty teen-age receptionist, saw Nancy frequently. Many years later, she remembered that she had orders that on Sunday morning Nancy was to be sent directly into Benny Thau's suite. Barbara nodded to Miss Davis as she walked into the vice-president's office; nodded again when she left later.' No wonder Nancy thinks the ERA is just plain silly."

That last sharp line is Vidal's signature. Vidal's prose is clean and crisp. Rarely do his sentences drift off into the abstract. He forever attacks fuzzy thinking, describing in great detail, for example, the making of movies. Far from the actual production academics tend to endow directors with magical gifts. In an attempt to set the warped record straight Vidal describes the part writers played in several films. Vidal's abhorrence of sloppy prose and slipshod thought may in part be responsible for his rarely writing about Nature. With its Wordworthian emphasis on worlds half-seen and then half-imagined, most contemporary writing about Nature is Romantic and sentimental. Distant objects please because they cannot be seen clearly and thus free the imagination and prose to strain after mood. Vidal does not try to create mood; instead he argues. In his essays he is a man of little doubt and much certainty. The labor of forty years of good writing has tightened Vidal's prose beyond doubt. Instead of the fashionable and critically alluring spectacle of a man struggling with himself, Vidal presents the hammered results of laborious thought. Instead of "process," readers get conclusion. In a time in which personality is more appealing than idea, Vidal's emphasis upon cause and effect may contribute to his small popularity with academics. To put it simply Vidal is very much an eighteenth-century writer. His sentences snap like couplets. His wit sparkles then explodes. Vidal does not blink at man's foolishness, and as a result a seam of lively melancholy runs through the essays. Behind the humor and anger is gloom, not the redemptive gloom of Johnson, the Christian Stoic, but that of the rational and the damned, that of the Byron who wrote *Don Juan*. Despite the laughter, Vidal is resigned to sadness, as indeed, almost all thinking men must be. The spectacles Byron describes bring laughter, even glee, but they chill the heart. Vidal's America is darkly hilarious, for at the center of the laughter is the realization that "things" will not get better. It is the nature of the beast not to improve. Infant damnation may be a thing of the past, but the smoke of our damnation is almost palpable in Vidal's essays.

Vidal's world is lonely. With the exception of the Wise Hack who knows all the Hollywood gossip, Vidal does not create characters. Fictional characters like Roger de Coverly and Will Honeycomb soften essays, giving them personality and place. For Vidal place is not very important. People move through places, but places don't shape people. Temptation shapes people, as does exerting the will and using the mind. Instead of fictional characters, though, actual individuals appear in several of Vidal's essays. Often these are people Vidal remembers from his childhood and youth: his father and grandfather, and then Eleanor Roosevelt for example. Often the people are literary characters, some known as friends, Tennessee Williams for instance, and others known through their books, probably the best example being Henry James. Unlike Mr. Spectator, Vidal describes the low comedy of actual not imaginary life, a subject that, for me at least, leads to spleen and melancholy. "Men," Montaigne wrote, "do not know the natural infirmity of their mind: it does nothing but ferret and quest, and keeps incessantly whirling around, building up and becoming entangled in its own work, like our silkworms, and is suffocated in it." Resisting the instinct to ferret about and suffocate in stifling conclusion is almost impossible. Essays are the swift products of moment and idea and portray as well as embody passing; yet it seems to me that Vidal's real companions are not writers or politicians, but books: cases of James, William Dean Howells, Edmund Wilson, Thomas Love Peacock, the shelves stretching through years of long reading.

Although Vidal writes crisply about our times, he seems out of place, occasionally sadly out of place. He would have been more at home, I think, in Queen Anne's London. In the heady coffeehouse society with its rich blend of politics, literature, and personality, he would have thrived. While his essays would have lost none of their edge, they might have gained familial warmth, not hot air puffed about by stuffy, embarrassing cousins from the country but the warmth which somehow develops in parlors filled with friends, writing friends. Still, that is the speculation of someone who has almost no writing friends but who has a family that often brings him joy and keeps him always fearful. "Our great and glorious masterpiece," Montaigne wrote, "is to live appropriately." What is a fitting life or literary method for me is not appropriate for someone else. Although Vidal rarely explores my domestic country, his essays are ever-alluring and always challenging, provoking one to wander far from the text, wondering and speculating. Vidal has written appropriately about our age, and he has written with style and courage, even as a moralist. Of few writers can so much be said.

12

On Gore Vidal: Wit and the Work of Criticism

ROBERT BOYERS

When he was nineteen, Gore Vidal fondly recalls, he was "the cleverest young fox ever to know how to disguise his ignorance and make a virtue of his limitations." The grown-up writer is considerably less alert to his limitations and less concerned to disguise his ignorance. A celebrity intellectual, popular novelist, and cultural entertainer with an appetite for the roguish and outré, he has for many years worked the line between wit and slander, haute journalism and preening self-advertisement. Armed with a supreme and often fatuous self-confidence, he has sought to make a final virtue of arrogance and a polished style based on disdain. Though he is surely the most amusing essayist on the American scene, he has rarely stooped to the work of analysis. The author of several books of essays and a regular contributor to the pages of such august publications as the *New York Review of Books*, he has attracted a following content to take him as he is, which is to say, as a provocateur principally noted for rebarbative displays of bilious one-upsmanship. To others he would seem to have made something less of his gifts, to have sacrificed criticism for effrontery, influence for notoriety. Whatever his stature as a novelist, his reputation as a critic probably far exceeds anything he deserves.

In many an essay by Gore Vidal we are informed that he has been unable to "actually finish reading" the material he is discussing. So often do we hear this that it is impossible not to conclude that he revels in his own ostensibly brave candor and rather prefers the effect it will make to anything he might have learned had he done the earnest book reviewer's duty. At any rate, we are rarely tempted to follow Gore's lead and skip past the pages of a Vidal essay. Once we have abandoned hope of learning much about the topic at hand and yielded ourselves to the prospect of ephemeral pleasures, we can read on with almost unimpeded if modest satisfaction. Convulsive cynicism can be very amusing in the right hands, and no one is nimbler than Vidal in bringing just about everything down to the level at which it becomes laughable. No matter whether he is dealing with Robert Coles or W. H. Auden, Donald Barthelme or Susan Sontag, Vidal can be counted on to get off memorable lines and to make us feel ever so superior. Of course we laugh hardest when the targets are our betters, those who write better, think harder, or take things more to heart than we do. High ambition is itself a goad to Vidalian rancor, and the dismissive wit is rarely so sharp as when animated by something like pique at the pretensions of those as gifted as the foxy master himself. It is also agreeable to laugh at the ponderous and powerful, at the "hacks of academe" and the political buffoons, and no one has been as adept as Vidal in sniffing out their soft spots.

Ridicule and contempt are more and more the crucial elements in Vidal's characteristic approach to his subjects, and laughter is the trophy most prized by his devout admirers. Does that laughter amount to much? Is the occasion of merriment such as to warrant the exercise of the prime Vidalian faculties? Is anything generated in the way of real insight, or is the laughter mostly the pure laughter of those for whom feeling superior is always preferable to the ignominy of taking things seriously?

Like other writers, including all manner of lesser wits, Vidal has his better moments, passages that eschew burlesque and high-spirited calumny for something approaching the ultimate real thing. These moments are more apt to occur in the political essays than in the literary reviews, though they are rare in either case. In one, reporting on the psychiatrist Robert Coles' *Children of Crisis* books, he reflects on Coles' unease in confronting bourgeois children—

"although they were my own kind"—after having spent a long time interviewing the children of the poor. "So Saint Francis must have felt," muses Gore, "whenever he stopped off in Assisi to visit the folks, only to find them still busy netting and eating those very same little birds he liked to chat with." in such a passage Vidal resists what he elsewhere in the same essay finds irresistible, namely, the temptation to mock one whom he also admires. Mostly Vidal feels "a warm glow" in the presence of a Coles article, and is embarrassed enough by his niceness to refer to him thereafter as "Thee" and "Bishop Coles," finally associating him with the birdman of Assisi. Yet it is possible to discern in the Assisi passage an element of almost reverent wonder that is complicated, not subverted, by the admixture of hyperbole and satire. In that tension lies Vidal at his best.

But Vidal's humor does not usually operate at that level. More often he travesties and jeers, and we are moved to laugh by the spectacle of a critic who says outrageous things without feeling that he has to justify them. So a contemporary critic who wants to renovate the tradition of the art novel is said to have an attitude which "reflects not so much the spirit of art as it does that of Detroit." Why Detroit? Never mind. So the humorlessness of American society is demonstrated, argued, in the sentence "what other culture could have produced someone like Hemingway and not seen the joke?" Such sentences are effective not simply because they exaggerate but because they convey no impulse to apologize or explain. Frequently they have little to do with the ostensive topic at hand. They surprise us because they are largely or entirely gratuitous expressions of something that looks like conviction but is closer to the will to deride.

From the first Vidal made a reputation as a moralist who bravely took down the powerful and went perpetually against the grain. It is not hard to see why such a reputation should have grown. For one thing, Vidal himself has long been at pains to make high claims for his fearlessness. Before it became fashionable for aspiring celebrity intellectuals to expose themselves and invite reprehension he spoke out against the heterosexual mafia in American literary culture and made no secret of his own exotic sexual proclivities. He also made it his business to say nasty things about famous writers, from Scott Fitzgerald to John Barth, and to dwell not only on the wickedness but the stupidity of most mid-century politicians. No doubt Vidal meant some of the things he wrote about Eisenhower and Nixon, Kennedy and Reagan; he may even have believed some of what he wrote about the writers he lampooned. But always it was clear that for Vidal a subject represented principally an occasion for display. Ever the opportunist, he sought novel ways of taking subjects on without succumbing to their allure. The moralist in Vidal's terms is one who need never apologize for his opinions, indeed who knows so entirely what to think and say that ambivalence and hesitation in others will always be read as signs of weakness, confusion and susceptibility to turpitude. Vidal's is the morality of the gamesman who knows himself to be a winner and complains about what others do and suffer without ever having to feel implicated. To read him on the corruptions of empire or on the careerism of avant-garde writers is to feel that human beings in general are a pretty awful lot and that Vidal almost alone has escaped the craven and the pathetic by refusing to make himself lovable. Motivated, as he more than once put it, "by an overdeveloped sense of justice," his morality resides in his insistence that things are not what they ought to be and are not apt to improve no matter what we do. Both compassion and hope are to be associated with the slow-witted and the credulous.

Though Vidal's essays sometimes seem as various as their occasions, they show much greater consistency of aim and manner than do the essays of comparably celebrated critics. This consistency goes well beyond Vidal's flashy locutions and pompadour vanities, his habit—as V. S. Pritchett deliciously put it—of seeming to go "romantically into action with one socialite arm tied behind his back." Of course a Vidal essay on French literary theorists will raise issues nowhere visible in a piece on the Kennedy dynasty or the Adams family. The posture of "hell's least kind recording angel"—Stephen Spender's rather admiring epithet—occasionally relaxes when the subject is not, say, an American President but a less imposing or rapacious figure. On occasion Vidal can be almost painstaking in setting up a target before aiming his lance and riding into action. On other occasions he dispenses with preliminaries and is decidedly less fastidious about representing the positions he means to ridicule or otherwise contend with. But however obvious the differences among the essays, they are mostly alike in their characteristic simplification of ideas, their suspicion of high seriousness as a form of humorless solemnity, and their worldliness. Whether he is writing about literature or politics, Vidal comes across always as a man who has seen and considered just about everything and has no time to entertain uneasy second thoughts. Though he fancies himself an inveterate truth-teller, the essays offer at most the truth about Gore. They are rarely reliable on the subjects they purport to discuss.

This has much to do with Vidal's aims as a satirist. It is not simply that he is notably more dogmatic than he likes to suppose and therefore willfully blind to a great deal that passes before his preter-naturally sensitive nose. His omissions and distortions are, inevitably, in the service of the effects he wishes to produce. Spender, like others, rightfully reminds us that "satire is unfair, simplifies those attitudes it attacks, and then expresses the simplification with an elegance and elaboration pleasing in themselves." If we care about the objects flattened or simplified by the witty satirist, we are apt to complain a little, though embarrassed at our high-mindedness and sorry not to enjoy what is given. To belong to a satirist like Vidal one must learn not to care too much about anything, to exercise one's wits not in order to arrive at a complex truth but to experience the enlargement of one's faculties. To make us smart, not wise, is the object of Vidalian satire. To submit to its spell is to be primed at any moment to receive and to savor the clever line. To demand fairness or circumspection is to place oneself outside the charmed circle, to prefer weight to lightness, sobriety to play.

A typical Vidal review or essay of the fifties or sixties was apt to be more or less responsible in its handling of facts and documents. Now and then the unexpected would be teased from the material, but in the main Vidal was content to do the critic's or reporter's mundane job of work, quoting sources, engaging topical issues, dispensing more or less sensible opinions. Though his ideas were not so fresh as Harold Rosenberg's, his grasp of literature nowhere so fine as Lionel Trilling's, his scholarly reach never as broad as Edmund Wilson's, he could be counted upon to move briskly, adroitly through a body of work. The prose was elegant, now and then arch, only rarely osten-tatious in the way it was later more and more to become. Much of the political criticism already seems to have been written in a very distant past, the issues no longer much with us. The literary essays are mostly thin, but tireless in exposing the vacuous and the mediocre. It no longer seems to matter much that John Hersey is a dull writer, or that Henry Miller produced a lot of amiable twaddle, though Vidal would seem in his reviews of their work to have built solid cases. The pieces occasionally betray the neo-aristocratic hauteur that was to color his later prose, but often the wit is not forced, the targets remain recognizable. So John Kenneth Galbraith is warmly applauded as "economic apostle to the middlebrows"; the infatuation of the Harvard intellectuals with the Kennedy brothers is characterized with the words "at this very moment beside the river Charles a thousand Aristotles dream of their young Alexanders, and the coming heady conquest of the earth." Amused by Henry Miller's empty prose poems, Vidal notes that, "lurking pale and wan in this jungle of rich prose, are the Thoughts." No egregious distortions here. In another essay Vidal even goes so far as to chastise Saul Bellow for overstating his case. A better-than-average reviewer, a thoughtful if finally unoriginal critic, Vidal was on his way to building a modest reputation as an essayist at a time when his standing as a novelist was very much in question.

In the years of Vidal's greatest celebrity, both as novelist and critic, his criticism changed dramatically. The pieces were at once more opinionated, more self-regarding, more calculated to wound, more cynical, and more diffuse. Even where Vidal was ostensibly reviewing a single book he would casually digress, strike poses, reminisce, emit articulate noises of dismay and disdain. More and more often the targets would be "the hacks of academe" or the avant-garde. In the political essays the enemy was often the "middle class," and liberalism came increasingly to look like a species of reaction. Everywhere Vidal saw himself surrounded by the middlebrow and the insipid, the sententious and the vatic, enemies all of wit and genius. Beset on all sides by mediocrity or pretension (so he proclaimed), Vidal had no choice but to tell the hard truths and to accept the censure that would follow. Now and then driven to celebrate the rare excellence of a Calvino or a Sciascia, he would mostly remind himself that their readers were unworthy, the literary scene a place governed by pious frauds and cultural gangsters. Though committed to the arch composure of the mostly smiling satirist, he was ever at pains to distinguish himself from the hateful "academics" and seemed frequently to be wrestling with unmastered obsessions. As good as ever in the preparation of capsule biographies and journalistic summaries, he showed no gift for sustained analysis, and his penchant for sneering condescension often led him to withdraw from discussion just where he should have persisted.

But Vidal's tendency to overstatement and distortion is surely the most distressing aspect of his work. If we sometimes consider it a gift, that is because it is responsible for some of his best lines, because he knows how to drop an overstatement so deftly that it has us laughing before we've had a chance to consider it. Light-footed, ever reluctant to dwell too long on a point, Vidal rarely anticipates rebuttal or rejoinder. When he asserts that "we do not, of course, write literary criticism at all now," he assumes that we will catch his drift and perhaps approve a little the severity of his disdain for the academic rot that disfigures the literary landscape. Presumably, confronted with the names of genuine critics, from Denis Donoghue to Robert Alter, he would understand but see no reason not to say the same thing again. No more would he be apt to apologize for deliberately misleading his reader in the sentence "In the sixties [Norman] Podhoretz wrote a celebrated piece in which he confessed that he didn't like niggers." So what if the word "niggers" belongs not to Podhoretz but to Vidal? What difference that Podhoretz's essay was written to express not a settled adult conviction but a deep conflict growing out of painful childhood memories? Podhoretz is in any case a political reactionary with a rotten record on important issues and therefore fair game for anything one might wish to suggest about him. What's more, his mother probably wore combat boots, and her son is widely reputed to have slandered his enemies and distorted their record. Why be fastidious in dealing with the likes of Norman?

Vidal's distortions are not limited to occasional passages. Though they do not fatally compromise all of his work, they are to be found in one essay after another. Does Vidal really believe that in ostensibly "serious" American novels "irony and wit are unknown while the preferred view of the human estate is standard American, which is to say positive"? Is it possible that, when he wrote that sentence, he just happened to forget about Saul Bellow and Flannery O'Connor, Philip Roth and John Updike? Even the sometimes lugubrious

Mr. Mailer has been known to demonstrate wit and irony, and there are other, rather less famous Americans, from Max Apple to William Gass, who offer precisely the virtues Vidal claims to miss. Vidal is on somewhat safer ground when he contends that "there is no serious American novelist who can write as well or as originally . . . as John Fowles or William Golding." This is, after all, only an opinion. One is free to reply that Vidal here betrays a strangely parochial view of originality, or that he typically acknowledges only the masters to which Vidal the novelist can plausibly measure up. Clearly, one needn't speak only of distortion or overstatement to contend that Vidal is less than a reliable witness, even when he writes about something he ought to know.

But the distortions are important and ought to trouble those for whom Vidal has seemed an entirely welcome figure on the scene. He is tolerably amusing when he writes that "the serious novel is of no actual interest to anyone including the sort of people who write them." That is the sort of smart remark no one is intended to follow up, a quip quite common in the routines of lesser wits. Though in essence it means almost nothing, it does allow Vidal to strike a pose, to assure readers that he would never take seriously something the professional literati solemnly debate. This empty posing seems especially harmless when set alongside plainly misleading statements that actually purport to say something. Consider, for example, the following:

> 1. "Americans will never accept any literature that does not plainly support the prejudices and aspirations of a powerful and bigoted middle class";
> 2. [At the universities] "what is said and thought and imagined is homogenized to a degree that teachers and students do not begin to suspect";
> 3. "Historical novels and political novels can never be taken seriously because true history and disturbing politics are not acceptable subjects."

The three passages together indicate how utterly Vidal counts on his reader to be charmed out of his socks by Gore's abrasive forthrightness and moved to consent by his way with wickedly dismissive epithets like "middle class," "bigoted," and "homogenized." Though he rarely offers evidence for his own brashly unequivocal assertions, he is forever accusing others of "vagueness" and overgeneralization; other critics are "congenitally short of data" or given to ignoring "contrary evidence." In an age of "academic hacks" and "slick journalism"—so Vidal never tires of telling us—elementary truths and niceties are ignored. Never does it occur to Vidal to associate himself with those who make little attempt to "prove a case," who write for a reader "not interested in analysis but opinion, preferably harsh and unexpected." Vidal pretends to be launching a high-minded attack on "literary gangsters" while describing his own standard practice. Indeed, Vidal counts on a reader who will not notice his frequent conflation of academic hacks—who are at the very least interested in analysis—and slick journalists—who are decidedly less fond of analysis and whose minds are not "slow and uncertain" in the way Vidal suggests. The truth is, Vidal has clearly learned a lesson by studying the so-called literary gangsters he loves to hate. That lesson—"the more violent and ad hominem the style, the more grateful his readers will be"—is increasingly apparent in Vidal's mature essayistic style. Why else the predilection for predictably resonant put-downs and ringing calls-to-comrades signifying only an instinct for correct sentiments? Why, in other words, the preternatural fondness for formulations like "a political system which is itself not only in crisis but the crisis" or "how the ruling class of an unjust society perpetuates itself through the indoctrination of its young" or "you don't have freedom in America if you don't have money and most people don't have very much"? If Vidal showed any willingness to substantiate such sentiments one would be ready to take them—and him—seriously. As it is, one credits only the accent with which he compulsively issues those elegant critical noises.

The numbered passages quoted from Vidal will of course inspire some readers to applaud, quite as others will understand his rhetorical flourishes on behalf of the poor, the lovers of freedom, and the victims everywhere of an unjust ruling class. For a writer not much given to currying favor, Vidal has a fine instinct for stirring just the sort of resentment favored by most of those who read his essays. The gratitude his readers feel—both for the light entertainment he provides and for the steady stream of venom he directs at approved targets—must typically incapacitate their critical faculties.

After all, it takes little talent to identify the weaknesses in Vidal's unapologetically sweeping generalizations. So:

1. When Vidal refers to "Americans," he cannot intend to speak of all Americans. He obviously has in mind Americans who read books, more especially those who at least pretend to be interested in serious literature. If this were not the case, he would need to say only that most Americans read no books and that most of the others read nothing good. Typically, though, Vidal in his literary essays is at odds with the ostensibly enlightened classes whose reading habits are contemptible and whose addiction to the usual forms of middle-class "bigotry" is at the very least disappointing. What puzzles us about this line of argument is that the readers Vidal condemns are hardly so conformist a lot as he pretends, and that the writers they teach or read are apt not to support the typical prejudices or aspirations of the middle class. One may rightly wonder in any case why Vidal should think the contemporary middle class so uniform in its values and assumptions, or why he should not know that an influential sector of the middle class may be said to constitute the principal guarantors of the freedoms Vidal most approves. But never mind that. The point here is that Vidal has apparently read a good deal of the fiction that matters most to American readers. Surely he knows that, in their attraction to the writing of Pynchon and Barthelme and Coover, sophisticated readers do not correspond to those he targets. Neither do the legions of readers who are drawn to more commercially successful novelists like Styron and Mailer and Doctorow. These novelists do not support the aspirations of a bigoted middle class, and in light of that fact, Vidal's assertion can only seem a smelly, and not very clever, fabrication.

2. Vidal pretends to know just about everything that is worth knowing, and so it is not surprising that he should turn his attention, if only in passing, to the university. Unfortunately, he knows not what he says. A case can be made, has been made, against a certain kind of conformity in the contemporary university. Though Vidal might have been worth hearing on that subject, his characterization of the phenomenon as a species of homogenization is grossly misleading. In an era notable for the proliferation of new specialties and subdisciplines, when the various academic jargons

produce something like an inharmonious cacophony, when even the so-called new historicists in literature departments may have very little in common with the deconstructionists or the feminists and almost nothing to say to their departmental colleagues in rhetoric or creative writing, to speak of homogenization is to miss the point. Of course one can always say that "at bottom," invisible to any eye but one, there is an awesome uniformity, but that hardly seems a plausible rejoinder even for one so game as Vidal. Homogenization is plainly not the issue in the university today.

3. Vidal believes that literate Americans are not interested in "true history" or "disturbing politics." So he says. And yet it cannot have escaped him that even ordinary readers of books show an extraordinary appetite for history. Serious works on the Civil War, on the Nazi period, on the Vietnam conflict, have been read by millions of people in recent years. Historical and political novels dealing with such subjects are among the most widely esteemed works of our day. One has only to mention novelists like William Styron, Robert Stone, and E. L. Doctorow to indicate that Americans can be interested in history and politics. Nor are such writers spokesmen for the American way of life or for an optimistic view of human progress. Whatever the limitations in their respective gifts, these are accomplished writers who have made it a part of their business to bring before readers deeply disturbing questions, to which readers have often responded with something like commensurate seriousness. Of course Vidal's own success as a historical novelist in the years since the original periodical publication of his sour reflections on "acceptable subjects" also serves as an answer to those willfully obtuse reflections.

If Vidal is often unreliable on the subjects he treats, and rather too pompous and self-assured to be taken for a moral thinker, is he in essence simply a comic writer? Do we admire mainly his ability to come up with punch lines and occasionally apt caricatures? In a piece on Norman Mailer, Vidal somewhat sententiously proclaimed that "what matters finally is not the world's judgment of oneself but one's own judgment of the world. Any writer who lacks this final arrogance will not survive very long in America." In such terms one might be tempted to make a case for Vidal as the embodiment of an imperial and sometimes bracing arrogance. So too might he be said to rise occasionally to the genuine work of the critic, distinguishing the merely pertinent from the true, the literary virtues from literature. Reading his best pieces, usually the more modest reviews of mid-cult writers like John O'Hara or the relentless send-ups of frankly commercial fiction or shabby politicians, we are less inclined than elsewhere to complain about the weak analysis or the reluctance to provide ample evidence. The more disfiguring obsessions and insupportable generalizations are less frequent or, in any case, less recognizable than they are in the patently ambitious pieces where Vidal takes on issues much too large for the virtues or instincts of a light, occasional essayist. His career as an essayist reminds us that endowments like wit, polish, fluency, and arrogance are not easy to control.

It doesn't help much, in thinking about Vidal, to judge him simply as a wit or, for that matter, as a literary journalist. He certainly regards himself as a critic, and would wish to be associated with the virtues of Wilson and V. S. Pritchett. Wilson's merits in this vein were recently said by one writer to include "the commitment to the language of the general, rather than the specialist, intelligence; the sophisticated curiosity that confronts the high and the popular, the new and the outré, with equal poise; most of all the ability . . . to give ideas the quality of actions." No doubt Vidal employs the language of the generalist, and shows to what a variety of expressive purposes it may be turned. But his curiosity is a very limited faculty which leads him neither to Wilson's scholarly commitments nor to the scrupulous examination of primary materials that we find in the best critics. He lacks patience as he lacks the courage to sit quietly, watching sympathetically the exertions of others neither so worldly nor so confident as he. His poise comes from his self-esteem and his refusal to be seduced away from his own settled attitudes and unwavering opinions. One never feels that Vidal will allow himself to learn much from his encounters, that his stance will in any way be affected, or that he will be moved to confess an important change of heart. His determination to look down on things guarantees that he will master what comes before him without ever submitting to it in a way that makes for genuine intimacy. His elegant, playful, always insouciant handling of ideas necessarily ensures that the ink will never come off on his fingers. By temperament mistrustful of ideas, he treats them as idle playthings or illusions before he has accorded them the provisional dignity of genuinely interesting or painfully tempting claimants. In no other writer of our day do we see so clear a gap between unimpeachable literary gifts and comparably drastic disabilities of mind, spirit, and purpose.

13

Vidal as Essayist: The Man Who Has Everything

Thomas M. Disch

"Vanity," wrote Lord Chesterfield to his bastard son, "or to call it by a gentler name, the desire of admiration and applause, is, perhaps, the most universal principle of human actions; I do not say that it is the best; and I will own that it is sometimes the cause of both foolish and criminal effects. But it is so much oftener the principle of right things, that though they ought to have a better, yet considering human nature, that principle is to be encouraged and cherished, in consideration of its effects."

Lord Chesterfield's *Letters* were published, posthumously, in 1774, thereby anticipating by two years Adam Smith's complementary formulation, that it is self-interest (or to call it by a less gentle name, greed) that is the great motivator, which, contrary to traditional moral doctrine, is to be "cherished in consideration of its effects." The difference between Chesterfield and Smith is the difference, simply, between the patrician and the bourgeois. The man who has everything needn't bother himself with mere money-getting, though he expects, in the natural course of things, to get money. His ambitions rather take the form, in Chesterfield's words, of "an insatiable thirst, a rage of popularity, applause, and admiration."

Gore Vidal is an American patrician with the same insatiable thirst and the same paradoxical penchant for spelling out, with often dismaying candor, the foundations on which patrician prestige and authority are based. Here, for instance, in his 1982 collection's title essay ("The Second American Revolution"), which calls for a new constitutional convention, is Vidal's summing-up of our whole socioeconomic shebang: "Those with large amounts of property control the parties which control the state which takes through taxes the people's money and gives a certain amount of it back in order to keep docile the populace while reserving a sizable part of tax revenue for the oligarchy's use in the form of 'purchases' for the defense department, which is the unnumbered, as it were, bank account of the rulers." Now, while most thinking people would not take grave exception to this assessment, it is rare for a thinking person of Vidal's class to give expression to it in so public and straightforward a way. One of the decorums the very rich are expected to observe— their way of paying, as it were, dues to the rest of us, who envy and resent their unearned privileges—is a hypocritical allegiance to the conventional morality of Sunday schools and civics classes. This allows those in the bleacher seats to enjoy the periodic spectacle of a scapegoat millionaire or senator squirming to maintain their evidence even as they are crushed by the evidence against them. The drollest of the essays in this collection, *The Second American Revolution* (Vidal's fifth), "How to Find God and Make Money," concerns the ritual sacrifice of Bert Lance and is so funny it had me laughing out loud while I waited in line at the supermarket. Short of their public flogging on satellite television, there's not a better way to savor the Lance's comeuppance than to read this patient paraphrase of LaBelle Lance's awesomely sanctimonious *This Too Shall Pass*.

Though Vidal is most entertaining as a prosecuting attorney or a debunker of inflated reputations (this collection kicks off with a jim-dandy demolition job on Scott Fitzgerald), Vidal has generous praise for such diverse figures as Edmund Wilson, Cecil Beaton, Thomas Love Peacock, and L. Frank Baum, who wrote the Oz books. Admittedly, it is mainly the illustrious dead and some few extremely senior statesmen of literature whom Vidal honors, while his peers are, by and large, ignored—as, by and large, they have ignored him, or at least his claims of preeminence. Though his books are on the bestseller lists, they seldom appear on prize lists. Vidal has said too many unkind things about literary academics to have been taken up as one of theirs, and in any case his work requires no more in the way of exegesis than Voltaire's.

Is this the secret of what makes Vidal run? That fame is the spur, and that so long as adequate laurels are denied him he must continue the pursuit? Vidal, of course, would never be so wanting in the right tone as to complain that he has been undervalued, but he does allow Random House to publicize his book with somewhat wistful quotes from the *New Statesman* ("America's finest essayist") and the Boston newspaper columnist George Frazier ("our greatest living man of letters").

Somehow I feel these are the wrong superlatives. John Gross has made a strong case, in *The Rise and Fall of the Man of Letters*, for declaring that particular species extinct, except in the shrunken domesticated form the literary journalist, i.e., a mere reviewer of books. As to Vidal's being our "finest" essayist, fine essayists of the first rank are as incommensurable as fine painters, or fine film directors or fine artists of whatever breed. "Finest," in such cases, usually boils down to the one I enjoy the most, or most agree with, or most would like to emulate, and in those three regards I would have to second the *New Statesman's* nomination. But that doesn't mean he has the cleanest prose style, for in lazier moments Vidal relies too much on his skill as a raconteur, and so meanders; nor has he the keenest nose for unexplored territory (Sontag Sontag excels in that); nor is his wit inerrant, for he's capable of cheap shots and false aphorisms. But that he's one of our best essayists is undeniable, and his faults rarely bulk so large as even to be visible unless you squint.

My own sense of the heap Vidal is legitimately and goldenly at the top of would be that of celebrity author, a much more select game with higher stakes and certifiable winners (and losers). In this arena, where the creation of an image is as important as the accretion of an oeuvre, Vidal's wit, common sense, and durable good looks stand him in good stead. It's hard to imagine him making a public spectacle of himself in quite the careless ways that Mailer and Sontag have recently done. Vidal may sometimes write in haste, but he is always deliberate in his judgments, if only from a profound horror (with which Lord Chesterfield would have sympathized) of being seen with egg on his face. I imagine him forever seated outside that trattoria in Fellini's *Roma*, delighting everyone about him with his conversation, the life of the party.

As I came to the end of *The Second American Revolution*, I found myself still hungry for more, and accordingly imagined two other genres of nonfiction (as the bestseller lists style all books that aren't novels) in which Vidal has yet to exercise his gifts and by which I think he might extend his man-of-letters claim. The obvious one is memoir-writing. His essays continually yield tantalizing glimpses of his family background, and his life away from the nest seems to have been equally rich in anecdote. I trust that he is only biding his time and that he has no illusions that authors of his celebrity will be able to preserve their privacy. If James could not escape Leon Edel, what hope has Vidal to keep a single secret?

The other possibility, which Vidal may not have considered, since the genre has fallen into such desuetude, is the etiquette book. Since Lord Chesterfield's *Letters to His Son* and Franklin's *Almanac*, no writer of the first rank has produced a guide to civilized comportment in all its aspects from good grooming to bedroom protocols. I can't think of any writer more certain to have exactly the right opinion on absolutely everything.

14

Gore Vidal: Private Eye

STEPHEN SPENDER

I first met Gore Vidal in 1947 (or was it 1497?). He was very young and looked spruce and golden. He had tawny hair and eyes that made me think of bees' abdomens drenched in pollen. The center of each eye, perhaps its iris, held a sting. He wore a bow tie to work, and a well-tailored, light-brown, English country-style suit. He discussed his success (he had just published *The City and the Pillar*) like a joke which we shared. He showed me an envelope on the inside cover of which an ardent fan had glued an ecstatic self-photograph. He could not have been more enviable.

Perhaps it was on this occasion that I made the priggish remark he quotes in his essay on Norman Mailer's *Advertisements for Myself*. The conversation had shifted for a moment from his success to some other young writer who had "unexpectedly failed, not gone on, blown up." Apparently I said, "The difference in England is that they want us to be distinguished, to be good." I should have added, of course, that in England success is supposed to be kept within the bounds of decency: that is to say, to bring your friends credit for knowing you, but not pushed to that extreme where they might become envious. I have always suspected that the real reason Forster gave up writing novels was in order not to provoke his English friends.

Just about this time there was an even younger American writer who, when we first met, looked at me coolly and said: "When I meet older writers I can just *smell* failure!" Fortunately I was able to get back some of my own minutes later when he asked me, as one infinitely acquainted with the sordid ways of the literary world, whether I considered that he should follow his publishers' advice and have himself photographed entering a brothel. I saw my chance and answered: "I assure you there isn't a brothel in the world that could do you more harm than your own publishers are already doing by promoting you." The remark went unheard.

The difference between Gore Vidal and the second writer was the sense in which Gore Vidal wasn't serious. Or perhaps I should have written "was serious." For he is one of those who care and learn "to care and not to care," and to discriminate between things that are worth and things that are not worth caring about. For all he talked about it, I do not think he really cared about success. Certainly someone mad about success would not achieve his most genuine effects in a form so modest as the essay; yet this is what Gore Vidal does. Not only are the individual essays excellent, the whole volume is more than the sum of its parts. For taken together Vidal's essays compose the features of the writer, complex and a bit mysterious, like a face mirrored in the darkened waters of a well.

There are at least two or three Gore Vidals. One is the earnest and attentive student of literature, doggedly informative about subjects such as the *nouveau roman*. The second is the tipster of the author's stakes: a great expert on the running form of Norman Mailer, and with much inside knowledge of the fixers and the rackets. And the third is the President-watcher, standing at a respectful distance while inspecting presidential candidates, but with a glint in an eye that is altogether too observant.

The essays about literature are probably the most studied and the least at ease with themselves, for Gore Vidal, superbly self-assured at his best, can be painfully painstaking, as he is in "French Letters: Theories of the New Novel." He is much happier when he moves from the written to the writer, as is shown in the first essay in the volume, "Novelists and Critics of the 1940's." This essay hardly counts as literary criticism, but that does not matter, for there is justification for an attack on the extraordinary pretensions of modern critics to make absolute judgments.

It is difficult, on internal evidence provided by the essays, to measure his learning, but in this first essay he already shows that he has access to an arsenal of random information about the ancient Romans and the church fathers (it may well have come out of Gibbon), which he draws on to make quick thrusts as an opponent. The arguments of new critics remind him of

> the semantic and doctrinal quarrels of the church fathers of the fourth century, when a diphthong was able to break the civilized world in half and spin civilization into nearly a millennium of darkness. One could invent a most agreeable game of drawing analogies between the fourth century and today. F. R. Leavis and St. Jerome are perfectly matched, while John Chrysostom and John Crowe Ransom suggest a possibility. The analogy works amusingly on all levels save one: the church fathers had a Christ to provide them with a primary source of revelation, while our own dogmatists must depend either upon private systems or else upon those proposed by such slender reeds as Matthew Arnold and T. S. Eliot, each despite his genius, ritual victim as well as a hero of literary fashion.

This is delightful and gives one a ringside feeling like that which the Israelites must have had watching their youthful David go out to meet Goliath. One wonders, a bit anxiously, how many of these learned pebbles Gore Vidal has in his sling. (He has mentioned earlier that doubt is cast on Matthew Arnold's enthusiasm for Dante on account of Arnold's inadequate Italian.)

The pleasure conveyed by the passage I have just quoted is not as elementary as it may seem. This is partly on account of its style, which is worth considering, for Gore Vidal is an elated stylist. He carries weights of packed allusion with a buoyant air. In so far as he has an argument, he is well on top of it. This is most characteristic of him in this passage as a kind of mock pomposity. The learning or the pseudolearning verges on the hectoring or lecturing manner. But just as he seems about to cross the line which divides riding high from pomposity, he wheels his charger around and turns the whole thing into a joke, just as he turned the talk about his success into a joke when we first met.

As Gore Vidal several times reminds us, his grandfather was a senator and he himself electioneered to become a congressman, as though to turn into his grandfather. That he should ever have wished to be in Congress is utterly absurd. His strength and his deepest seriousness are that he himself sees the absurdity. He has turned pomposity manqué into a lifestyle. The charm of his essays when he describes important people in public life is that the description seems constantly to inflate little balloons of importance—and then to stick pins into them.

The underlying activity, which he sees to be common to the academic, the literary, and the political life is a success game. He does not forget, of course, that games can be serious, especially in politics; the fascination of his President-watching essays is that he sees in Washington the interlocking games of high seriousness and low comedy.

A game which he rather enjoys playing himself is that which he calls, in an essay of that name, "Literary Gangsters." Stung by opening a number of *Playbill* and reading some remarks by Mr. Richard Gilman in which Gore Vidal is referred to as "a culture hero of the Fifties," he launches forth into a wonderful attack on certain theatrical and literary journalists. It is written with such relish that sometimes it reads like Advice to a Graduate Student about to Embark on a Literary Career. He lists the rules for his hectic infighting, and concludes:

> Finally, the gangster can never go wrong if, while appearing to uphold the highest standards (but never define those standards or say just when it was that the theater, for instance, was "relevant"), he attacks indiscriminately the artists of the day, popular on the ground that to give pleasure to the many is a sign of corruption, and the much-admired on the ground that since all values now held by this society are false (for obvious reasons don't present alternative values), any culture hero must reflect perfectly the folly of those who worship him.

His account of some of those he labels gangsters is so boisterous that I can hardly believe they could be offended. In a swift summation, he relates one writer's career: how Mr. John W. Aldridge, Jr., set up in 1947 "as a legitimate literary business man, opening shop with a piece describing the writers of the postwar generation to which he warmly praised John Horne Burns and myself. The praise made us think he was not a hood, his shop a legitimate business, not a front." Alas, though, it was all a monstrous plot, even including the move to Connecticut "in order to be close to certain of his victims." It turned out that

> he was thoroughly casing the territory. Then he struck. The blaze of publicity, Mr. Aldridge bit one by one those very asses he had with such cunning kissed, earning himself an editorial in *Life* magazine congratulating him for having shown up the decadence and immortality of the post-war writers. He has long since faded from the literary scene . . . as have, fortunately, those scars on which we sit.

Gore Vidal is brash, but in a passage such as this, he elevates brashness to satire through the style. Satire is unfair, simplifies those attitudes it attacks, and then expresses the simplification with an elegance and elaboration pleasing in itself. What he does to the literary gangsters is to cut through the Gordian knots of their style and show that it often conceals a brashness less justified than his own plan (he is very good at playing his opponent's games better than he does himself).

Memories of having been the young lion who shook out his mane before ten thousand glowing sophomores, who leaped from the circus floor to jump through the same hoops as Norman Mailer, and whose scorn to be thought whelped of the same litter as Truman Capote—these are aspects of Vidal's self-mockery, which does not call his whole personality into play. It is when he is writing about politicians that he becomes like one of those "opposites" in a Yeatsian world of antinomies, the perfect negation of his own secret self-image. The negative of his positive Senator Vidal, but also deep down the projection of him, he looks with the glare of an unthinkably powerful search light at Ronald Reagan, illuminates every pore and wrinkle exposed under the grease paint, and writes the description down with the diamond lens of hell's least kind recording angel:

> Ronald Reagan is a well-preserved not young man. Close-to, the painted face is webbed with delicate lines while the dyed hair, eyebrows, and eye lashes contrast oddly with a sagging muscle beneath the as yet unlifted chin, soft earnest of wattle-to-be. The effect, in repose, suggests the work of a skillful embalmer. Animated, the face is quite attractive and at a distance youthful; particularly engaging is

the crooked smile full of large porcelain-capped teeth. The eyes are interesting: small, narrow, apparently dark, they glitter in the hot light, alert to every move, for this is enemy country—the liberal Eastern press who are so notoriously immune to that warm and folksy performance which Reagan quite deliberately projects over their heads to some legendary constituency at the far end of the tube, some shining Carverville where good Lewis Stone forever lectures Andy Hardy on the virtues of thrift and the wisdom of the contract system at Metro-Godwin-Mayer.

It is description of this kind, done with the fervor of a scientist exploring a strange land and making a description of its fauna of such accuracy that the language itself acquires the clarity of cells magnified under a microscope, that Gore Vidal does best. The language becomes an apparatus designed to capture very rare specimens observed in highly characteristic but not often reported situations, like that of camels in heat—

> Ordinarily Rockefeller's face is veal-white, as though no blood courses through that thick skin. But now, responding to the lowering day, he has turned a delicate conch pink. What is he saying? "Well, let's face it, there's been some disagreement among the pollsters."

Just as Vidal is even better on writers than on writing, so he is better on politicians than on politics, about which he is always interesting. But as President-watcher, he comes to be either frolicsome or satiric; he is contributing to knowledge in describing with great attention a new American species: the public man seen as a fusion of all the external forces of publicity, presentation, and advertising media concentrated upon him in the extraordinary transformation of the inner man into mechanical will and perpetual guardedness which is the result of exposure to these conditions.

Joseph Alsop, also a President-watcher, once explained to me that men like Johnson and Nixon are not at all like the rest of us. They think of power unceasingly, and they tap resources of will and duplicity which by ordinary standards are unthinkable. Obviously, politicians like Adlai Stevenson "to whom, humanly, Hugh Gaitskell was a close equivalent" are too nice and cultivated for such a task. Occasionally they think of something other than power, and this is debilitating to a system which ought to be fueled on nothing but high-octane publicity. Some men have energy that is human and some have energy that is inhuman, but they rarely have both at once. Increasingly, Presidents tend to conscript the inhuman or superhuman in themselves (perhaps Nietzsche's Superman is really a mid-twentieth-century American president).

Descriptions such as those of Governors Reagan and Rockefeller are cruel not because they are satirical and malicious, but because they are true. As President-watcher, Gore Vidal is personally quite sympathetic to the objects of his attention. Of course, failure, like absence, lends enchantment to the view, and his portrait of Barry Goldwater renders him positively charming.

In his famous essay on the Kennedys, "The Holy Family," he combines satire with observation. The satiric idea that the Kennedys projected onto the American public their sense of family which derives from Ireland, "priest-ridden, superstitious, clannish," is worked out to the point where the satire is superseded by the tragedy:

> Meanwhile, the source of the Holy Family's power is the legend of the dead brother. . . . Yet the myth that JFK was a philosopher-king will continue as long as the Kennedys remain in politics. And much of the power they exert over the national imagination is a direct result of the ghastliness of what happened in Dallas. But though the world's grief and shock were genuine, they were not entirely for JFK himself. The death of a young leader necessarily strikes an atavistic cord. For thousands of years the man-God was sacrificed to ensure with blood the harvest; there is always an element of ecstasy as well as awe in our collective grief. Also, Jack Kennedy was a television star, more seen by most people than their friends or relatives.

The modern world absorbs the atavism and legends of the past and transforms the Fisher King into its own terms—hence Jesus Christ Superstar. Gore Vidal, President-watching, expresses this process with exceptional vigor, but where he is most original is in his insight into the qualities of personality (or lack of it) required today of the holders of highest office. The public does not require the President to be, as a person, trustworthy. What they do require is that they can trust him never to stop thinking about the presidency.

Hypocrisy and self-deception are the traditional characteristics of the middle class in any place and time, and the United States today is the paradigmatic middle-class society. Therefore we can hardly blame our political gamesmen for being, literally, representative. Any public man has every right to try and trick us, not only for his good but, if he is honorable, for ours as well. Trust in this context means not trusting the President to refrain from trickery during elections, but trusting him to be wired into, *powered* by his own ambition unceasingly like a dynamo.

When he writes about power one is impressed by something authoritative in Gore Vidal's manner. The features reflected on the surface of the well have muscles compressed to seriousness, yet they do not loose the self-awareness which includes a trace of self-mockery. The writer who can quote to such effect in parenthesis ("It all began in the cold": Arthur M. Schlesinger, Jr., A *Thousand Days*) is not likely to fall into the trap of solemnity.

Gore Vidal is by now obviously irremediably saved from his public persona. His essays celebrate the triumphs of private values over the public ones of power. They represent the drama of the private face perpetually laughing at, and through, the public one. At the same time, their seriousness lies very largely in his grasp of the conditions and characteristics which make up the public world. What makes an essayist? It is curious to reflect that the greatest essayist, Francis Bacon, was also a man with the strongest sense of public values consistently questioned in his essays by those of the private human condition, and that Montaigne was a magistrate who retired from public life to his country estate and thought much about the world, and about power, and about friendship.

15

My O My O Myra

CATHARINE R. STIMPSON

My o my o Myra, my o my o Myron. Myra rides and Myron clowns through *Myra Breckinridge* and *Myron*, Gore Vidal's wild, steely, and amazing rodeos of the word.[1] Vidal has coupled Myra and Myron as tightly as Jack and Jill, then filled their names to the rim and brimmed them with meanings. Surely Myra, my "ra," is at once: a deity; the symbol for radium, a radioactive element; and a cheer, Bronx-inflected (think Yankee Stadium). "M," inverted, is "W," the lead letter in "Woman." Surely Myron, my "ron," invokes the Hollywood actor/politician Ronald Reagan, who served as governor of California while Vidal was thinking Myra and Myron up. All this is possible and more. Amid such plenitude, I will focus on Myra as self-willed woman and divinity, as self-named "eternal feminine" and goddess. In brief, *Myra* and *Myron* are narratives of the godhead in the secular Space Age. Indeed, in such an age, we must create divinity for ourselves. If zoosemiotics is "the scientific study of signalling behavior in and across animal species," and anthroposemiotics the subordinate study of signaling systems specific to the human species,[2] then this essay will contribute to "theosemiotics" (my neologism for the study of communications from, with, and about the gods).

General opinion, the go-cart of critical judgment, considers *Myra* a better novel than *Myron*.[3] *Myra* is, I believe, fresher, more ebullient, unleashing Myra first on a heedless, needy world. *Myron* must stick with Myron, who whines, atheistically fights the divinity, and like an unhappy camper gets homesick away from wife and pets. Nevertheless, the novels are faithful to each other in their fashion. (So, too, are the books in another Vidalian narrative sequence, the story of Senator James Burden Day and the Sanford family.)[4] Together, *Myra* and *Myron* apparently have their nineteenth-century ancestry. Vidal compares *Myra* to *Tom Sawyer*, *Myron* to *Huck Finn*.[5] Just as ironically, I might compare *Myra* to *Little Women* and *Myron* to *Little Men*. More soberly, another critic finds a parallel to the Alice books as "twin exercises in cerebral fantasy."[6] Like the Alice books (especially *Through the Looking Glass*), the Myra books (especially *Myron*) set up a situation that must seem, at best, a merely intellectual possibility to the ordinary reader. (Think, for example, of a child behind a looking glass or a transsexual goddess time-traveling to a movie set.) These books are funny because their characters responds to such situations with a mixture of improvisation and earnest devotion to the everyday logic they bring with them.

Connecting *Myra* to *Myron* are the reliable staples of plot, theme, and character. To recapitulate these for those unfamiliar with the novels: In 1968, the year of Richard Nixon's first election as President of the United States, Myra Breckinridge lands in Los Angeles.[7] Apparently, she is the widow of Myron Breckinridge, a film critic with homosexual habits who has been writing a book about Parker Tyler and the films of the 1940s.[8] Myra is claiming her share of the estate of Myron's mother, a practical nurse named Gertrude (a Shakespearean allusion that hints at the nature of Breckinridge family ties). Gertrude's brother, Buck Loner, also wants the property. Once a cut-rate singing cowboy, he is now the proprietor of the Academy of Drama and Modeling. To stall Myra, Buck gives her a job teaching Empathy and Posture. Eventually, Myra must reveal to him that once upon a time she was Myron, before a thrilling sex-change operation in Copenhagen. The ancient comic figure of the transvestite, thanks to modern surgery, now mutates into the comic figure of the transsexual.[9]

Myra, however, has an identity far greater than property-owner and pedagogue. Although she occasionally suffers a mortal pang, she is the spirit of femininity, the perfection of a human type, *and* Robert Graves' White Goddess, a superhuman being. If she were an ordinary woman, she would be egomaniacal. Since she is Woman Incarnate and Woman Divine, her claims to power and her powers come with the territory. Myra gives herself the names of deities from a jumble of cultures: Cybele, the great Mother Goddess, the Great Goddess, even Jesus and Buddha (only the goody-goody Virgin Mary seems exempt from Myra's claims). Embracing multitudes, she is contradictory: cruel but gentle, exacting but forgiving, demanding of human sacrifices but giving of life, prepared to command but respectful of democratic rights. Though she might believe in equal rights under the boring old law, feminism is as relevant to her as theories of social justice would be to Dionysus on a toot.

In the seesaw of the pagan heavens, one deity's ascent foredooms another's fall. Serving as the prophet of her own coming, Myra decrees, "the cock-worshipping Dorians enslaved the West, impiously replacing *the* Goddess with a god. Happily his days are nearly over; the phallus cracks; the uterus opens" (*Myra and Myron*, p. 6). In large part, the god is falling because the male role is declining. The cosmos chains sacred and secular together. What Robert Bly now preaches to a mass audience, Myra has foretold: "[Women have] no ritual testing of . . . manhood through imitation or personal contest, no physical struggle to survive or mate" (*Myra and Myron*, p. 57).

Exquisitely sensitive to the calibrations of power, Vidal distinguishes between a brutal machismo, cocky or sullen before the complexities of the world, and virility, a sculpted muscularity that flexes itself handsomely in the world. Vidal is happy to discard machismo, a "keep 'em barefoot and pregnant" attitude toward women. He loathes the conjunction of domineering patriarchal god, patriarchal state, and patriarchal pop culture too much to mourn their passing. However, he is ambivalent about the loss of virility. On the one hand, he believes that men must change if the human species is to avoid an apocalyptic doom and manage the great danger of the late twentieth century: overpopulation. Myra's messianic task is to struggle against overpopulation. She preaches that "efforts must still be made to preserve life. . . . There is an off chance that my mission may yet succeed (*Myra and Myron*, p. 123). Her path to salvation is to change the sexes, "to re-create Man" by asking men to imitate Myron the First or Myra, the harbingers of a new race. So doing, men will snip off the heterosexual activity that equates sexuality with reproduction. This will stop the release of the countless spermatozoa that swarm toward the less plentiful (but plentiful enough) ova. Vidal's fear of overpopulation pervades his work beyond the Breckinridge books, often articulated as lectures to the Roman Catholic Church and the Third World. In "On Pornography," Vidal declares, "Man plus woman equals baby equals famine. If the human race is to survive, population will have to be reduced drastically."[10]

On the other hand, the virile is a source of physical and aesthetic beauty. Moreover, curbing masculinity will join with social and economic hierarchies to deprive most men of any outlet for their power drive. Unable to prevail in work or battle, men may subliminate this lust in two ways: first, into sexual violence and bondage, and next, into a pathetic theatricality. Myra predicts to her therapist, Randolph Spenser Montag, that men will masquerade as traditional men. They will stand tall in the saddle in an urban bar. This anxiety has its plausibility. Intensifying it is a second fear about the price of population control, which quick-witted Myra also recognizes: the loss of civil liberties it may entail.

Myra first experiments with a hunk, one Rusty Godowski, raping him in body and soul. She next takes over his girlfriend, sweet songbird Mary-Ann Pringle. So plotting and scheming, Myra embodies, indeed encourages, all those garish, atavistic fears that liberating a woman is tantamount to crawling before La Belle Dame Sans Merci, whetting the castrator's knife, cracking the dominatrix's whip, getting out the nanny's ruler and the nurse's enema tube, howling vainly to the Bacchae in blood-spattered wilds. Tough luck, Myra might say, Power to the Powerful. Fortunately for the fearful, a hit-and-run driver smashes into Myra. Perhaps Buck is taking his revenge; perhaps Rusty is. Perhaps it is simply an accident. Whatever the cause, the effect is clear. Myra's female body vanishes and Myron's male body returns, a stunning reversal, a corporeal and literal peripeteia. "Where are my breasts? *Where are my breasts?*"

shrieks Myra (*Myra and Myron*, p. 210), recalling Ronald Reagan's anguished "Where's the rest of me?" in the 1941 *King's Row*.

From this wreckage, Myron the Second struggles forth. The end of *Myra* recapitulates and then bends the generic rules of the domestic comedy. Myron the Second, with a surgically devised phallus, marries Mary-Ann. They are happy and good. They have each other for sex and love, the television industry for work, Planned Parenthood for civic activity, and the God of Christian Science for worship. However, despite the best efforts of his medical team and nonmedical faith, Myron the Second cannot have children and enact the promise of the final scene of traditional domestic comedy: the renewal of the household and family. Myron the Second and Mary-Ann must content themselves with oodles of dogs. However, if the survival of the species depends on population control, their happiness is an exemplary conclusion for the domestic comedy of the late twentieth century: a virtuous couple, no kids.

Myron further domesticates the Breckinridges. Square as square can be, anti-Commie as anti-Commie can be, they now cater Chinese food in Orange County. The only residue of Myron's homosexuality is a warm, cozy, avuncular feeling for a well-built adolescent boy. Unfortunately for them, that old trickster, History, is feeling his oats. For it is 1973, the year of Watergate and Nixon's resignation from the presidency; of *Miller v. California*, the Supreme Court case that legally defined obscenity; and of the death of so many movie stars that a virtual Götterdämmerung has occurred. Among the dead is Fay Holden, who played Mom Hardy, the matriarch of MGM's Andy Hardy clan. To Myra, the Hardy family is *the* peerless symbol of American virtue (a moral quality) and American innocence (a moral *and* a cognitive quality). America threw both away when it dropped those atomic bombs on Japan, "two mushroom shapes set like terminal punctuation marks against the Asian sky" (*Myra and Myron*, p. 29). Since then, the honor of World War II has given way to the tortures of the Vietnamese War, the strength of President Roosevelt to the slyness of President Nixon, the clean-cut GI to the Green Beret.

In the midst of such decay and turmoil, Myra miraculously reappears, trilling and jilling and throwing her lead-weighted pocket-book around, a General Douglas MacArthur in drag. Psychologically, Myron's "repressed feminine" has returned. Culturally, the competition to inscribe the narrative of America's soul has a new champion. Politically and socially, the battle is rejoined between the Majoritarian American, one of the gang (Myron), and the American Individual, a mad minority of one on a self-scripted Mission Impossible (Myra). Vidal's preference is clearly for the minority of one.[11] Mythically, the stage curtains of the sky have opened to reveal the Goddess, who has been hiding in the wings.

The agon of *Myron* is the subsequent struggle between Myron and Myra, two mutually loathing souls imprisoned in a single body. Myra is determined to wrest "her" body away from Myron, drink hormone cocktails, and restore its feminine charms. The fight begins when "that bitch Myra" pushes Myron through a TV set while he is watching a Late Late rerun of *Siren of Babylon*, a 1948 production starring Bruce Cabot and Maria Montez (whose name also doubles the letter "M"). Unhappily bound together, Myra and Myron, M&M candies without any sweetness, emerge on three strips: the strip of celluloid of the original film; the strip of TV commercials added to the original strip; and, finally, the Hollywood Strip of 1948, where *Siren of Babylon* is being shot. (Myra also compels men to strip and striptease before her. The puns on "strip" speak to Vidal's interconnected explorations of power, representations of reality, and reality. Power, obviously, resides in controlling as many "strips" as possible.) Meanwhile, Myron spends his energies trying to escape from the celluloid strip and return to his 1973 life in front of the TV set. Myra spends her energies trying to remain in 1948 in order to manipulate "reel life" in ways that will alter and redeem the "real life" of TV-ridden 1973.

The savior's first goal is to keep Louis B. Mayer in charge of MGM and his brand of movies in distribution. In so doing, she will foil the ascendancy of such crude directors as Sam Peckinpah (peck-and-paw). However, this is but a means to a larger end. Even more radically than the Myra of *Myra*, the Myra of *Myron* seeks to alter human reproduction, this time by giving all men the drastic excitement Myron the First experienced in his Danish surgery. She will abolish not simply male heterosexual desire but the male heterosexual body. She will substitute sperm banks for the penis and scrotum;

fun-loving Amazons for men. MGM movies will convince America that all this is swell. With her silicone, knives, and little bottle of Lysol, Myra begins by transforming red-headed Steve Dude, Rusty's successor, into Stefanie Dude. "Once I have restored Hollywood to its ancient glory (and myself to what I was!)," she gloats with habitual exuberance, "I shall very simply restructure the human race. This will entail the reduction of world population through a complete change in man's sexual image" (*Myra and Myron*, p. 250).

Unlike Uncle Buck, Myra *has* read the "Great Books," though often in translation. She exults in rewriting Plato (that "dumb Greek"). In the *Symposium*, a lovely narrative about an Athenian banquet that has its share of homosexual flirting, Aristophanes tells his famous fable about the three original human creatures: one female, one male, one female/male or androgynous. The gods split each of them in half as punishment for their arrogance, and then, relenting, permitted each half to reunite with its partner. The female couple is the prototype of the lesbian, the male couple of the male homosexual, and the androgyne of the heterosexual dyad. Myra's mission is to cut the androgyne apart again.

For Myra to revise Plato, *Myron's* final scenes must alter the conventions of ancient comedy, which affirm the renewal of life's great cycles. Myron—back home with his barbecue, backyard, and Barbie-doll wife, "darned proud" to belong to the "highly articulately silent majority" (*Myra and Myron*, p. 416)—is sure that he has won out, that order is restored. Foolish Myron. For the divine Myra lives, well beyond his petty domestic and social order. In Vidal's theophany, she appears, neither in masque nor pageant, but in mirror-writing on the novel's last page. She has guaranteed the cosmic survival of the species by beginning to block life's outmoded reproductive techniques. The new fertility goddess is an antifertility goddess. "Stefanie Dude," that "fun-loving Amazon," is the governor of California. Myron, blind to Stefanie's origins in the womb of Myra's plot, complacently predicts that she will be the next Republican president of the United States. Whoopee.

Perhaps the best-known result of *Myra / Myron's* search-and-enjoy missions among the classics is its debt to the *Satyricon* of Petronius. This title may be a pun on *saturika*, a "lecherous, randy" work concerned with satyrs, and "satura, a satire, a potpourri of

subjects and styles.[12] *Myra/Myron* makes hay with this double identity.[13] If Encolpius, "The Crotch," is the narrator of the *Satyricon*,
then Myra, Buck Loner, and Myron the Second, the squabbling
narrators of the Breckinridge books, embody the spectrum of genital
possibilities in the late twentieth century: heterosexual biological
male, homosexual biological male who has become a medically
created but ardent female, who in turn becomes prosthetic male
(the dildo), medically created male. Like the *Satyricon*, *Myra/My-
ron* blithely accepts polymorphous sexual experiences, including
the orgiastic masochism of Letitia Van Allen, killer agent and feminist nightmare of a career woman.

Myra's insouciance about sexual difference has obscured the interesting difficulties of the novel's ideas about sex, sexuality, and
gender, ideas that Vidal anticipated in his 1966 essay "On Pornography."[14] Unlike many contemporary historians of sexuality, Vidal is
no social constructionist—that is, one who interprets sexual desires,
activities, and codes as the product of specific historical periods.
Rather, for Vidal, sexuality has at least three constants.

First, we are a bisexual species. The mixture of Myra and the two
Myrons symbolizes the potential human norm, not a perversion
from it. Once released, bisexuality is the field on which both sexes
play in their sensual games. In these, each of us will be top and
bottom, male and female, transcendent and fleshly. Polytheistic
deities know this better than monotheistic prigs. In one operatic
passage, Myra glows:

> I am . . . at heart . . . a mere woman. One who wishes to love
> and be loved. To hold out my hand to a masterful man, to let him
> draw me close to his powerful chest, to feel strong arms about my
> beautiful if not entirely re-equipped-for-action body, to look up into
> his strong face and say, "I love you!" And then fuck his ass off. Yes, I,
> too, am vulnerable, tender, insecure. (*Myra and Myron*, pp. 333–
> 34)

Yet, read strictly, this passage reveals a contradiction in Vidal's
dramas of sex and gender. Yes, Vidal believes in bisexuality. Yes, he
delights in the spectacle of the female taking on the male's body and
gender role. Bisexuality entails equal opportunity for hedonists. The
Breckinridge duet, however, takes more interest in the spectacle of
the male taking on a female body and/or gender role—in Myron the

First becoming Myra, the woman who has *willed* her femininity,
then enters into competition with the less determined woman whose
femininity is a birthright. As the "gobbling queen" brings another
man to climax, he extracts "the ultimate elixir of victory . . . not
meant for him but for . . . [a] wife or girl of simply Woman" (*Myra
and Myron*, p. 78).

Such a weighting of interests is compatible with Vidal's projection of the second constant of sexuality: aggression as the motor of
eros and the will to power as the the the starting mechanism and fuel of
this motor. As Alfred Adler teaches Myra, we yearn to dominate.
We prefer power to submission, hate to love. If we did not, Myra
notes, we would have no satire, no Juvenal, Pope, or Billy Wilder.
Some women do have a will to power (Myra, her buddy Letitia);
some men are gentle. Nevertheless, Vidal masculinizes the "ag-
gressive/creative drive" and feminizes pliability and tenderness.
Myra first goes soft in her relationship with Mary-Ann—woman
with woman—though both squeamishly deny being lesbian, one of
Les Girls. To penetrate sexually is the high, historic sign of domination; to be penetrated, especially anally, the historic sign of submission. "Real men" despise it. "Myra," Steve Dude tells her after her
assault on him, "I hated every last minute of what you did, and
that's the absolute truth so help me God, sincerely" (*Myra and
Myron*, p. 344). "Getting fucked" has often humiliated Myron the
First, a pain for which Myra seeks revenge through the anal rape of
guys who show off as guys. However, some gay men, like Myron the
First, also reverse the power relationship of tough guy and queen.
They only appear to be submissive, when actually, they are calling
the shots, manipulating Big Butch into believing that he is in
charge.

The third constant is fully a trait of both sexes: the marriage of
mind and body. We are members of a fantasizing species that en-
folds, infiltrates, and interprets its sexual activity with mental images. A passage in *Myron* dramatizes this coupling. Myra stumbles
over "two guys making it" in a "pleasant bosky dell." Staring at their
penises, Myra calls the tips "a pair of standard American rosebuds."
Metaphor, here ironically formulaic, reveals the mind's seizure of
the flesh. Myra then adds graciously, "to be fair to the American
rosebud, like a Christmas present, it is not the actual tiny gift but

the thought *behind* the erection that counts" (*Myra and Myron*, p. 334). The individuality of human minds guarantees an infinite, heterogeneous variety of sexual activities. Or, as Vidal puns in "On Pornography," one man's meat is another man's poison. In turn, this variety ensures that the theory and practice of bisexuality will be fluid rather than strict. "Sex," Myra teaches, "is the union of two things. *Any* two things whether concave or convex or in any combination or number in order to provide more joy for all or any concerned with the one proviso that no little stranger appear as the result of hetero high jinks" (*Myra and Myron*, p. 301). The orgy scene in *Myra* (sect. 20), an echo of the *Satyricon*, is funny because of Myra's vivid descriptions and initial prudishness. It also illustrates a free-floating, polymorphous, often sweetly silly joy, "the Dionysian . . . [as] necessity in our lives" (*Myra and Myron*, p. 89).

Destructively, the "monstrous tribal norm" of the West represses the teeming energies of sexuality and presses us between the cold sheets of the heterosexual nuclear family. So tucked in, we learn to forget that a homosexual lives in every heterosexual, a heterosexual in every homosexual. Our structures are strictures. Because Myra has been a gay man (Myron the First), mostly but not exclusively a straight woman (Myra), and a boringly normal man at heart but not in body (Myron the Second), her experiences replicate the Western conflict between repressive sex roles and the range of human sexual drives. So do her disagreements with Montag, a puritanical Jew in religion and culture, once a dentist by profession and still orally fixated.

Myra is also the goddess. In her divine mode, she affirms two cosmologies of sexuality, which simultaneously praise its glory and satirize such literary prophets of heterosexuality as Lawrence, Miller, and Mailer. In the first cosmology, sexual bliss with a woman will permit Myra to triumph over time, its cycles of life and death, its passages from womb to tomb. Fingering Mary-Ann's "blonde silky thatch," she raves, "if I am to prevail I must soon come face to face with the Minotaur of dreams . . . in our heroic coupling know the last mystery: total power achieved not over man, not over woman but over the heraldic beast, the devouring monster, the maw of creation itself that spews us forth and sucks us back into the black oblivion where stars are made" (*Myra and Myron*, p. 189). Her second cosmology is even grander. In a daisy chain she drives across the galaxies, Myra links creativity, divinity, anality, homosexuality, filmmaking, and her mission of guaranteeing the survival of "the regnant species." She is the new "Creatrix," the creator who is also a trickster. Extending the literary and conversational tradition of homosexual slang, Vidal puns in order to link "respectable" discourses with that of homosexuality. Thus, a "tearoom" is a nice cafe or a subway lavatory where men pick each other up; a "spout" pours tea and semen. In an astonishing soliloquy that chaotically compresses ancient and modern, mythic and scientific, explanations of the origins of the universe, Myra vows

> it is not possible for me to fail. In this I resemble God at the moment he created the universe with a single fart. Yes, I am happy to give my imprimatur to the big-band theory that is generally accepted as being the first movement of music of this and all the other spheres.
>
> But I have now begun to outdo the prime mover himself as I weave this cage of old time, salvaged from cloacal confusions of that mindless universe the first mover has so wisely surrended to me. Slowly, carefully, I now draw to myself the very stuff and essence of all time . . . sucked into the last FADE OUT which is FADE IN to the other . . . the negative universe beyond the quasars and pulsars of our knowing." (*Myra and Myron*, p. 359)

Myra/Myron is, then, a series of collisions among sexual codes and rebellious sexual realities, epistemological codes and our heads, sacred codes and profane aspirations to appropriate them, sacred codes that deny sexuality, and sacred codes that enshrine it, "good taste" and flamboyant sexual performances that defy its criteria. *Myra's* "high baroque comedy of bad taste" is the proper literary form for these clashes. For the baroque "is the art of wreaking an explosion deep inside the classical structure and re-assorting the classical elements back into an incongruity grotesque, ironic, comic, barbarically majestic or all at once, but always—by virtue of the discipline which creates a new form to hold the . . . elements together—beautiful."[15] As a comedy of bad taste, *Myra/Myron* commandeers our ridicule of a rigid decorum and promises that the loss of decorum will permit structures that are deeper and more flexible: in life, bisexuality; in fiction, deftly controlled narrative form.

If there are more things in our sexual heaven and earth than our moralists permit, pornographers are our sexual realists. "They recognize that the only sexual norm is that there is none."[16] Given this definition, which neither social conservatives nor some radical feminists would accept, *Myra* is willful pornography. Moreover, Vidal is satirizing the pornographic tradition and at the same time correcting its errors. The novelist is not only "doing" literary criticism, he is performing a literary service. Has this tradition neglected two "modest yet entirely tangible archetypes, the girl and boy next door, two creatures far more apt to figure in the heated theater of the mind than the voluptuous grotesques of the pulp writer's imagination"?[17] Vidal will therefore provide Rusty Godowski and Mary-Ann Pringle, two supreme next-door types in love. Perhaps Vidal's plumpest target is the Marquis deSade. If Sade, a boring village overexplainer, calls on Nature to justify harmful behavior, Myra will glory in being "unnatural," a transsexual. If Sade, as boringly, reiterates his syllogism of power (the strong must violate the weak; men are strong; women are weak; therefore men must violate women), Myra will be a strong woman who violates men. Some of Myra's rodomontade also mimics the "tirades" of Sade that "often strike the Marlovian note."[18] In one scene, for example, she imagines the bliss she will feel when she transforms the obnoxious Half-Cherokee into an Amazon. Myra exults, "It is plain that nature and I are on a collision course. Happily, nature is at a disadvantage, for nature is mindless and I am pure mind. . . . I alone can save the human race" (*Myra and Myron*, p. 293).

Half-Cherokee is obnoxious because he chillingly acts out Eldredge Cleaver's theory of sex-as-racial-vengeance in *Soul on Ice*. Half-Cherokee wants to rape and humiliate "white bitches" because of Wounded Knee. However, Myra has her own grisly plans for him. Their encounter is a slapstick variant on the theme of the conflict between two wills to power, that of the castrator and the rapist. Simultaneously, Half-Cherokee is a sketch of a Native American as a smug, dumb stud. Throughout *Myra/Myron*, Vidal claims the privilege of the satirist and refuses to exempt any person or group, no matter how disadvantaged, from his mockery. An affirmative-action employer would dread his treatment of minorities (the figures of Half-Cherokee, Irving Amadeus, Mr. Williams), lesbians (sporty Miss Cluff), and religions (Judaism and Catholicism).

Myra/Myron is, then, a direct challenge to the American culture's ability to accept freewheeling satire as well as polymorphoussexualities.

Not surprisingly, the presence of *Myra* as revisionist pornography eluded many of its initial reviewers in the United States. Nearly all agreed that it was camp, and that Myra's rhetoric took a particular homosexual style as one linguistic model. They disagreed whether *Myra* was unreconstructed pornography (to them a genre that putatively focuses on sex for the sake of sex) or just dirty-minded (to them a childish perspective that sights sex everywhere). "Some of this wild fantasy . . . is funny," *Publishers Weekly* huffed, "but most of it just seems sniggering, like a small boy delighting in writing dirty words on a wall."[19] Joining together two American obsessions—proper sex and business—the reviews also stressed *Myra's* unusual marketing plan, a sudden dramatic appearance with no previews, advance review copies, or advertising.

Today, the sexualities of *Myra/Myron* seem almost tame, more game than gamey. Myra's rape of Rusty is still ugly, but it is Myra's sadistic shouts of ecstasy as she rides her "sweating stallion into forbidden country" that revolt us, not her dildo. She, too, is ultimately "saddened and repelled" by this power trip in pain-giving overdrive (*Myra and Myron*, p. 150). This is the one touch of guilt from the goddess; a blessing of divinity is the exemption it grants from secular moral codes and punitive superegos.

Of course, America today (even after Ronald Reagan) is a more open, a more Petronian landscape than it was in 1968. This is a boon for criticism, for the fuss over sex then deflected attention from the ingenuity with which Vidal fulfills the second formal mandate in the word *satyricon*—to provide a "potpourri of subjects and styles." Vidal mixes fewer subjects than styles. The trajectory of the divine Myra's mission gives *Myra/Myron* a taut thematic coherence. It is her voice, almost by itself, that provides the variety show of style. This mouth is a carnival of registers—from cosmic rants to autodidactic allusions to anthropology, film, and Alduous Huxley; from cajoleries and commandments to bitchy pungencies. She is also something of an echo chamber for Myron the First's smarts and whimsies. In brief, her rhetoric moves from high drama to low colloquialism as quickly and easily as sexual desire could zip around if it were liberated. To increase diversity, Vidal offers two other narrators: in *Myron* we have Myron the Second's written banalities; in *Myra*, the far more agrammatical, nonlinear, taped musings of Buck Loner. His "recording discs" are the tablets of the future. Ominously, they begin, "Other matters to be taken up by board in reference to purchases for new closed circuit TV period paragraph I sort of remember that Gertrudes boy was married some years ago and I recall being surprised as he was a fag" (*Myra and Myron*, p. 20). Though only Myra has explicit sociolinguistic interests, these three narrators encompass speech that captures the patterns of Late Imperial America.

Vidal also picks over the various narrative forms available to the twentieth-century writer: the *nouveau roman*;[20] the memoir, written or taped; the client's confession to the therapist/analyst;[21] the Hollywood star biography/autobiography;[22] the Hollywood novel; and the female impersonator's monologue, which both pays lavish tribute to traditional femininity and tosses acid at the world. The stiletto heel of the drag queen is a stiletto. Not accidentally, "Myra" is both an anagram of "Mary," a generic name for a homosexual queen[23] as well as the stage name of a female impersonator Vidal knew.[24] Like Jean Genet, Vidal is taking the language of a subculture out of the bars, baths, and streets and transcribing it for publication. Significantly, only the Hollywood novel and the homosexual queen's monologue permit fiction the social role of entertaining an audience while instructing it about the ways of the world. The *nouveau roman* is too fretful about language; the memoir and client's confession too self-centered; the Hollywood autobiography too giddily self-serving.

Like that of many contemporary writers, Vidal's catalogue of narrative possibilities is a tough-minded elegy for literary culture composed in a visual culture that reads little or nothing, that writes little or nothing except its autograph. The late twentieth century, Vidal realizes, is the post-Gutenberg age. Literary genius can never be wholly extinguished. The ability to provide narratives, stories, zooms across all media. Nevertheless, literary genres have withered. Poetry has given way to the novel, the novel to the visual media, literary criticism to book-chat (even *Myra* the novel briefly succumbed to a film adaptation that Vidal scorned and repudiated).

Inseparable from the decline of writing is the decline of speaking, of verbal wit and eloquence. Language itself, the basis of literature and speech, is deteriorating—dissolving like classical and neoclassical architecture in the polluted air of modern cities. Plato's *Symposium* and Petronius' banquet scene are now fodder for Myra's conversations about gender and population control with Rusty and Mary-Ann in the Cock and Bull Restaurant on the Hollywood Strip. (On this street of dreams, Myra's linguistic force is as singular as her body.)

Myron is a most glittering and gay obituary for contemporary literature. There, inside a Westinghouse television set, may be found Vidal's contemporaries and rivals: Maude, a gossipy hairdresser, a "fat small man with a big, bald pug-dog head" (*Myra and Myron*, p. 225) is a parody of Truman Capote; Whittaker Kaiser, a drunken cook from Philadelphia, is a fag-hating, woman-hating nutcase (a parody of Norman Mailer); and Mel and Gene, two Beat boys from New York, are parodies of Jack Kerouac and Neal Cassady. There, too, is their master and leader, Mr. Williams (a "dinge queen" from Albany in communion with Louis B. Mayer), who is himself as furtive and omnipotent as an omniscient narrator, attempting to sabotage the march of culture (Vidal's iconoclastic caricature of Henry James as a devotee of the art of *reel*politik).

Self-determinedly optimistic, Myra is much more cheerful about the evolution of modern culture than is her creator. Let Hollywood triumph over the novel! Hollywood gives us our myths and dreams. It is our paradise, our heaven, our pantheon of deities. At one point Myra asks a rhetorical question, then answers it bluntly: "Could the actual Christ have possessed a fraction of the radiance and mystery of H. B. Warner in the first *King of Kings*? . . . No" (*Myra and Myron*, p. 32). Like martyrs in training, the students in Buck's academy will submit even to torture in order to achieve the apotheosis of stardom and enter the Kingdom of Hollywood. Myra's happiest and most lavish self-praise is to compare herself to a star from Hollywood's classic period: her chuckle to Irene Dunne, her pursed lips to Ann Sothern, her baby talk to Ginger Rogers, her toughness to Barbara Stanwyck. Indeed, her drive pays homage to that of the great female stars, Joan Crawford or Bette Davis.

Brazenly ambitious, Myra seeks to be even more than a goddess/star. She aspires to industry mogulhood, to be a maker of myths, a producer of dreams, a god's god. Her surreptitious but titanic battle with Mr. Williams is between The Word and The Image for the control of the studios of culture and the collective unconscious. However, the goddess recognizes (most acutely in *Myra*) that television, especially its commercials, has usurped the throne of the Hollywood movies. Like McLuhan, she predicts that the new medium will create "a new kind of person who will then create a new kind of art." She writes in her notebook, "It is a thrilling moment to be alive!" (*Myra and Myron*, p. 95). Culturally promiscuous, she soars on. A writer can but dramatize her flight.

Since Myra's birth in a satiric novel, an apocryphal story has been alive in the land, told in health clubs and meetings, printed on T-shirts and cards. It consists of two brief sentences separated, in the telling, by a pause: "God has come back to earth" / "And is she ever mad!" (In more vulgar versions, the second sentence substitutes "pissed" for "mad.") Is Myra this deity? Vengeful but tender? Irate but amusing? Dotty but shrewd? A touch too tyrannical but smitten with democratic virtues? Human of feature but superhuman in will? Female and male? Homosexual and heterosexual? If she is, few may bring offerings to her temple. Our reticence is less the consequence of her delirious and comic monstrosity than of her birth. If we are to believe her creator, in a post-Gutenberg age our most popular gods and goddesses will be born and borne from celluloid, not paper. Our new interpreters of signs and symbols will huddle around television or movie screens. For those of us who still read, there yet remains the glow of pleasurable embers that Vidal throws on his pages—the occasional graffiti, the provocations of satire, and the risible comfort of the Myra/Myronic cult figures.

16

The Romanitas of Gore Vidal

JAMES TATUM

*Duluth! Love it or loathe it, you can
never leave it or lose it.*
—Gore Vidal, *Duluth*

Historians of Latin literature are fond of observing that most Roman
writers did not come from Rome. Another way to state that curious
fact, and one more flattering to the capital, would be to say that any
writer of promise made sure he got to Rome as soon as possible.
Urban life in the original *urbs* being what it was, there was a no less
powerful impulse in these same writers to flee from the center of
empire, once they were established there. They loved it, and then
they hated it.

Any nation that models itself on Rome can acquire these Roman
passions. So will those writers who understand what an acquired
Roman identity means. Like Vergil or Ovid, they will be drawn to
the center of empire, only to develop an even more powerful revul-
sion at the realization of the imperial dream. These contradictory
feelings are what the neon sign atop *Duluth's* McKinley Communications Center is all about. It is a perfect fusion of Roman tag and
American bumper sticker: "Love it or loathe it, you can never leave
it or lose it," *odi et amo* ("I hate and I love"), *nec tecum possum
vivere, nec sine te* ("I can't live with you or without you").

In American letters and politics it was once commonplace to link
the new republic with the original *res publica*. A historian of the

United States Capitol, George C. Hazelton, Jr., declared in 1903 that, just as all roads once led to Rome, so now all roads led to Theodore Roosevelt's Washington. He shared the imperial enthusiasms of a forgotten poet of the capital city, Tom Moore.

> In fancy now, beneath the twilight gloom,
> Come, let me lead thee o'er this "second Rome."

Well before the age of the first Roosevelt, Nathaniel Hawthorne's *Marble Faun* taught Americans how to acquire their Roman identity; they can get it as much from the books they read, as from the place itself. By the time Hawthorne's well-read pilgrims reach the city, they already know the Rome they want to see, before they see it:

> We stand in the Forum, or on the height of the Capitol, and seem to see the Roman epoch close at hand. We forget that a chasm extends between it and ourselves, in which lie all those dark, rude, unlettered centuries, around the birth-time of Christianity, as well as the age of chivalry and romance, the feudal system, and the infancy of a better civilization than that of Rome. Or, if we remember these medieval times, they look farther off than the Augustan age. The reason may be, that the old Roman literature survives, and creates for us an intimacy with the classic ages, which we have no means of forming with the subsequent ones. (*The Marble Faun*, ch. 18)

This view of an American citizen's Roman past has had an enduring appeal, and not just for tourists visiting Italy. In academic circles it is once again fashionable to celebrate the virtues of a republic that turned into an empire. For some Americans today, our Second Rome is essentially the same as the one envisioned by George C. Hazelton, Tom Moore, Theodore Roosevelt, or Nathaniel Hawthorne.

There are other ways to return to Rome, and for different reasons. Among writers outside of academe, none has done more to make that city and its history his point of reference than Gore Vidal. In this respect he was well ahead of the present game of recovering the classical world for America: "Americans in general are not concerned with anything that happened before yesterday. Even in 'serious' quarters, an interest in the Roman empire is regarded as a sign of deep irrelevance." This is a typical expression of Vidal's *Ro-*

manitas, a word the Christian Tertullian used in disparaging reference to Rome's cultural legacy. Vidal has been equally critical of that legacy, though he is no Christian. He uses Rome to create an ironic mode, a powerful weapon for dissent from the tendency of those who govern America to be at once ignorant and arrogant about the realities underlying our national identity.

This acquired Romanness is not simply a knowledge about the past, or a desire to recover it or relive it. For those seeking political power, the ideal of Rome has been used time after time to define and legitimize authoritarian and imperial destinies—typically, with little regard for the potential costs of assuming those identities. But the heritage is not so easily controlled. One gains not only the republic of Cincinnatus or Brutus, but the empire that their republic became. Whatever Rome and its destiny meant to the original Romans—and it could be very troubling to those who seem to us to be most essentially Roman, like Vergil or Tacitus—it is a complicated legacy to acquire. To grasp it fully is to go far beyond the kind of naive reading that is content simply to identify one's present republic (or empire) with Rome's. The rise of Rome drew on energies that were as destructive as they were creative. The costs, like the achievements, were very high. To be endowed with a Roman consciousness may lead one to be at once at the center of the things of empire, and appalled to be there. The more informed one's *Romanitas* is, in short, the more complex and ambivalent that identity becomes: a great love struggling with a great hate, at once patriotic and dissenting, even despairing.

Vidal's engagement with Rome is to be found not merely in books with classical themes, like *The Judgment of Paris*, or *Julian*. It is also central to fiction that, at first glance, does not seem to be Roman at all: the continuing chronicle of American history in *Washington D.C.*, *Lincoln*, and *Hollywood*, and many other novels, as well as comic fantasies like *Myra Breckinridge*, *Myron*, and *Duluth*. Loving and loathing are what empires most inspire, and about both of them Vidal has had much to say. This is a sketch of that *Romanitas*: whence it came and what it has to say about this Second Rome in which we live.

For a long time the heart of the dark business of turning anyone into a Roman was the elementary Latin textbook. It taught the language of the Romans, the surest way for the future rulers of a world to acquire an authentic, literate *Romanitas*. And there were other uses. Beginning Latin could be as much a founding text in the politics of recovering the past as an introduction to the language of the past. Elementary Latin courses have long been esteemed for the discipline and punishment they offered the teachers of the young. Ordeal by Latin was considered an effective initiation into masculinity, a pedagogic introduction to the agonistic values that Walter Ong has nicely termed a Western male's "fighting for life."

A Latin inscription on the front of the Academy building in Exeter, New Hampshire, promises just such a transformation:

> HVC VENITE PVERI VT VIRI SITIS.
> Come hither boys that ye be men.

When Gore Vidal was a pupil there in the early 1940s, induction into Hawthorne's old Roman literature began with *An Introduction to Latin*, first published in 1914 by John Copeland Kirtland and George Benjamin Rogers. This no-nonsense, austere textbook marches its pupils through basic Latin grammar and ends with the first book of Caesar's *Commentaries on the Gallic War*, doubtless chosen for its satisfying account of the way Rome crushed an incursion of Helvetians. Along the way, students are required to translate into Latin such sentences as

> If he should throw himself from this high building, he would be killed instantly.

> If you should change your opinion again, as you are wont to do, I should not know what you wish.

> I know that I cannot change my nature by increasing my knowledge.

> I am not going to boast about my prosperity.

Here are virtues to be cultivated in the future members of a ruling class: a sense of the fragility of life, candor about the boring habits of friends, acknowledgment of the vanities of learning, the need to mask how much money one has, and, not the least, an impressive command of the subjunctive mood.

Vidal's response to the higher uses of a classical education is instructive. Although he completed no more than two years of Latin at Exeter, he got what he needed, and what he needed was not quite what Kirtland and Rogers had in mind. In an essay unpublished until 1972 (until then it was, evidently, unpublishable), there is a brief memoir of Vidal's early Roman days.

> Tiberius. Capri. Pool of water. Small children. So far so good. One's laborious translation was making awful sense. Then . . . fish. Fish? The erotic mental image became surreal. Another victory for the Loeb Library's sly translator, J. C. Rolfe, who, correctly anticipating the prurience of schoolboy readers, left Suetonius's gaudier passages in the hard original. One failed to crack these intriguing footnotes not because the syntax was so difficult (though it was not easy for students drilled in military rather than civilian Latin), but because the range of vices revealed was considerably beyond the imagination of even the most depraved schoolboy. There was a point at which one rejected one's own translation. Tiberius and the fish, for example.

Tiberius' term of endearment for his fish was indeed colorful: *pisciculi*, in that context, has the flavor of "itty-bitty fish," "fishy-wishies," or, more prosaically, "minnows." By happy coincidence, Rolfe issued his discreet version of Tiberius' antics in 1914, the same year as the first edition of Kirtland and Rogers. The publication of Robert Graves' translation of *The Lives of the Twelve Caesars* in 1957 inspired the above reverie and revealed most of what had been hidden from an inquiring Latinist. "Some aspects of Tiberius' criminal obscenity are almost too vile to discuss, much less believe!" Thus Graves' Suetonius, who, as usual, turns at once to speak about what he has just said is unspeakable:

> Imagine training little boys, whom he called his "minnows," to chase him while he went swimming and get between his legs to lick and nibble him! Or letting babies not yet weaned from their mother's breast suck at his breast or groin—such a filthy old man he had become!

Not even Graves discloses everything. What he renders as a moral outburst ("such a filthy old . . . ") masks Suetonius' thoughtful explanation of just why the emperor employed unweaned babies: *pronior sane ad id genus libidinis et natura et aetate* ("all the readier for that kind of sex, of course, because of their natural disposition at that time of life"). The syntax of Suetonius is not beyond the student of Kirtland and Rogers, but Vidal is right: the thoughts that syntax leads to are indeed very different from anything Caesar has to offer.

About the same time Vidal confronted Kirtland, Rogers, and Suetonius, there appeared the first edition of what was ultimately Ullman, Henderson, and Henry's *Latin for Americans*. Unlike Kirtland and Rogers, *Latin for Americans* passed through many revisions, with ever more elaborate appeals to its prospective pupils' imagination. Following the lead of *The Marble Faun*, an edition from the early 1960s opens with an essay on "Our Roman Heritage," illustrated with a picture of the arch of Septimius Severus in the Roman Forum.

> The Romans used great arches as monuments to celebrate military victories or famous heroes. All over the world other peoples have built triumphal arches in imitation of this Roman custom.
> Arches are also gateways, and the Latin language is the arch through which countless generations of Western men have been able to enter into their past and discover the ideas and traditions that have shaped their lives. . . . Now you too stand before the arch. Step right ahead! Just through that arch is the rich inheritance the Romans have left you. It is yours—and all men's—to share.

This is not for the captive, privileged audience of Kirtland and Rogers. Where their brief preface addresses only experienced teachers, this one aims at consumers, at American students and their worried parents, citizens who need not buy a product unless they can be persuaded to buy it. Why step right ahead? Because if you do, you can rest assured that what you are about to learn is practical.

> But why study Latin and Rome rather than a modern language and a modern city? Because no other language and no other city have had so much influence—and for so long a time—upon our own culture.

This kind of pitch became increasingly necessary because Latin was shifting from its place in the center of the curriculum, as the masculine initiation rite par excellence, to what academic critics would now call its margins. Instead of being freighted with obligations to a ruling class or the niceties of the English subjunctive, the translation exercises of *Latin for Americans* steer their charges firmly toward the topical and the patriotic.

> We put a senator in charge of affairs; he desired to send men to the moon.

Even an exercise on the imperative mood and the relative pronoun can reflect tensions of urban high-school life.

> Show him your new books; he will not do harm to them.

> Next month I shall find a house in which there are no bodies.

There are many Latin songs to learn.

> *O, potestne cerni, praefulgente die,*
> *Satutatum signum, circa noctis adventum?*

> Oh, can it be seen, at the first gleam of day,
> That standard we hailed, near the onset of night?

And there are questions about the ties between today's American world and its Roman past.

> Why did the Romans emphasize a boy's entry into adult life? Can you think of any parallels in modern times?

Boys, entry, adult life: it is not hard to imagine what answers a young decoder of *The Life of Tiberius* could have devised for such questions.

No experienced Latin teacher would be fazed by Vidal's inventiveness. Unless they turn professional Classicists, most veterans of Latin survive by playing just such games, then leave those childhood scenes behind them. There can be interesting consequences if these first responses to our Roman heritage are carried forward into adult life. By straying from the Caesarean forced marches of Kirtland and Rogers into the luxuriant thickets of Suetonius, Vidal found a Rome that he has studied, in one form or another, ever since. His Rome became everything that Kirtland and Rogers' Rome was not: the source of a *Romanitas* that began by rejecting the unimaginative puberty rites to which Latin was intended to lead.

Unlike Kirtland and Rogers, *Latin for Americans* is a comprehensive book, not only an introduction to the ancient language, but a guide written to accompany its pupils throughout life, leaving little to their imagination. It is the foundation for a *Romanitas* that celebrates not just America's Roman origins, but America's Roman destiny. Turn from its pages to the grown-up profession of Classics as it is sometimes practiced in the United States today, and you will find much the same view of our Second Rome as the one that *Latin for Americans* so vigorously expounds.

This vision of American *Romanitas* can be found in many places, at this moment perhaps nowhere better than in Boston, at the Institute for the Classical Tradition, newly founded at Boston University: "a clearinghouse," as a recent brochure declares, "for research and teaching in the Classical Tradition." On occasion the Institute can be more than a clearinghouse. Its president presided over a conference in 1989 on "The Classical Tradition and the American Constitution," where one could hear papers on such timely topics as "The Classics at the States' Ratification Conventions," "Classical Perspectives on the Bill of Rights," "Greek Influences on Southern Responses to the Constitution," "Athenian Democracy in American Thought," and "Aspects of the Athenian Democracy During the Last Two Centuries." Timely, because shortly thereafter that same president announced his candidacy for the governorship of Massachusetts. He is widely known to revere the classics, with frequent calls for a return to the antique virtues that the classical world seems to exemplify.

Now, apart from the intrinsic interest of such topics or the exigencies of democratic politics in the Commonwealth, what is striking about a theme like "The Classical Tradition and the American Constitution" is how faithfully it follows the lead of *Latin for Americans*. That textbook ends its first year with an enthusiastic peroration that does not let up for a moment on the basic pitch: all things Roman are alive today, all things Roman are good.

> Non iam vivunt Lucius et eius amici, non iam vivunt Caesar et Cicero, principes summae auctoritatis, sed lingua eorum vivit, vivunt eorum dicta et facta, leges et mores, gloria et fama. Haec omnia in eorum libri inveniuntur. Eis qui itinera parva per illos libros faciunt Romani ipsi vivere videntur.
>
> Lucius and his friends are no longer alive, Caesar and Cicero are no longer alive, leaders of the highest prestige, but their language

lives, their words and deeds live, their laws and their character, their glory and their fame. All these things can be found in their books. To those who make little excursions through those books, the Romans themselves seem to be alive.

Rome and its empire are equally alive for Gore Vidal, though his Rome does not seem quite the city *Latin for Americans* has in mind, or, for that matter, anything the Institute for the Classical Tradition seems destined to hold a conference about.

> "Jesus, you'll split me!" The voice was treble with fear. As I approached him, dildo in front of me like the god Priapus personified, he tried to wrench free of his bonds, but failed. Then he did the next best thing, and brought his knees together in an attempt to deny me entrance. But it was no use. I spread him wide and put my battering ram to the gate.
>
> . . . I pushed. The pink lips opened. The tip of the head entered and stopped.
>
> "I can't," Rusty moaned. "Honestly I can't. It's too big."
>
> "Just relax, and you'll stretch. Don't worry."
>
> He made whatever effort was necessary and the pursed lips became a grin allowing the head to enter, but not without a gasp of pain and shock.
>
> Once inside, I savored my triumph. I had avenged Myron. A lifetime of being penetrated had brought him only misery. Now, in the person of Rusty, I was able, as Woman Triumphant, to destroy the adored destroyer.
>
> . . . Oh, it was a holy moment! I was one with the Bacchae, with all the priestesses of the dark bloody cults, with the great goddess herself for whom Attis unmanned himself.

Someday Myra and her dildo may take their rightful place in histories of the American classical tradition and its *Rezeptionaesthetik*. A heroine who can allude so learnedly to Priapus, the Bacchae, and Attis at the climactic scene of her novel deserves nothing less.

Myra Breckinridge offended some readers when it first appeared in 1968. If the recent persecution of the work of Robert Mapplethorpe and other artists is any guide, it would stir up far nastier responses now. In fact Vidal's celebrated novel has a distinguished literary pedigree; a scene like this one could be exchanged for any number of similar passages in such venerated Roman writers as

Apuleius, Juvenal, or Petronius. In this respect *Myra* builds on the classical education its author started with his researches into Tiberius and his little fishes, in much the same way that *Latin for Americans* finds its scholarly apotheosis in a conference on the Classical tradition and the American constitution.

The different uses of the past are, of course, striking. On the one hand, a conference that reflects an unbroken line from elementary textbook to mature academic scholarship, presided over by a soon-to-be announced candidate for high office; on the other, a learned, priapic assault on banal notions of sexual and literary decorum that, brilliant as it is, would not seem to have been designed to win its author an office of any kind. How is it that those who were following the lead of *Latin for Americans* so faithfully could apparently get the Classical Tradition so right, while Vidal, carrying his youthful naughtiness into adult life, was getting it all so, well, left—or, at least, not straight?

Present debates about the condition of the American mind are part of the answer. Nothing better serves the purposes of those who want to deny present injustice and its probable consequence than to turn back to the imagined "origins" of our world, in antiquity. These days Boston University seems to have become very much the university for the Cradle of Liberty. About the same time its president presided over that gathering of classicists in the Back Bay, he also published a precampaign manifesto called *Straight Shooting*, yet another contribution to the growing number of badly written academic treatises that aim to fix all that has gone wrong with modern America. (Appropriately for the post-Reagan era, *Straight Shooting* had already served as the title for an autobiography by the Hollywood actor Robert Stack.) A conference on the classical tradition and the American constitution was clearly a step in the right direction, so far as Boston was concerned.

More generally, such divergent evocations of a Roman past are always possible, because Rome offers at least two different paradigms for would-be Romans: at one end of the scale is the Republican image, the founding city that is the Rome of Brutus, Cincinnatus, and the early books of Livy's history; at the other end, the imperial Rome of Vergil, Ovid, Tacitus, Petronius, and Suetonius. That later, imperial Rome is a far less reassuring model for political or spiritual life. Understanding the difference between these Roman images is as crucial to understanding other nations' love affairs with *Romanitas*, as it is to understanding our own; it is the way to measure the political difference, for example, between Jacques Louis David's republican "Oath of the Horatii" and the same artist's later "Coronation of Napoleon I," a quintessential image of imperialism. For Vidal, the classical world of republican Rome that once supplied the United States its founding texts has always been no more than a point of departure, an imagined past not nearly as relevant to the present day as the imperial Rome of the Caesars.

For the formation of that *Romanitas*, the Roman images of Washington, D.C., were as important as Roman letters. Well before he came to Kirtland and Rogers, Vidal had a Roman mind that was grounded as much in that city and its politics as in literature. As the narrator of *Two Sisters* says,

> My childhood was spent between the library of the house in Rock Creek Park and the Capitol, where I used to roam about in the cellars, committee rooms, even on the floor of the Senate, where I sometimes sat in my grandfather's chair while he was in the cloak-room, conspiring against whoever happened to be president.

In the Washington of 1940, images of Rome abounded, and nowhere was the *Romanitas* of the United States more manifest than in the seat of government itself.

By both name and design Capitol Hill recreates the *Mons Capitolium*. For more than a century its architects and sculptors worked to turn the vision of the Capitol poet Tom Moore into a reality.

> Where tribunes rule, where dusky Davi bow,
> And what was Goose-Creek once is Tiber now.

Most of them were Italian artisans or aspiring American artists living in Italy. All were inspired by Roman art: Constantino Brumidi's canopy for the ceiling of the Rotunda, Carlo Fanzoni's "Car of History" in Statuary Hall, Luigi Persico's "Mars" at the East Pediment, Enrico Causici's "Life of Daniel Boone," in marble panels, as well as works by Giuseppe Valaperti, Giuseppe Franzoni, Giovanni Andrei, Antonio Capellano, and Francesco Iardella. And from the American artists in Rome there was Thomas Crawford (the East Pediment of the Senate, as well as its bronze doors), William H. Rinehart (the Indian and Pioneer who support the clock in the House of Representatives), and Randolph Rogers (the Columbus Doors at the east entrance to the Rotunda). The United States Capitol refashions much of American history into Roman images—an iconographical crash-course on the evolution of American republican ideals.

Vidal was not the first American writer to reflect on the cumulating imperial vision. The Civil War veteran general Lew Wallace published *Ben Hur: A Tale of the Christ* in 1880, about the same time Italian artists and their American disciples were finishing their work on the Capitol of the Second Rome. His successful novel has been read many ways—not the least interesting being the veiled homoeroticism of its two Hollywood versions, starring Francis X. Bushman and Ramon Navarro (1925) and Charlton Heston and Stephen Boyd (1959). To begin with, however, *Ben Hur* was a discreet, Christian response to the imperial rhetoric of the Second Rome and its capital city, a center of an empire which by the time Wallace published his novel was obviously beginning to get out of hand.

Disillusionment with Rome and *Romanitas* appears early in the novel; in the writing of it Wallace was much assisted, as have been most of Rome's critics, by testimony from the Romans themselves. Thus Ben Hur's mother consoles him after an unpleasant reunion with his boyhood friend, the Roman Massala:

> "There never has been a people who did not think themselves at least equal to any other—never a great nation, my son, which did not believe itself the very superior. When the Roman looks down upon Israel and laughs, he merely repeats the folly of the Egyptian, the Assyrian, and the Macedonian."

Wars and conquests, the annihilation of foes, and, from time to time, mercy to the downtrodden are pervasive themes for the artists of the United States Capitol, as they also are in the famous speech of Aeneas' father Anchises in the *Aeneid*. Not for the Romans as the mother of Ben Hur depicts them: "'In nothing but war, I say again, has Rome any claim to originality. Her games and spectacles are Greek inventions, dashed with blood to gratify the ferocity of her rabble.'"

Also in the novel there is a recycling of Calgacus' much-quoted indictment in Tacitus' *Agricola* of the Roman penchant for making a wilderness and calling it peace: "'To the excellences of other peoples the egotism of a Roman is a blindfold, impenetrable as his breast-plate. Oh, the ruthless robbers! under their trampling the earth trembles like a floor beaten with flails.'"

Neither Massala nor any other Roman of his class would have found this criticism upsetting. The people who invented the model *imperium* also came up with some of the earliest and most effective attacks on it. Whether Roman models come from the Rome of the republic or the empire, they always have within them the potential for their own subversion. Ben Hur's mother says as much—the Romans themselves found it difficult not to write burlesques of life in the capital: "'Rome, her poets, orators, senators, courtiers, are mad with affection of what they call *satire.*'"

Early exposure to the realities of political life in the Second Rome made it equally difficult for Vidal not to write satire. By returning to the source of all *Romanitas*, he recovered the original version of what the artists and politicians of Washington's Capitol had sought to re-create.

In *America's Rome* William Vance observes that American artists in Europe do not forget who they are or where they come from; with rare exceptions, "they labor as Americans for America." Whether Vidal's fellow citizens can see this patriotic side to him is debatable. Europeans certainly do. When the Italian edition of *Lincoln* was published, the reviewer for the *Corriere della Sera* noted just this quality in his work, finding it as political as it is artistic. Everywhere, along with the satire, appear signs of Vidal's *grand'amore* for his country.

Thus Washington and its empire are at once a source of Vidal's political identity and a center of his writing. In commenting on the career of Upton Sinclair, another politically engaged writer, he speaks of the comparative rarity of that kind of commitment: "A few of our writers have written on public themes, but as they were not taken seriously, they have ended by not taking themselves seriously, at least as citizens of a republic."

Unlike most expatriot writers, he took himself seriously enough as a citizen to run for office in 1960 for the House of Representatives from New York, and again in 1982, for the Senate from California. A video documentary about the California campaign portrays a candidate whose main strategy was, first, to spell out in considerable detail America's imperial identity, then to point out the consequences of that empire for the poor, the elderly, and the disadvantaged. The rhetoric of the campaign was everywhere inspired by the example of ancient Rome: before World War II the United States was a "consul-ruled republic"; afterward, "the empire of the west." This was a classic example of an imperial transformation, whereby a few profited at the expense of the many. Vidal did not win political office by this kind of argument, but did in fact come surprisingly closer to winning than anyone had supposed he would, himself included.

Much of the force of Vidal's perceptions about our Second Rome comes from personal acquaintance with that imperial transformation. When he began to live and write in Italy in the five years between 1945 and 1950, there were abundant reasons for an American writer to think about the Second Rome and its relation to the first. As he has often observed, that was the time American nuclear power made its empire worthy of its ancient example; briefly, it was supreme. Beyond that, there was much to be learned from the juxtaposition of American and Italian culture. The Fascists had made their link with ancient Rome quite explicit, so that a visitor to Rome in the 1940s, as today, could inspect the images of that recent attempt at empire superimposed on the ruins of others. In his first novel *The Gallery*, Vidal's contemporary John Horne Burns captured beautifully the collision of the emerging American empire with that older civilization.

> In those young men of Italy I'd seen something centuries old. An American is only as old as his years. A long line of something was hidden behind the bright eyes of the Italians. And then and there I decided to learn something of the modern world. There was some-

thing abroad which we Americans couldn't or wouldn't understand. But unless we make some attempt to realize that everyone in the world isn't American, and that everything American isn't good, we'd all perish together, and in this century.

At the end of his story, Burns learns the most important of all war's lessons: "Everything in life is a delusion, all happiness is simply a desire for, and unhappiness a repining of, love. Nothing else matters."

Moments like this raise Burns' book out of his particular experience, giving it wider scope. For him and most of the characters he created, the discovery of love came tragically too late. Writing some years after Burns' early death, Vidal found only *The Gallery* to be an authentic re-creation of its times; other books were "too redolent of ambition and literature." The comment at first seems surprising, since they are very different writers. Burns was the discoverer who wrote as if encountering Europe and its older traditions for the first time; Vidal, never anything less than the writer who is returning to a place and a tradition he already knows. Yet the affinity is there. Burns' tortured perception of American attitudes about love and imperial power was hard-won but complements Vidal's satiric view of the same themes.

Neither Burns' response to Italy nor his innocent tone were possible for Vidal. From the first he cultivates a fine Roman disdain for American innocence and all of its discoveries. In *The Judgment of Paris*, published five years after *The Gallery*, Vidal's agreeably sophisticated hero Philip Warren walks toward the Roman Forum as though he were returning to the center of a familiar place, a copy of *The Marble Faun* in hand.

> Suddenly the modern buildings ceased and on either side he saw dark canyons a dozen feet lower than the street, and he could see dimly by starlight the ruins of the Forum, pale familiar shapes of broken buildings, shattered columns and arches, an occasional dark massive section of some government building still intact, reminiscent in style of nearly every railroad station in every American city.

The Colosseum appears just as he imagines it would from books in his school days—perhaps in supplements to Kirtland and Rogers. Warren is impatient with the intervening Christian centuries separating him from imperial Rome. He is in the process of ridding himself of a Puritan consciousness that believes all pleasure to be evil and only pain to be good.

> Now though the churches themselves had died of their own victory long before the last of the wars of religion began, the fear of pleasure and the hate of loving persisted, a withering frost at the heart of summer, and all the martyrs, clinging upside down like bats from the rafters of heaven, no doubt felt that their work had survived the vicissitudes of knowledge better than even they might reasonably have suspected.

Vidal's early opposition of pagan and Christian would eventually come to full flower in *Julian*. Though an historical novel set in the fourth century, the subject was chosen for its connections to the present: "During the fifty years between the accession of Julian's uncle Constantine the Great and Julian's death at thirty-two, Christianity was established. For better or worse, we are today very much the result of what they were then." The story that unfolds is strongly reminiscent of twentieth-century America, giving early Christianity an unmistakably American, fundamentalist voice.

> Callistus offered me dinner but I chose to take nothing more from him. I said I must go. He accompanied me to the vestibule. He was all grace and tact, even when he chided me for never having acknowledged the "Ode to Julian" he had sent me.
> I apologized for my negligence. But then I said, "How could you write such an affectionate work about the man you murdered?"
> Callistus was perfect in his astonishment. "But I admired him tremendously! He was always kind to me. Every word I wrote about him was from the heart. After all, I am a good Christian, or try to be. Every day I pray for his soul!"

The murderous sanctimoniousness will sound familiar to those who can recall *Elmer Gantry* or *Inherit the Wind*. *Julian's* conflict between pagan values and Christian intolerance transfers from the first Rome, where it began, to the second, so that a story about the fourth century becomes a parable for the twentieth.

The historical novels from *Burr* onward work in similar ways. When Vidal writes about ancient Rome, he makes you think of modern America; when he writes about modern America, he makes you think of ancient Rome. The further the chronicle goes, the more the nation it portrays comes to resemble the Roman *imperium* of Suetonius and Tacitus. In *Lincoln*, for example, the president and his general are as much concerned about the stability of the new empire they are creating as they are about the war they want to end.

"It is a good thing," said Grant, as he prepared to go to the front, "that Sherman will take no part in the last battle."

Lincoln gazed down at the small general with some surprise. "Surely," he said, "there is glory enough for all."

"There isn't," said Grant. "That's the problem. The army we have here is the Eastern army. More important, it is the *Northern* army. But this army has always failed. If Sherman were to join us, the country will say that the east starts wars that westerners have to finish."

"You know, General," said Lincoln thoughtfully, "you have the makings of a very superior politician."

Grant nearly smiled. "Just as you, sir, have the makings of a very superior military tactician."

Thus American generals turn themselves into presidents, and American presidents, into generals. The transition from republic to empire may be imperceptible to those who live through it, but not to these two. Both Lincoln and Grant were well aware of the imperial direction American power had taken since the beginning of their careers. The Tacitean irony is that Congressman Abraham Lincoln and Lieutenant Ulysses S. Grant had been American republicans, strongly opposed to the imperial Mexican War of President James K. Polk.

The precise locus for our transformation from a republic into an empire continually shifts throughout Vidal's writings. When was it that America really lost its republican innocence? After the Second World War, as Vidal claimed in his race for the Senate? After the Civil War, as *Lincoln, 1876,* or *Empire* seem to suggest? Or was it as early as the American Revolution, as *Burr* slyly hints? Similar shifts of opinion can be found in Roman imperial history and literature, where the decisive battle or the political figure most fatal to liberty is subject to revision by Lucan, Seneca, Tacitus, and their modern

216 JAMES TATUM

followers. What remains constant in both Vidal's writing and his
Roman predecessors is the idea that the present regime is a betrayal
of its citizens. The game of identifying the Second Rome with the
first remains unchanged.

That same game of reading American political life as a reenact-
ment of Roman experience enables Vidal to explore sexuality and
private morality in ways that no American politician ever could.
Myra, Duluth, and the historical novels demonstrate with Roman
clarity the connections between American notions of sexuality and
American political practice. In the United States, gay sensibilities—
Vidal's preferred term would be "homosexualist"—are as subversive
to those who have ambitions of ruling this Second Rome as is the
exposure of the imperial reality underlying its republican veneer.
American love is, by legislation, straight shooting, the projection of
an image of power quite as deliberate as the projection of power
required for the realization of an imperial dream. For their part, the
Romans tended to be less evasive about the links between love and
empire than we are. Venus the goddess of love was the guiding deity
for Caesar and the mother of Aeneas, the founder of Rome. When
Vergil turns to the wars in Italy at the beginning of the second half of
the *Aeneid,* he invokes Erato, the muse of love poetry, to inspire his
song.

This aspect of Vidal's *Romanitas,* linking the political and the
erotic, is what lies behind his disposition to pull apart and reex-
amine American sexuality and American political power. He has
devoted some of his most amusing, scandalous writing to the topic;
in fact, that same writing is also Vidal at his most serious. Officially,
the separation of sexual and political desires is thought to be as firm
in our Second Rome as the separation of church and state. Both
conventions are observed with equal hypocrisy. Thereby the domi-
nating conventions of both love and the republic in which it is
supposed to stand became equally fit subjects for Vidal's satire. The
political fictions of *Lincoln* and the outrageous burlesque of American sexuality in *Myra Breckenridge* are two sides of the same erotic
coin.

In antiquity a Latin tetragram linked these related erotic energies
by a palindrome of the names of the city and its god: Roma and
Amor, Rome and Love:

R   O   M   A
O   M
M   O
A   M   O   R

There in essence is the logic of Vidal's *opera omnia*, with its progress
from a novel about Washington, the center of political power, to a
novel about Hollywood, the center of imaginary and real erotic
power. Writing toward the end of the presidency of our first actor-
president, Vidal represents the first generation of moviemakers in
Hollywood, shrewd students of the American scene who have already grasped the possibilities of linking the politics of Washington
with the new entertainment industry.

> Hays—or some other high federal officer—could act as a bridge
> between politics and the movies. If Caroline and Tim, somehow,
> could capture the bridge, the impulses that now came to Hollywood
> from Washington would be reversed and Mr. Hays, or whoever,
> would be *their* transmitter from West to East, from the governed to
> the governors.

It is thus as Roman as it can be for Vidal to have written a rape
scene like the earlier quoted passage from *Myra Breckenridge*. Both
Ovid and Livy (never thought to be an especially erotic writer) make
the rape of the Sabine women integral to their works. For Livy, that
occasion is solemnly justified as the first legitimate expansion of
Roman power under Romulus; for Ovid, it is the opportunity for a
witty reflection on the amorous uses of the public games in the *Art
of Love*. In both their Rome and Vidal's Second Rome, rapes are an
essential part of empire-building. The difference between global
conquest and private aggression is, for the Romans, mainly one of
scale. The erotic energy that creates empires is channeled against an
individual victim instead of a nation; the *amor* that rules the art of
love is also the word that Cicero uses to characterize the Romans'
love for conquest and dominance, *amor habendi*.

This erotic conception of empire explains why Ovid made rape
central to the plot of his *Metamorphoses*. Roman *amor* is what
makes that poem—seemingly apolitical, a handbook for modern
courses in mythology—a text every bit as political as the *Aeneid* or
Lucan's *Civil War*. The poem's central figure of political power,

Jupiter, governor of gods and men, is also the chief rapist of the poem. At several crucial moments he is likened to the emperor Augustus, who was deeply committed to what American politicians and their fundamentalist allies are fond of calling "family values." Augustus exiled Ovid to the Black Sea shortly after the publication of his poem.

That Roman conception of erotics brought Vidal to *Duluth*, the most rape-filled of all his books, and his angriest. When an illegal alien intent on raping Sergeant Darlene Ecks of the Duluth police department is subjected to a strip-search, the ensuing scene reverses more than the roles of rapist and victim.

> Darlene pulls up a crate and sits on it in such a way that the area of most interest to her is now at eye level. Then, gingerly, she moves her fingers up the quivering left thigh to the point where the sturdy legs join the thin torso. Victory! Hidden in the wiry thicket are two miniature prunes, removed from view by terror and cold.
>
> "So you had them all along," she says, squeezing the prunes together. She is rewarded with a whimper. Next she removes her comb from her Mainbocher uniform pocket and, carefully, she parts the pubic bush in the middle. As she combs the hair to each side of the central parting, she is rewarded with a highly privileged close-up view of what proves to be easily the smallest and greenest—well, more bluish, she concedes—okra that she has yet found. It sticks out, the one eye shut tight with terror.
>
> "For a rapist, boy, you're a non-starter."
>
> "What?"
>
> On impulse, Darlene pushed the okra back inside the alien, who screams. "Now you see it!" she shouts, "Not you don't!"
>
> Little does Darlene Ecks dream that at this moment of her greatest triumph to date, she has just created the merciless chief of what will soon be known worldwide as the Aztec Terrorists Society, whose cry "The fire this time!" (in Spanish) will demoralize and destabilize Greater Duluth.

There are symmetries with the earlier scene in *Myra Breckinridge*. As easily as *Roma* reverses *Amor*, Sergeant Ecks turns Myra's rape of Rusty inside out. Now you see it, now you don't. From grotesque penetration to even more grotesque exposure: a policewoman's strip-search of a suspect turns into a pet owner's search for a tomcat's balls.

Duluth seems to have been calculated to offend every audience that *Myra Breckinridge* did not. Sergeant Ecks shows no more regard for the sensitivity of so-called minorities—a typical American category that *Duluth* demonstrates will soon be incorrect—than Myra Breckinridge did for American notions of sexual propriety. But in the course of offending everyone, Vidal makes the connection between American sexual fantasies and images of American political power ludicrously explicit: not at the top of the American heap, as in *Washington, D.C.* or *Hollywood*, but at the bottom, in the emblematic city of the despised American Midwest, which is at the same time a border city of the American Southwest—all places where the fire this time is already under way. Outrageous as it is, *Duluth* has the sharp bite of a satirist like Juvenal: not pleasant, often not even funny, and thoroughly Roman.

A classicist would be inclined to measure the authenticity of Vidal's *Romanitas* by the way it comments on what that remote world now means to those Americans who still think it worth knowing. In a recent essay on Vergil and the Romans, one of their more perceptive American students nicely sums up the burdens of living in that empire, and the way we view that empire today:

> When they looked on their city, the Romans felt delight, felt pride in the grandeur of her monuments in which the grandeur of her history was visible. But they felt other things, things they could not quite bring themselves to say, that they could, most of them, only hint at, could only bring to light by speaking of *amor habendi.* Vergil saw something else. Until fairly recently, it had not been the fashion to pay much attention to the last half of Vergil's strange foundation epic. Why is it that in recent years we have become more interested than before in Aeneas when he arrives in Italy, in the last six books, where, not the promise of *imperium* and its grandeurs, but their complex ambivalent fulfillments are hauntingly evoked?

If a comprehensive answer to Ralph Johnson's question were to be found anywhere in American letters, it would be in the loved and loathed worlds we have come to know, thanks to the *Romanitas* of Gore Vidal.

But Vidal's *Romanitas* offers much more than an understanding of how some of us presently read classics like the *Aeneid*. He brings an authentic Roman view to bear on the American scene, one developed over a lifetime of writing and thinking, not something cooked up at short order; in the process, he reveals with great clarity what our once exemplary republic has actually become. To focus uncritically on the classical "origins" of the United States at this late moment in our imperial history is to miss the possible relevance of classical antiquity to contemporary America altogether. It is as if one were living in the America of James K. Polk or Theodore Roosevelt, rather than in the world where a Bostonian who murdered his pregnant wife could easily persuade the Boston police and most of white Boston that an African-American man was the culprit—an act that led to much police harassment of black communities and many racist attacks before the fraud was discovered. Search through reactionary manifestos like *Straight Shooting* or Allan Bloom's *Closing of the American Mind*, and you will never see the society that kind of incident bespeaks, let alone a way of beginning to confront it. By contrast, in Vidal's essays, *Duluth*, *Myra Breckinridge*, the chronicle of American history, and his campaign for office in California, there emerges an accurate image of imperial America that puts to shame the kind of distorted, partial uses of the past that have appeared with more and more frequency in this country, exposing them for the shallow stratagems they really are.

Vidal's mastery of the ironic and the erotic modes in both fiction and politics makes his work a powerful counterstatement to the mean spirits that abound in America at present. For both the ironic and the erotic modes, the wit and irreverent spirit, are anathema to those who would rule a country their way. That is the kind of perception one gains of our Second Rome, thanks to the *Romanitas* of Gore Vidal. It is something that Ovid, in his exile, would have understood very well.

Duluth! Loved. Loathed. Left. Lost.
Duluth (end)

17

The Central Man: On Gore Vidal's Lincoln

HAROLD BLOOM

Walt Whitman elegized Lincoln as "the sweetest, wisest soul of all my days and land." "The actual Lincoln was cold and deliberate, reflected and brilliant," according to Gore Vidal's brief meditation on the martyr president in *The Second American Revolution and Other Essays: 1976–1982*. The somber "Note" by Vidal gave us a Lincoln at heart . . . a fatalist, "a materialist" who "knew when to wait; when to act." This is the Lincoln of Vidal's superb novel, celebrated by the author as the master politician who invented what is now in crisis, the American nation-state.

If I count accurately, this is Vidal's nineteenth novel and thirtieth book and he is (or is going on) 59. I have read thirteen of the novels and two books of essays, which may be enough to yield some reasonable estimates about at least the relative nature of his achievement, if only to see how his work might be placed, so far. Though Vidal has a substantial audience, which certainly will be augmented by *Lincoln*, he has had rather mixed esteem among the most serious readers whom I know. I myself found his fiction very readable but not greatly memorable until the appearance of his ninth novel, *Julian*, which seems to me still a beautifully persuasive historical tale, a poignant portrait of the Emperor Julian, known forever as the Apostate by the Christian tradition that he rejected and abandoned.

Of the earlier novels, I had read only the first, *Williwaw*, and the third, *The City and the Pillar*, both refreshing, but then I was disappointed by the book just before *Julian*, an ambitious yet sketchy work that courageously was titled *Messiah*. What the far more powerful *Julian* showed, I thought, was that Vidal lacked invention, and so was most gifted at reimagining history. The political and historical *Washington, D.C.*, which followed *Julian*, seemed to confirm this estimation, since everything and everyone weakest in it was of Vidal's own creation, but I underestimated Vidal badly. *Myra Breckinridge* followed, an apocalyptic farce that rivaled Nathanael West's *A Cool Million* and Evelyn Waugh's *Scoop*, three outrageous travesties that will outlive many of the more celebrated visions of our century. After many readings, *Myra Breckinridge* continues to give wicked pleasure, and still seems to have fixed the limit beyond which the most advanced aesthetic neopornography ever can go.

Myra compelled a revisionary estimate of Vidal, who had powerfully demonstrated that superb invention was his strength, provided that the modes were farce and fantasy. The polemic of *Myra* remains the best embodiment of Vidal's most useful insistence as a moralist, which is that we ought to cease speaking of homosexuals and heterosexuals. There are only women and men, some of whom prefer their own sex, some the other, and some both. This is the burden of *Myra Breckinridge*, but a burden borne with lightness, wildness, abandon, joy, skill. It was a little difficult to see just how the author of *Julian* was one with the creator of *Myra*, but that increased a sense of expectation for what was to come.

I have never encountered a copy of *Two Sisters*, which followed *Myra*, I have read the half-dozen intervening novels before *Lincoln*, with some appreciation and much puzzlement, until now. *Myron* and the recent *Duluth* seem to me failures in the exhuberant mode of *Myra Breckinridge*, though I was stimulated by the references in *Duluth* to the egregious Thornton Bloom, author of *The Kabbalah*. The fictions of political history, *Burr* and *1876*, were far better, and indeed *Burr* stands with *Julian* and *Myra Breckinridge* as Vidal's truest contributions before *Lincoln*. But *Kalki* was another *Messiah*, contrived and perfunctory, in the religious mode that Vidal should perhaps handle only historically, while *Creation*, a civilized and learned narrative, showed that Vidal, even working historically, is simply not a philosophical novelist. *Creation*, unlike *Julian*, reduces to a series of essays, which are always provocative, but almost never very consequential. Vidal, reimagining our cultural origins, or rather our imaginations of those origins, is no Burckhardt and no Nietzsche, but then why should he be?

What he is, in *Lincoln*, is a masterly American historical novelist, now wholly matured, who has found his truest subject, which is our national political history during precisely those years when our political and military histories were as one, one thing and one thing only: the unwavering will of Abraham Lincoln to keep the states united. Vidal's imagination of American politics, then and now, is so powerful as to compel awe. Lincoln is to our national political mythology what Whitman is to our literary mythology: the figure that Emerson prophesied as the Central Man. No biographer has been able to give us a complete and convincing account of the evasive and enigmatic Whitman. No biographer, and until now no novelist, has had the precision of imagination to show us a plausible and human Lincoln, one of us and yet beyond us. Vidal, with his book, does just that, and more: he gives us the tragedy of American political history, with its most authentic tragic hero at the center, which is to say, at our center.

Lincoln: A Novel begins in the early, frozen morning of February 23, 1861, as Lincoln, flanked by the detective Pinkerton and by his presidential bodyguard, slips into Washington so as to avoid being murdered before his inauguration. A minority President, elected with less than 40 percent of the total vote, he confronts a crisis that no predecessor, and no American head of state since, could even envision. Though his election committed him only to barring the extension of slavery to the new states, and though he was a moderate Republican and not an Abolitionist, Lincoln was violently feared by most of the South. Vidal's opening irony, never stated but effectively implied, is that the South beheld the true Lincoln long before Lincoln's own cabinet had begun to regard the will and power of the political genius who so evasively manipulated them. Vidal's Lincoln is the most ambitious of all American presidents. The South feared an American Cromwell, and in Vidal's vision, the South actually helped produce an American Bismarck.

But there is no Southern perspective in Vidal's novel, nor should there be. Lincoln, the first Westerner (Illinois) to be elected since Andrew Jackson, is presented as the heir of Jackson and Polk. (Polk, was, of course, a believer in the strong executive tradition and a respecter of neither the states, nor the Congress, nor the Court, nor the parties, nor even the Constitution itself.) This Lincoln, rather enigmatically, is transcendental and idealist only in the mode of the later Emerson, author of the grim essay "Power" in his superb *The Conduct of Life*. "Power" works by the dialectic of Emerson's Lear-like revision of Coleridge's compensatory imagination. Coleridge thought (or hoped) that experiential loss can be transformed into imaginative gain. Emerson rephrased this formula as "nothing is got for nothing," which seems the secret motto of Vidal's Lincoln, who follows another great essay, "Fate," in *The Conduct of Life*, by worshipping, not Jehovah nor Jesus, but only what Emerson called the Beautiful Necessity, the American tragedy of the struggle between freedom and fate, in which the heroic agonist secretly loves neither freedom nor fate, but only power. Vidal's strong Lincoln, triumphant at last over the South and his own cabinet and party, is such an agonist, a dialectician of power, and finally a kind of self-willed Orphic sacrifice who, in the closing words of Vidal's book, "had willed his own murder as a form of atonement for the great and terrible thing that he had done by giving so bloody and absolute a rebirth to his nation."

It is Vidal's skill as a narrator, and his art as a reimaginer of historical personages, that makes plausible this curiously nihilistic rebirth. The book's narrative principle is a highly traditional one: deferred revelation, and enacted throughout by Lincoln's brilliant alternation of an endless, almost passive waiting with sudden overwhelming acts of decision. What is perpetually deferred is a full awareness of Lincoln's preternatural ability to prophesy the moves of every other politician, as well as his uncanny sense of his own greatness, his own central place in national and world history. That this savage greatness paradoxically has been revised by American mythology into Whitman's "sweetest, wisest soul" and later debased into Carl Sandburg's homespun sentimentalist may be the provocation for Vidal's novel, yet one senses that Vidal's motives are more immediate. With the likely, impending reelection of Reagan (1984), the nation confirms what might become the final crisis of Lincoln's presidential creation. If our system is, as Vidal contends, Lincoln's invention, then the American age of Lincoln finally approaches its apocalypse. Should Vidal prove correct, his tragic vision of Lincoln as Orphic dictator may serve also as an elegy for the one hundred and twenty years of Lincoln's invented America.

On its surface, Vidal's novel is a grand entertainment, maintaining a total intensity that might be called humorously somber. Lincoln himself is presented as the master of evasions, strongest as he strives to appear weakest, and a purposive self-mythologizer. Vidal cunningly contributes to the mythologizing by adding "the Tycoon" and "the Ancient" to "Old Abe" and "Father Abraham" as presidential nicknames. The crucial name probably is "the Ancient," who indeed is what Emerson called "spontaneity or instinct" in the crucial essay, "Self-Reliance." Lincoln falls back continually upon what is best and oldest in his own self, an ancient spark that seems to have originated not only before the creation of the Union, but before the Creation itself. More than Whitman, this Lincoln is Emerson's American Adam, post-Christian and self-begotten, who knows no time when he was not as now. If this is Vidal's ontological Lincoln, the imperial Lincoln, archetypal politician yet tragic sufferer, nevertheless more winningly dominates the novel.

Vidal demystifies Lincoln to the rather frightening degree of suggesting that he had transferred unknowingly a venereal infection, contracted in his youth, and supposedly cured, to his wife, Mary Todd, and through her to his sons. The gradually developing madness of Mrs. Lincoln, and the related early deaths of two of the boys, form one of the dark undertones of this novel, plausibly suggesting a more than temperamental basis for Lincoln's profound melancholia. Counterpointed against this sadness is Lincoln's celebrated humor, conveyed by Vidal with authentic verve, but always with a Freudian sense of wit, in which the laughter carries the burden of double or antithetical meanings:

> "Sometimes I say those things and don't even know I've said them. When there is so much you *cannot* say, it's always a good idea to have a story ready. I do it now from habit," Lincoln sighed. "In my predicament, it is a good thing to know all sorts of stories because the truth of the whole matter is now almost unsayable; and so cruel."

The "predicament" here overtly refers to the Southern rebellion and the "truth of the whole matter" perhaps to the endless catastrophe of the sequence of incompetent Northern generals, but the underlying references are to Lincoln's inner despairs. Vidal seems to be suggesting, quite subtley, throughout the novel, that Lincoln's obsessive drive to preserve and restore the Union of the states was a grand restitution or compensation for what never could be healed in his own personal and familial life. Combined with a metaphysical will to power, this results in the gradual emergence of Lincoln as the first and most forceful dictator-president, forerunner of the Roosevelts and of Lyndon Johnson.

It seems to me an astonishing achievement that Vidal makes us love his Lincoln, "cold and deliberate, reflective and brilliant," qualities that do not often engender affection whether in fact or fiction—particularly because we have to struggle also against our mystified sense of the Sandburgian or Hollywood saintly Lincoln. I suspect that Vidal succeeds because his Lincoln is an authentic image of authority. Freud taught us that love reduces to love of authority, love of the father image that seems not to love us in return. But Vidal's Lincoln is Shakespearean, not just in his recurrent quotations from the plays, but in his lonely and heroic fatalism. He inspires love partly because he seems to be beyond needing it.

Surrounding Vidal's Lincoln swarms an almost Dickensian roster of fabulistic caricatures: politicians, generals, White House aides, Washington ladies, newspapermen, Northern and Southern conspirators, and amiably evil bankers, including Jay Cooke himself. These are Vidal's Americans, then and now, and they are rendered with an almost invariable and unfailing gusto. The most memora-

ble and entertaining is the sanctimonious Salmon P. Chase: archetypal Republican, pious Abolitionist, hero of bankers, endless plot-
ter to seize power from Lincoln, and forever ungrateful to the
President for his appointments as Secretary of the Treasury and
Chief Justice. Vidal's Chase is a comic foil to Vidal's tragic Lincoln,
for Chase has every quality except aesthetic dignity. Inwardly hum-
ble, but in the Dickensian mode, Chase pursues greatness, to the
parodistic extent of obsessively yielding to a ruling passion for col-
lecting the autographs of famous writers.

In a finely rendered scene of comic pathos, Chase confronts the
job-seeking and highly disreputable Walt Whitman, who's devoting
himself to the care of sick and wounded soldiers. Since Whitman
bears with him a letter of recommendation from Emerson, Chase's
sole concern is to extract the desired letter while rejecting the
obscene bard. Whitman splendidly starts off wrong by comparing
the inside of the Capitol to "the interiors of Taylor's saloon in the
Broadway, which you doubtless know." Chase shudders at thus
encountering a populist beast, and proceeds to his triumph:

> "In Mr. Emerson's letter, does he mention *what* you might do in
> the government's service?" Chase thought this approach subtle in the
> extreme.
>
> "Well, here it is," said Whitman. He gave Chase the letter. On
> the envelope was written "The Honorable S. P. Chase." Inside was
> a letter dated January 10, endorsing Walt Whitman highly for any
> sort of government post; and signed, Chase excitedly saw, with the
> longed-for-but-never-owned autograph "R. W. Emerson."
>
> "I shall give Mr. Emerson, and yourself, Sir, every sort of consid-
> eration," said Chase, putting the letter in his pocket where it seemed
> to him to irradiate his whole being as if it were some holy relick.
>
> "I shall be truly grateful. As will Mr. Emerson, of course." Chase
> shook Whitman's hand at the door and let him out, then Chase
> placed the letter square in the middle of his desk and pondered what
> sort of frame would set it off best.

As the novel progresses, Vidal's exuberance in depicting Chase
increases, and the reader begins to share the author's dialectical
sympathy for this comic monster who nevertheless is the clear ancestor of all sanctimonious Republicans since, down to the menag-
erie currently staffing the White House. Though a paragon of selfishness, Chase nevertheless is sincere in behalf of the slaves, while

Lincoln frees them only reluctantly, and then idly dreams of shipping them off to the West Indies or back to Africa. Chase seeks power, for presumably idealistic purposes; Lincoln, with the single purpose of keeping his nation unified, stalks power with no concern whatsoever for human rights.

Vidal does not celebrate Lincoln's destruction of civil liberties, but shows a certain admiration for the skill with which the President subverts the Constitution he is sworn to defend. There is a split in Vidal between the man of letters who has a friendly contempt for politicians and the born political man who would make a remarkable senator, if only even California was quite ready for him. The audacity that distinguishes Vidal as visionary politician, amiably and sensibly urging us to withdraw tax-exempt status from churches, synagogues, foundations, and universities, is matched by his audacity as political novelist, urging us to see Lincoln plain while giving us a Lincoln that our mythological needs cannot quite accept.

I return to the still ambiguous question of Vidal's strength or perhaps competing strengths as a novelist. *Lincoln*, together with the curiously assorted trio of *Julian*, *Myra Breckinridge*, and *Burr*, demonstrates that his narrative achievement is vastly underestimated by American academic criticism, an injustice he has repaid amply in his essayistic attacks upon the academy, and in the sordid intensities of *Duluth*. But even *Lincoln* (unlike the slighter but flawless *Myra Breckinridge*) has its disappointments. Booth's conspiracy against Lincoln's life was melodramatic enough in mere actuality, but that does not justify Vidal's rendering of it as a quite perfunctory melodrama. The difficulty appears again to be Vidal's relative weakness, except in farce, for inventing characters, as opposed to his immense gift for revisualizing historical personae. David Herold, upon whom the Booth conspiracy is made to center, remains a name upon these pages; he simply does not stimulate Vidal's imagination, unlike Lincoln, Chase, and the other personages of our common past. Lincoln's striking Epicurean fatalism is asserted rather than dramatized; the ideological and religious vigor that portrayed Julian the Apostate so memorably is simply absent here. And though Vidal's humor is a pleasure throughout, he restrains himself too strictly from relying upon his genius for farce. This may be just as well, since the author of *Myra Breckinridge* is also the author of *Duluth*. But it does prompt the critical question: will it ever be possible for Vidal to reconcile all of his talents within the dimensions of a single novel?

The question would be unjust or misleading if *Lincoln* did not testify so persuasively that Vidal, in his late fifties, remains the developing rather than an unfolding novelist, to borrow a useful distinction from Northrop Frye. There are several extant American novelists, more highly regarded by critics than Vidal, who nevertheless will never surprise us. Vidal, like the very different Norman Mailer, has the capacity to confound our expectations. Such a capacity, in so bad a time for the Republic, both of letters and of politics, scarcely can be overpraised.

18

Vidal's Empire

RICHARD POIRIER

With *Empire*, Gore Vidal has taken his vast chronicle of American history from *Burr* (1973) to *Lincoln* (1984) and *1876* (1976), then on to *Washington, D.C.* (1967) and the onset of World War II. *Empire* fills in the turn of the century, from 1898 with William McKinley's administration, to 1906, when Theodore Roosevelt, who came to office after McKinley's assassination in 1901, had reached the middle of his first elected term. Roosevelt had already helped set the course of American empire as McKinley's assistant secretary of the Navy. Presiding in that capacity over the buildup of the American fleet, he was strongly persuaded by the views of Captain Alfred Thayer Mahan, author in 1890 of *The Influence of Sea Power upon History*, and those of his friend Brooks Adams, who argued in *Law of Civilization and Decay* (1895) that political supremacy depended largely on the control of trade routes.

Roosevelt did not need much persuading. He had reached similar conclusions in 1882 with his own *The Naval War of 1812*. An ardent supporter of American expansion, he agreed with the Brooks Adams of *America's Economic Supremacy* (1900) that "supremacy has always entailed sacrifices as well as triumphs, and fortune has seldom smiled on those who, besides being energetic and industrious, have not been armed, organized, and bold." "Bully," as Roosevelt is apt to say several times too often in this novel, clicking his ever visible "tombstone teeth."

Roosevelt had a large element of the ridiculous in him, but as presidents go, he was unusually smart. Because of him America was "armed, organized, and bold" at the right time and place. So that while the American people may have been taken by surprise, Roosevelt and the fleet were ready when the battleship *Maine* was blown up in the harbor of Havana, Cuba, then a Spanish possession. The fleet had already been positioned so close to the Philippines that William James, one of the teachers exasperated by Teddy's loquacity at Harvard, and later an officer of the Anti-Imperialist League—he is absent from Vidal's glittering cast of characters—was among those who wondered just how surprised anyone had a right to be. James could not then have known that Roosevelt, while briefly replacing his superior at Navy, had secretly ordered Admiral Dewey to assemble his ships at Hong Kong, from which they could steam into Manila and destroy the Spanish Armada.

In a mere ten weeks America had come into possession of a world empire that included Cuba (to which independence of a sort was granted), Puerto Rico, Guam, and the Philippines. The Philippines resisted for a time, requiring the brutal suppression of an independence movement originally armed and inspired by the islands' new conquerors, and at a cost in lives, fortune, and honor greater than the cost of the war with Spain. All told it had been, in John Hay's phrase, "a splendid little war."

Empire opens with a house party at Surrenden Dering, deep in the English countryside, a day after the war has ended. The hosts are the recently retired senator from Pennsylvania, Don Cameron, and his wife, Elizabeth, niece of General Sherman, the hero of an earlier war (though not a hero if you lived in Atlanta). Elizabeth is the adored confidante here, as she was in life, of another house guest, the historian and novelist Henry Adams. The opening is in the mode of Henry James, who in fact drops by for lunch. Vidal's James is more convincingly portrayed even than he is in Edith Wharton's *A Backward Glance* or in Simon Nowell-Smith's invaluable compilation of reminiscences, *The Legend of the Master*. And while Vidal may have depended on such sources for help in catching the great novelist's manner and cadences of speech, he greatly enriches these by qualities of sharpness, worldly perception, confidence, and toughness, which he has inferred from reading James' fiction and critical writings.

Vidal's James is a figure of benign, alert majesty who will prove more than a match for the effusive conversational aggressions of President Roosevelt at a White House dinner (such a dinner actually did take place). How appropriate to James' life, and signally to the theme of Vidal's novel (though outside its time frame) that a novelist who brought two continents under his authorial sovereignty should, in the delirium of his final illness, have begun signing his letters with the name "Napoleone," using, as Leon Edel points out, the old Corsican spelling. With his relaxed, receptive skeptical style, James in these opening chapters is an early indication of how Vidal's novel will itself deal with its powerful and famous characters. James is allowed gently to demolish the assertive pomposities of Brooks Adams, who on this as on other occasions manages to irritate his brother Henry, and to deride affectionately the patriotic, sentimental dialect poems composed by another guest, John Hay, the ambassador to the Court of Saint James, the former assistant secretary to Lincoln, and soon to be called back to Washington as McKinley's secretary of state.

Also introduced in this first chapter is the fictional heroine of the book, Caroline Sanford. Like Isabel Archer in James' *Portrait of a Lady*, Caroline intends to be a "free" woman. But where James' heroines have an unfortunate habit of renunciation, Caroline will have none of it. In her own mind she doesn't rule out sleeping with a woman as readily as with a man; she will manage to seize the inheritance that her brother Blaise tries to deny her; and she determines on a career in Washington, as yet unheard of for a woman. She transforms a respectable but impoverished newspaper into a sensationalist and politically powerful one, while acquiring an illegitimate daughter during her (and the book's) one extended sexual affair—an emotionally cool one—with a married congressman named James Burden Day.

It will be obvious that in *Empire* Vidal manages inextricably to mix the fictive and the historical, the social and the legendary. These elements are so fused in his style that none can be differentiated from the others. All partake of the same issues of inheritance, legitimacy, rivalry, deception, and ambition. Such mixtures can of course be found in many good historical novels, but in Vidal the mixtures are brewed in a particularly potent way. He means to suggest that historical position and achievement notwithstanding, the historically great are no different from the fictive persons with whom he surrounds them. Part of Vidal's originality derives from the attendant assurance that he can create and command the American history of his novels all as much as any imaginary components. No other American writer has Vidal's sense of national proprietorship, and his presumptions work marvelously well both for his novelistic intentions and, for reasons that I'll get to in a moment, for the political point he wants to make.

Taking any position involves limitations, however, and these include for Vidal a reluctance to confront anything that can't be brought within the control of his high urbanities. He has none of the humility claimed, for example, by Henry James in his own *The American Scene*, of 1907, the very period of this novel. Speaking of New York City and its awesome differences from the New York of his youth, James admits that

> the reflecting surface of the ironic, of the epic order, suspended in the New York atmosphere, have yet to show symptoms of shining out, and the monstrous phenomena themselves, meanwhile, strike me as having, with their immense momentum, got the start, got ahead of, in proper parlance, any possibility of poetic, of dramatic capture.

There are similar evidences that America is beyond "capture" in Mailer, Bellow, or Pynchon when they try to express the obscure nature of the national identity as it exists in poor, marginal, or inarticulate people. So far, Vidal has relegated such scenes and human types almost exclusively to the series that includes *Myra Breckinridge*, *Myron*, and *Duluth*, novels that reveal how, parodistically at least, he chooses to invent an American unconscious. In *Empire*, as in other novels in the chronicle, he limits himself to highly self-conscious people of the governing and dominant classes. The implication is clear: from the first exchanges between Hay, Henry James, and the Adams brothers, with Caroline and her fiancé

Del Hay listening in, it is to be assumed that polite conversation can fully account for national, international, or geopolitical reality.

While such an approach might easily foreclose "any possibility of poetic, of dramatic capture" of those elements that yield only to more exploratory ones, the danger is mostly outweighed, I think, by the political as well as literary benefits that accrue to Vidal's directness, clarity, and purposiveness of style. It is as if he shares in part at least the perception of Hay, "who thought of the [White House]—the city, too, and the republic beyond—as a theater, with a somewhat limited repertory of plays; and types."

The positive accomplishment of Vidal's style is that it proves an effective instrument to clear away the verbal mumbo jumbo that often accompanies the idea of "empire," to dispel any metaphysics about the kinds of power necessary to imperial acquisition, and to expose the mythologies that have made "empire" palatable, especially to a country that recoils incredulously when the word is applied to itself. Even the admirable McKinley wants to believe that only on his knees and in prayer could he convince himself to annex the Philippines. We had a duty to Christianize it, he says of a country already 80 percent Christian.

On the subject of "empire," that is, Vidal is writing outside the dominant stylistic traditions in which imperial power is usually represented in English. Melville, Conrad, and, later, Faulkner, Mailer, and Pynchon write about the imperial quest as if its source, movements, and results are necessarily concealed. It is evoked by them as a mystery, something that calls for a style correspondingly elaborate and suggestive, and that cannot ever be fully exposed to view. *Heart of Darkness* treats imperialism in the way *The Turn of the Screw* treats its ghosts. By contrast Vidal's prose is intended to strip American imperialism of any shrouded majesty and to erase from the American political landscape the "hieroglyphic sense of concealed meaning" that Pynchon finds even in a configuration of California lights.

I confess a preference for a prose that carries a greater sense of the inexpressive, of imponderables, than Vidal's characteristically does, and for the reason that even while it allows for Vidal's quizzical sense of politics and history it can enrich it more than he does. *Moby-Dick*, arguably the greatest novel written by an American, is also a critique of nineteenth-century capitalistic imperialism, especially toward colonial people. And yet Melville's critique is inseparable from the density of his style, suggesting as it does that imperialism is concealed in a rhetoric of mystification even from its main actors. Vidal's offhand comment in an article on Anthony Burgess—that people do not find Ahab nearly comic enough—is not so much wrong as myopic, and an indication of how resolute he is in opposing anything less than the clearest possible exposure of a betrayal of the country's purpose that, beginning with the founders themselves, was, as he sees it, intensified with the Louisiana Purchase.

However, a fact often lost sight of is that Vidal, like Santayana, refuses to treat American imperialism as if it were something that shouldn't have happened. I mean the Santayana who refers contemptuously to William James' bellyaching about the American seizure of empire from Santayana's native Spain. In *Persons and Places* he complains that James

> cried disconsolately that he had lost his country, when his country, just beginning to play its part in the history of the world, appeared to ignore an ideal that he had innocently expected would always guide it, because this ideal *had* been eloquently expressed in the Declaration of Independence. But the Declaration of Independence was a piece of literature, a salad of illusions. . . . The American Colonies were rehearsing independence and were ready for it; that was what gave their declaration of their independence timeliness and political weight. In 1898 the United States were rehearsing domination over tropical America and were ready to organize and to legalise it; it served their commercial and military interests and their imaginative passions. Such antecedents and such facilities made intervention sooner or later inevitable. . . . James's displeasure at the seizure of the Philippines was therefore, from my point of view, merely accidental. It did not indicate any sympathy with Spain, or with anything in history that interests and delights me. On the contrary, it was an expression of principles entirely opposed to mine; much more so than the impulses of young, ambitious, enterprising America.

Santayana is here expressing Vidal's own hard-nosed worldliness, along with an appreciation, which Vidal's fiction also shares, of "young, ambitious, enterprising America." Myra Breckinridge is herself a thwarted evidence of this appreciation, and Caroline Sanford is an historically earlier, more respectable version of Myra. Caroline will have her way and do the best she can for herself despite those who try to crush her. She is no less charmingly Luciferian than Burr, another aspirant to empire outside the officially sanctioned one. Pregnant by Congressman Day, she gets herself a husband—a hapless lawyer who is her cousin and whose bed she will never share—by in return agreeing to pay his debts; threatened by her half and only brother, Blaise, with a takeover of her newspaper, and guessing that he is secretly of her own same-sex inclinations, she gets Congressman Day to seduce him, thereby giving her the leverage of blackmail over both of them. And yet Henry Adams endorses Vidal's high opinion of Caroline. As in *The Education*, where he is charmed by Clarence King as "the ideal American they all want to be," Adams is admiring here of someone with the energy and knowledge equal to the accelerating demands of a new age, while persevering in the ideals of the old. Neither Adams nor Vidal asks that so capable a person would also be a nice one.

Vidal is not in any simple way against American "empire." He has spoken nostalgically about the ten-year period after World War II, when America was the most powerful empire the world has ever known, calling it "the golden age," which is the promised title of the summary volume in his America history chronicle. "What potential there was for the Republic and how we blew it," he laments in *Interview* for June 1974. Rather, he opposes the brutal and self-defeating ways of getting and managing an empire, one example of which is the McCarthyist brand of anticommunism that helped bring "the golden age" to an early end. Nor is he complaining that America, like other countries, creates fictional apologias for expansion. It is not the fictions themselves, but their proliferation, mechanization, and shabbiness that, in his view, have sickened and corrupted the nation. *Empire* locates this process of corruption in the conjunction, at the turn of the century, of Roosevelt's jingoism with Hearst's yellow journalism, a term derived from the yellow ink used in printing a cartoon strip called "The Yellow Kid," in Hearst's *New York Journal*.

Roosevelt and Hearst are, by the end of the novel, the leading contenders for control of the new "empire," and in the meeting that brings the novel to its close, the President must grotesquely shove his rival aside in order to secure his own designated chair at the head of the cabinet table. There are several exquisitely managed scenes in this novel between peoples of immense personal force, as when Hay and the supercilious Elihu Root gradually bait the aspiring Roosevelt into the admission, "I hate irony." But perhaps the best such scene is the final one in which Roosevelt and Hearst each claim to have invented the American empire. Hearst says at one point that "the future's with the common man, and there are a whole lot more of them than there are of you." "Or you," Roosevelt replies.

Who is the "common man"? After Roosevelt and Hearst use this exhausted rhetorical expression the issue is dropped. By letting it pass, Vidal probably means to suggest that in the America dominated by these two, "the common man" is effectively passing out of existence, already at century's turn about to disappear into the combination of mass press and governmental brainwashing that, having to some extent shaped "the common man," now largely produce him. This invites us, I think, to read *Myra Breckinridge*, along with *Myron* and *Duluth*, as post-Hearstian comedies, in which human beings have devolved into grotesque assemblages, patched together out of images created by television series and B movies. The three books are to be read as comic-nightmare versions of Vidal's more realistic historical novels.

Is history fiction? Is fiction history? Roosevelt jeeringly remarks to Hearst at the end of *Empire* that "I was aware of your pretentions as a publisher, but I never realized that you are the sole inventor of us all." "Oh, I wouldn't put it so grandly," Hearst replies with impressive calm. "I just make up this country pretty much as it happens to be at the moment." The two are clearly not practiced in analytic philosophy—what does it mean to "make up" something if the something already "happens to be"?—but Hearst brings as much discrimination to the issue as it deserves. Fiction making is and always has been an essential part of the making of history, essential, that is, even to the decision that something, and not some other thing, deserves to be called "history." The fictionizing occurs not only retrospectively but on the spot, as in Greek mythology, allusions to which are frequent in this book. The ancients, too, needed the mythologies they gave themselves before handing them on to us, for our eager adaptations. In life fiction is no less inseparable from history than it is in Vidal's historical novels. He confirms this with a technical brilliance the more impressive for being nearly invisible, especially in his characterization of McKinley.

Along with recent revisionist historians, Vidal regards McKinley as the first great president since Lincoln. In the novel, the revisionist process is transferred from later historical interpretations and given to the actually engaged figures in McKinley's own circle. Driven by events, and by their own quest for historical importance, the men around him feel compelled to displace one fiction about the President—that he is a pawn of Mark Hanna, the Ohio millionaire who helped him to the White House—with another, in which he is, as Brooks Adams describes him, "our Alexander. Our Caesar. Our Lincoln reborn." Meanwhile, McKinley, in Vidal's portrait, is quietly occupied with his wife, with food in great quantities, and with small-town musings on "whether we are really going to set up in the empire business or not." He is an endearing rather than a grand enigma, and becomes enigmatic at all only because he is involved in a new political situation that asks him to be more than he knows himself to be. Events require a figure commensurately imposing. McKinley's true greatness for Vidal consists in his modest but crafty demurrals, and the space his modesty gives him for sanity, flexibility, and independence. What better "empire," the novel seems wistfully to suggest, than that.

19

Babylon Revisited

Louis Auchincloss

In the beginning of Gore Vidal's new novel, *Hollywood*, the "duchess," as the consort of Ohio Senator Warren G. Harding is affectionately known, visits the Washington salon of the astrologist Madame Marcia to read her husband's horoscope. The visit has been arranged by Harding's henchman, Harry Daugherty, who is pushing him for the Republican nomination in 1920. Daugherty believes that his candidate will be nominated and elected, and he expects that Madame Marcia, who is consulted by the greatest in the last, will predict this, and that her prediction will be a good way of preparing the Duchess for her future role. Only Harding's hour and date of birth have been supplied to the functioning sorceress, but since she has instant access to the Congressional Directory, a glance could allow her to match the date to the man. Or has Daugherty fixed her in advance?

Madame Marcia duly foresees the presidency in the stars and rampant lion of the horoscope. But she also sees a darker fate. In answer to the question: "He'll die?" she replies:

"We all do that. No. I see something far more terrible than mere death." Madame Marcia discarded her toothpick like an empress letting go her sceptre. "President Harding—of course I know exactly who he is—will be murdered."

We are now in the world of Gore Vidal. Many years ago, although an avid reader of his novels, I was uneasy in some parts of that world. I remember waxing a bit hot under the collar, reading *Burr*, at what I considered a travesty of the character of my hero, Thomas Jefferson. But since that time the bottom has fallen out of my old world. We have undergone Watergate and Irangate; we have seen a president resign from office under fire and a daydreaming movie star occupy the White House. If I hear the truth spoken by an elected official or his representative, I wonder if he has had no inducement to lie. I have had to face the nasty fact that the world is—and probably always was—a good deal closer to the one so brilliantly savaged by Vidal than any that I had fondly imagined.

And even now, as I pause in writing this piece to glance at the newspaper, I read that the second volume of Robert Caro's heavily documented life of LBJ will attempt to prove that that lauded Texas liberal was the greatest and most unabashed rigger of elections in our political history. We may yet live to see Vidal branded a sentimentalist!

Vidal has said that *Hollywood* is the last (though not the last chronologically) of a sequence of novels loosely called his History of the United States, starting with *Burr*, which deals with Aaron Burr's conspiracy, jumping forward to *Lincoln* and the Civil War, pausing in *1876* to cover the scandal of the Hayes-Tilden election, then moving in *Empire* to the imperialism of Theodore Roosevelt, and ending in *Washington, D.C.* with Joe McCarthy's reign of terror. *Hollywood* fills in the First World War and the Harding administration. But if the novels are all stars, at least in the brightness of their dialogue and character delineation, they do not form a true constellation. I doubt that they were really conceived as such before the writing of *Lincoln*. I find a true unit only in the trilogy of *Lincoln*, *Empire*, and *Hollywood*, which relate the grim, dramatic story of the forging, for a good deal worse than better, according to Vidal, of the American empire and its ultimate conversion into the celluloid of the moving picture, which is all he deems it to be worth.

In *Lincoln* he finds the only man in his epic to whom he is willing to concede true greatness, and his portrait of this man raises the novel a head above the others of the trilogy and may even make it a significant addition to the mountain of books on the emancipator, many of which, in Vidal's opinion, are packed with lies. His Lincoln is not so much concerned with freeing the slaves; he wants to save the union in order to turn it into a huge, world-dominating state, the "empire" that will be the subject of the next two novels. The book ends with John Hay musing on the question of whether the assassinated president might not have willed his own murder "as a form of atonement for the great and terrible thing that he had done by giving so bloody and absolute a rebirth to his nation."

Vidal admires the creator but not the creation. He is constantly fascinated with the subject of power. Money, oratory, muscle, wit, and sex (the latter when not used exclusively for brief physical pleasure) are devoted to the domination of one's fellow man. For what purpose? For the fun of the game. Vidal is something of an existentialist, suggesting as he does the absurdity of grand projects. Theodore Roosevelt in *Empire* exults in blood and guts and accomplishes nothing. The question is raised at the end of the novel if it is even he who has effected the things he has purported to effect. In a scene between the rough rider and the newspaper despot William Randolph Hearst, the latter suggests that the President has been his puppet.

> "True history," said Hearst, with a smile that was, for once, almost charming, "is the final fiction. I thought even you knew that." Then Hearst was gone, leaving the President alone in the Cabinet room, with its great table, leather armchairs, and the full-length painting of Abraham Lincoln, eyes fixed on some far distance beyond the viewer's range, a prospect unknown and unknowable to the mere observer, at sea in present time.

The two main characters, who weave the episodes of history into the narrative of *Hollywood*, Blaise Sanford and his half sister, Caroline Sanford Sanford, have settled an old family feud by agreeing to comanage a Washington newspaper of wide circulation and great political importance. They have a genealogical connection with Charles Schermerhorn Schuyler, the narrator of *Burr* and *1876*, who dies at the end of the eponymous year, which is worthy of a Jacobean tragedian. Schuyler's daughter Emma, widow of the

French Prince d'Agrigente, has plotted to marry the wealthy Colonel William Sanford after his wife has died giving birth to a child whose conception Emma knows will be fatal to her but which she has nonetheless wickedly encouraged. Mrs. Sanford duly dies giving birth to Blaise, and the next year Emma, now her successor, is justly punished by expiring at the birth of her own child, Caroline. The two babies are given a genetic head start to face the rigors of life in a Vidalian world.

Their creator has chosen the appropriate interpreters for his cool and unsentimental story. They are dedicated sophisticates, devoid of any prejudice and of any religious or even political bias, brilliant, charming, and quite as decent to others as others are to them, with wit, delightful manners, and a fixed determination to do anything they choose to do as well as it can be done. Above all, they aim to see the world as it is, no matter what conclusion that vision may entail. Caroline has been married to and divorced from a Sanford cousin, but her dismal, right-wing, Red-baiting daughter and only child, whom she understandably dislikes, is the child of a former lover, U.S. Senator Burden Day, another detached interpreter of the political scene. Sex in Vidalian fiction rarely gets out of hand. It is entirely physical, entirely for pleasure, and is indulged in with both sexes. Oddly enough, it is just the opposite of what it is in Proust, whom Vidal deeply admires, where it is identified with pain.

Caroline's brother Blaise, who is married to an heiress, has a brief homosexual encounter in Paris with a *poilu* turned prostitute, an episode that might be deemed the trademark of a Vidal novel, like the fox hunt in Trollope or the appearance of Hitchcock as an extra in each of his films.

Caroline takes leave of the Sanford-owned newspaper to explore the new phenomenon of Hollywood in 1917, where she becomes not only the mistress of a director, Tim Farrell, but the leading lady of his films, under the name of Emma Traxler. That a middle-aged, world-famous newspaperwoman should become a movie star without anyone recognizing her surely lacks verisimilitude, but in the dreamlike reality that Vidal so successfully evokes we are only too happy to accept it. Blaise remains, for the most part, in Washington, which allows the reader to follow two of the three themes of the novel: the involvement of America in war and the rise of Hollywood to world power, each through the eyes of a Sanford. The third theme, the why and wherefore of the election of Warren Gamaliel Harding, we follow through the mind of one of his crooked henchmen, Jesse Smith.

The Sanfords, of course, know everybody. Caroline fills us in on Hearst, Marion Davies, Elinor Glyn, Douglas Fairbanks, Mary Pickford, the murdered William Desmond Taylor, and hosts of others, while Blaise introduces us to everyone of note in the capital from President Wilson down. It is an entrancing gallery of portraits, as funny as it is acute.

Wilson is the best, "an odd combination of college professor unused to being contradicted in a world that he took to be his classroom and of Presbyterian pastor unable to question that divine truth which inspired him at all times." Eleanor Roosevelt, then wife of the assistant secretary of the Navy, is "the Lucrezia Borgia of Washington—none survived her table." The malice of her cousin Alice Longworth, TR's daughter, has "the same sort of joyous generalized spontaneity as did her father's hypocrisy." As it was an article of faith that the American public could not fall in love with a screen star who was married in real life, Francis X. Bushman, the father of five, is "obliged to pretend to be a virtuous bachelor, living alone, waiting, wistfully, for Miss Right to leap from the darkened audience onto the bright screen to share with him the glamor of his life."

We see Wilson on board the SS *George Washington*, confiding to Blaise that he could have done well in vaudeville, and, to prove it, letting his face go slack and his body droop as he performs a kind of scarecrow dance across the deck singing: "I'm Dopey Dan, and I'm married to Midnight Mary." We see Charlie Chaplin and Douglas Fairbanks naked in a steam room discussing how they should have used some of their surplus earnings to buy the press and bury such Hollywood-damaging scandals as the Fatty Arbuckle affair. We see Mrs. Harding, hurling furniture at her husband's mistress, and Alice Longworth doing handsprings before her father's admirers.

Whether we believe it all or not, it is always in character, always more than possible. When a character suggests that a woman as plain as Eleanor Roosevelt would never have hired as her secretary as beautiful a woman as Lucy Mercer to be brought in constant contact with her handsome husband unless she had been attracted to her herself, one's first reaction may be one of shocked indignation, but then, when one pauses to consider it . . . It is always that way with Vidal.

There are moments when a gathering of his characters takes on some of the features of a fancy dress party. One tries to identify each newcomer before he is introduced. Sometimes the characters are not. I think I spotted Rudolph Valentino in the young extra in a Hearst private movie who had "a square crude face" and eyebrows that grew together in a straight line "like those of an archaic Minoan athlete."

Through conversations with the capital's power wielders Blaise and Senator Day follow the slow enmeshing of a peace-loving president in the imbroglio of European war. "I do believe the Germans must be the stupidest people on earth," Wilson groans as the submarine sinkings mount. But he is helpless against the U-boat and Allied propaganda, as he will be helpless against the Republican Senate majority to save his league. Vidal sees our involvement in the war of empires as a mistake and one that cost us essential liberties in the Red-baiting era that followed, but he does not see how the mistake could have been avoided. America in his view, ever since Lincoln forged his new union, has been ineluctably committed to the course of empire. Empires are not good things: they ruthlessly exploit weaker tribes, but at least in Europe, with its aristocratic traditions, the process is carried out to its inevitable dissolution with a certain style. America, on the other hand, being a mix of peasant emigrations, is easily victimized by any sort of propaganda and doomed to make an imperial fool of itself.

Caroline, the author's primary spokesman, like her mentor Henry Adams (one of Vidal's finest portraits) believes in nothing but "the prevailing fact of force in human affairs." In Washington, where the game of force is played for its own sake and where morality is always relative to need, "one man's Gethesmane might be another's Coney Island." In Hollywood she finds things even worse. Now the Administration has invited Caroline herself to bully the movie business into creating ever more simplistic rationales of what she has come, privately, despite her French bias, to think of as the pointless war. Nevertheless, she is astonished that someone has actually gone to prison for making a film. Where was the much-worshipped Constitution in all of this? Or was it never more than a document to be used by the country's rulers when it suited them and otherwise ignored?

She finds a new source of national power in the movies and begins to wonder if Hollywood might not even be able to persuade a defeated country that its army had been victorious, at least abroad.

> A moving picture was, to begin with, a picture of something that had really happened. She had really clubbed a French actor with a wooden crucifix on a certain day and at a certain time and now there existed, presumably forever, a record of that stirring event. But Caroline Sanford was not the person millions of people had watched in that ruined French church. They had watched the fictitious Emma Traxler impersonate Madeleine Giroux, a Franco-American mother, as she picked up a crucifix that looked to be metal but was not and struck a French actor impersonating a German officer in a ruined French church that was actually a state-set in Santa Monica. The audience knew, of course, that the story was made up as they knew that stage plays were imitations of life, but the fact that an entire story could so surround them as a moving picture did and so, literally, inhabit their dreams, both waking and sleeping, made for another reality parallel to the one they lived in. . . . Reality could now be entirely invented and history revised. Suddenly, she knew what God must have felt when he gazed upon chaos, with nothing but himself upon his mind.

She finds the war unpopular in California until the people succumb to every "anti-German, anti-Red, anti-negro demagogue," and she resolves, when peace comes, to use the new power of the film to offset some of the damage done. Whether she will enjoy success in her project is far from clear at the end of her tale.

The parts of the novel that deal with the handsome and amiable Warren Harding and the gang of crooks with whom he is too easygoing not to associate are highly amusing, but on a lower level. They are like the play put on by the mechanicals in A Midsummer Night's Dream, though considerably more ominous. Harding is shown as shrewd enough to see that if he is every delegation's second choice he will be nominated in a convention deadlocked over bigger men. I suppose the reason his story lacks the impact of the two other themes of the novel is that here Vidal has little to bring to our already settled conviction of its sordidness. He adds a murder or so for zest, but it is not essential. We know those men would have been capable of anything.

In *Hollywood*, as in many of Vidal's novels (*Lincoln* and *Julian* excepted), the parts are greater than the whole. But that is what he would say of the universe. In a senseless mosaic are not the beautiful details all the more precious? His highly polished prose style, in part the fruit of his classical training, is a constant delight. One might even go so far as to call him a modern La Rochefoucauld. I suppose it is a mistake to take sentences out of context to illustrate this, but I submit a few.

The Irish lover of a society girl "had entered her life like a sudden high wind at a Newport picnic, and everything was in a state of disorder."

Wilson, asked what was the worst thing about being president, replies: "All day long people tell you things that you already know, and you must act as if you were hearing their news for the first time."

And here is the end of the court of Henry Adams:

> In the twenty years that Caroline had known Adams, neither the beautiful room, with its small Adams-scale furniture nor its owner had much changed; only many of the occupants of the chairs were gone, either through death, like John and Clara Hay, joint builders of this double Romanesque palace in Lafayette Park, or through removal to Europe, like Lizzie Cameron, beloved by Adams, now in the high summer of her days, furiously courting young poets in the green spring of theirs.

20

America and the Vidal Chronicles

DONALD E. PEASE

An account of Vidal's fictional history of America should begin with the following remarkable information from his personal history. Gore Vidal is the most prolific and arguably the most talented writer of his generation. His writing career began at age twenty with the publication of *Williwaw* in 1946. Written out of Vidal's wartime experience as first mate on a ship stationed in Alaska, *Williwaw* was often cited, along with Norman Mailer's *The Naked and the Dead* (1948), as the best novel of a new generation of American writers.[1] Since 1946 Vidal has at this writing published twenty-three novels, five plays, six volumes of essays, and a volume of short stories. A brief inventory of the literary and dramatic forms Vidal has mastered—the novel, biography, political oration, satire, essay, play, interview, history, screenplay—indicates the range of his accomplishments. Yet despite his early success and lifelong achievement, Vidal's work has (since the publication of *The City and the Pillar* in 1948) remained virtually unrecognized within the academy.[2]

While his novels remain untaught in American Literature courses, Vidal has since 1967 been writing a comprehensive fictional history of the United States that includes an important revisionist understanding of the relationship between American history and its literature. In a passage that calls attention to the discrepancy between his project's ambition and his literary standing, Vidal renders the fact of his academic exile into a precondition for writing his "American Chronicles":

> The fact that there is still a public eager to find out who we are and what we did ought to encourage others to join me but by and large, the universities have made that impossible. They have established an hegemony over every aspect of literature—except the ability to make any. They have also come to believe that a senior novelist deals only with what he knows, and since our educational system is what it is, he is not apt to know much about anything; and since our class system is uncommonly rigid, he is not going to have much chance to find out about any world other than the one he was born into—and the school he went to. Certainly he will never, like his predecessors, be able to deal with his nation's rulers. They prefer shadows.[3]

In this passage, Vidal affiliates exclusion from the academic establishment with a freedom from its limitations, and claims for his project the capacity to gratify the public's demand for historical understanding ("who we are and what we did"), which academic history cannot do, and to educate the public in the difference between what it wants and the ruling academic narratives. In realizing his project's ambitions, Vidal does not internalize the distinction (between imaginative reconstructions of experiences and accurately recorded facts) that makes American literature and American history separate fields of inquiry; rather he reshapes the materials of the past into structures of discourse and arrangements of social practices more inclusive and instructive than either academic discipline. Because he does not honor this distinction, Vidal's chronicles include various literary figures (Washington Irving, Mark Twain, Henry James, and others with whom professors of American literature have denied him association) in a context he believes makes readers better able to judge the comparative importance of these writers. When rescued from official literary history and resituated within Vidal's narrative, these writers encounter actual historical figures— Aaron Burr, Abraham Lincoln, Theodore Roosevelt, for example— as well as characters out of Vidal's imagination and his family's genealogy.

At the time Vidal published the first of his chronicles, *Wash-*

ington, D.C., in 1967, the controversy surrounding the Vietnam War resulted in widespread recognition of the difference between actual historical events and the official versions the nation told itself about them, a situation that eventually would lead to a reevaluation of their true place within the national allegory. Throughout the sixties, revisionist accounts of American history challenged the received view of the relationship between historical fact and the literary imagination. Vidal's ongoing project was but one example of this reconsideration. Others included Norman Mailer's nonfiction account of the 1967 Washington peace march, *The Armies of the Night*, and the counterculture. While the counterculture was a relatively short-lived phenomenon on the streets, the questions it raised concerning the historicity of literature would later result in the formation of an academic discipline called the New Historicism (whose relationship to Vidal's American chronicles I will consider when I argue their importance to American literature). At present I want to draw a distinction between Mailer's work and Vidal's.

The projects Vidal and Mailer undertook in the 1960s were as different as their literary careers (whose trajectories partially explain Vidal's exclusion from the academy). Mailer published *The Naked and the Dead* two years after Vidal's *Williwaw*. Following the critics' favorable comparison of both novelists with Hemingway, Mailer and Vidal became representatives of their generation's collective need to recover from their experience of war.

In the two novels he published after *The Naked and the Dead* (*Barbary Shore*, 1951; *The Deer Park*, 1954), Mailer did not eradicate the combat soldier from his narrative consciousness but adapted his readiness for military action to the psychology of invented social types—the hipster, the sociopath, the "white negro"—who proposed new styles of postwar survival out of the residual energies of the battlefield. Mailer's novels presupposed the continued existence of a combat soldier within, for whom World War II was an imaginary alternative to everyday life during the Cold War. Experiencing demands urged on by perceptions, thoughts, and instincts that seemed to emerge out of a pervasive but invisible battlefield, Mailer's "existential heroes" were designed to meet the "enemy within" on familiar ground. Unlike Vidal's early novels, Mailer's novels did not replace the battlefield with a generalized system of symbolic exchange whereby its shocks became reflective experiences and its aleatory intensities narrative sequences. Every event Mailer's characters engaged in instead threatened to turn back into incidents of war. "Literary form in general," as Mailer explained his literary code, "is the record of war. It is the record, as seen in a moment of rest; yet it is the record of a war which has been taking place. Don't you see whatever is alive, or intent, or obsessed, must wage an actual war: it creates the possibility for form in its environment, by its every attempt to shape the environment. Whenever the environment resists, the result is form."[4]

In this and related accounts of his writing, Mailer proposes to continue the war in the substitute formations his novels provided. As the record of an ongoing war, Mailer's literary form does not recall what took place in battle but reinvests life-threatening sensations and impulses (which when experienced in battle were utterly beyond his representational capacity) in an activity reassuringly separable from actual combat. When he describes this as the record of a war, Mailer claims for his writing the power to separate the fragmented self from the shattering intensities of battle and resituate it within a medium where it can recover its psychic integrity.

On the battlefield the self was required for purposes of survival to respond with the entire sensibility pitched to a level of complete psychological alertness. Mailer superimposed this battlefield self onto the postwar environment to accrue related capacities of response for his characters. Because Mailer generalized this imaginary battlefield onto the collective arena of their actions, each of the social types Mailer invented after the war elevated the incomplete socialization of the veteran's war mentality into an enabling social power. Instead of surrendering their battlefield instincts, Mailer's hipsters spontaneously reactivated them in their war of survival within a threatening environment. Unable to release their instincts in violent actions, Mailer's hipsters came into deeper possession of their combat energies through symbolic actions—new kicks, highs, riffs, ecstasies—they could voluntarily recall.

Situated in a world where the corporate ladder had displaced the military chain of command, Mailer's characters did not participate in that world except through psychic states they had created to replace it. Literary form, Mailer explained, was the result of his successful substitution of psychic states for historical reality. His account of literary form as a symbolic record of war matched an analogous substitution taking place in the world of realpolitik, where the Cold War supplanted an actual war with a symbolic opposition between global superpowers. While the scope for the actions taking place in the Cold War exceeded any single individual's capabilities, Mailer's existential heroes nevertheless seemed empowered as agents within that invisible war: they displaced actual events with hypertrophied powers of response and established imaginary relations with imagined persons within this make-believe war. Because their relations to the Cold War were imaginary rather than actual, Mailer's hipsters enabled a related discrimination of their heightened states of psychic awareness from others' political actions. And this discrimination, insofar as it incorporated a fundamental tenet of literary criticism, eventually resulted in the acknowledgment of Mailer's work as serious Literature.

Constructed on the site of the generalized rejection of the political, Literature, in the early years of the Cold War, was also institutionalized as a permanent state of cultural warfare. While the specific assignment of the political was communist ideology, the term was generalized to include any form of politics. To facilitate rejection of political entanglements, instruction in Literature was believed to develop a mental faculty immune to all things political. Lionel Trilling described this faculty, after Keats, as a negative capability. When acted upon, this faculty denied the wish to realize literary impulses in the public world and redirected those impulses to the alternate cultural domain that had been constructed out of this powerful denial. On this imaginary site, literary subjects underwent a complex gratification of negative literary appetites—for density, nuance, variousness of register—whose preference for deferred gratification rendered them immune to ideological capture. Having previously described all ideological beliefs as submissive to alien powers, these critics then idealized Literature as a release from political captivity. When the characters in Mailer's novels experienced their negation of political action as a recovery of primitive energies, they supplemented Literature's release from captivity with a masculinist mythology. When construed from within the imaginary America of Mailer's novels, the struggle for the integrity of the literary subject became indistinguishable from defending the integrity of the nation-state.

Literary critics substituted a negative literary utopia for realpolitik, but Mailer represented the act of literary substitution as if it were itself a combat zone where the massive self-denial required to achieve the literary substitute formation was displaced into collective opposition to a composite figure—the homosexual totalitarian. The rationale for Mailer's choice of a composite villain derives from his understanding of the psychology of literary politics. Because literature was defined in psychological terms as a substitute gratification for political action, it included the denial of threatening sexual as well as political drives. Whereas ideological understandings of Literature were generally construed as politically threatening, the nature of that threat underwent psychosexual substitution in Mailer's novels into a perceived related danger: the feminization of the male. Because ideological allegiances were identified as forms of submission to an alien psychological power, becoming communist or becoming homosexual were, Mailer believed, interchangeable effects of the enemy within. As Mailer's characters overcame both threats, they enabled his readers to reexperience their separation from the political realm as the successful mastery of their homosexual drives. Along with the hipsters in his novels, Mailer developed a public persona who described the power to distinguish literary from political activities as a recovery of his masculinity. Able to transmute the sphere of significant action from political events to his heroic literary experience of them, Mailer engaged the separation of realms as an occasion for the construction of a masculinist public persona for the man of letters.

In his second novel, In a Yellow Wood (1947), Vidal also sanctioned the social importance of the separation of realms by representing it as the crucial decision in the life of his fictional war veteran, Robert Holton. But the realms Vidal separated were as different from Mailer's as their literary rationales. In Vidal's novel, the fact that Holton chooses work in a brokerage firm over the soldier-adventurer's life he shared with his army buddy during the Italian campaign is not as important to this decision as Vidal's representation of a homosexual underworld as the alternative path. When Holton finds the routines of corporate America preferable to the comparatively sordid adventures in a homosexual underground, Vidal associates literary culture with the values represented by corporate America. We have already observed the political importance of these alternatives. Following World War II, the socialization process entailed the replacement of corporate for military values with an attendant projection of the psychological subordination the process involved onto a homosexual scapegoat. American literature sanctioned this socialization process when it associated its power to organize experience into a literary order with the larger demands of reintegrating the nation-state. In several sociological accounts (including Mailer's "The Homosexual as Villain"), the homosexual underworld emerged as a symptomatic effect of the separation of literary culture from national politics. Because characteristics typically assigned to homosexuals (irresoluteness, preference for reflection over action, effeminacy, and so on) were transferred in these accounts to a literary culture reconceptualized as an underground social movement, literary culture had to distinguish its activities from homosexuals'. Whereas Mailer's hipsters readily overcame homosexuality as a psychic inhibition, Vidal's Robert Holton found this subculture disturbing enough psychologically to confuse it with the war he needed to forget.

Whatever their differences in characterization, Vidal's and Mailer's second novels ratified the same composite villain. But in his third novel, *The City and the Pillar* (1948), Vidal revised his account of the war veteran's readjustment in a manner also best explained in its difference from Mailer's. In his two postwar novels, Mailer conceptualized World War II as the social unconscious of the Cold War, and demanded from his characters the manly attributes of the soldier at war. Vidal's understanding of the relationship between military and civilian life addressed a more complex psychology. Becoming a soldier in Vidal's novels involved an internal division separating a partial self who underwent submission to military authority from a whole self. Following the completion of military training the submissive self was subordinated to an internalized commanding officer who identified all forms of submission with feminization. Soldiers overcame this internal division on the battlefield where the negative image of their submissive selves was redirected onto the enemy, and the positive image projected onto the comrade. Whereas the enemy became the locus of their collective rage, the comrade represented what was memorable in the military ordeal they shared. Rather than taking on the explicit content of that shared ordeal (helplessness, fear, submission, trauma, rage), the comrade idealized the partial (feminized) self that the enemy demonized. Because the battlefield drew upon instinctual urges otherwise indistinguishable from those discharged in sexual excitement, aggressive and erotic drives coexisted within the soldiers' psyche. The complex identification of the enemy with their enforced feminization divided the objects of combat soldiers' erotic drives into women and buddies. When women were the actual objects of the combat soldiers' drives, they were also representative of their complex internal division. Like the enemy, the women who existed within the combat soldiers' psyche literalized the feminization that the comrade idealized.

When they returned home from war, Vidal's veterans underwent readjustments answerable to this complex psychology. In *In a Yellow Wood*, Robert Holton simply represses his memory of the war, but in *The City and the Pillar*, Jim Willard finds military comradeship to be an unsatisfying substitute for the homosexual relationship he had experienced as an adolescent. During his military training Willard elevates that earlier relationship into a homoerotic ideal that he tries unsuccessfully to rediscover in his military friendships. An athletic, purposeful idealist Willard has nothing in common with the homosexual stereotype in the popular imagination, and his homoerotic passion is indistinguishable from that of a heterosexual male who measures his erotic reactions to others against an idealized first love.

Whereas Mailer represented World War II as the social unconscious of the Cold War, Vidal represented homosexuality as the social unconscious of military training. Consequently when Jim Willard, after his return home from war, is unable to continue the homosexual relationship with his high school friend, he cannot distinguish erotic from aggressive drives, and, as if acting against his own drives, in the original version of the novel he kills the friend (Vidal later revised this ending; see above, chapter 3).

The literary reaction to Vidal's third novel ranged from expressions of outrage to personal betrayal. Instead of substituting literature for the gratification of political instincts, Vidal had turned the homosexual activities that literary critics associated with political scandal into a legitimate literary subject and the homosexual into a possibly heroic ideal. Having formerly designated Vidal as an exemplary figure in the substitution of complex literary experiences for partisan politics effected after World War II, many literary critics now believed him guilty of nothing less than a crime against American culture. In the early years of cold war liberalism, critics had indignantly resisted accounts of Literature as a feminized or otherwise subordinated cultural activity and considered the publication of works susceptible to such characterizations as occasions ritually to exclude their authors from cultural membership. They took Vidal's publication of *The City and the Pillar* as just such an occasion.

Vidal's banishment is important for understanding the cultural persona he subsequently developed to reappropriate that event. During his ten-year exile from literature, Vidal worked primarily in television, writing original scripts and dramatic adaptations of stories for such programs as *Philco Playhouse, Omnibus, Studio One,* and *Suspense.* His success with television drama encouraged him to try his hand at full-length plays. In 1960, *The Best Man*, his second full-length drama, played for 520 performances on Broadway. The play follows the rise to power and subsequent fall of Joe Cantwell, an utterly self-serving political opportunist. A central event in the play involves Cantwell's being falsely charged with homosexual activity.

The inclusion of the charge that had been directed against his own work as an element in his political play completed Vidal's separation of his imaginative project from the rules governing the literary realm. In *The Best Man* Vidal did not condemn homosexuality but exposed the accusation as a political enforcement of psychosocial norms that had supplanted political debate with a politics of scandal. In returning to the topic of homosexuality as a weapon in the cultural politics of scandal, Vidal, as a previous victim of such politics, refused to submit to those norms.

In his move from literature to television, Vidal, like dozens of formerly blacklisted Hollywood actors, was rehabilitated from political disgrace by the television audience. The scripts Vidal wrote helped make the television audience into an alternative cultural realm with a different understanding of the relationship between cultural and political matters. The ideological concept of the privacy of a television audience was, as Lynn Spiegel has observed, more than simply an experiential retreat from the public sphere. That experience of privacy detached viewers from political factions but also gave people the paradoxical sense of belonging to a larger community with shared values. By purchasing homes in newly formed suburbs, young American couples of the 1950s developed a sense of themselves as a new political community at once bound together yet separated by the television programs they watched:

> There was an odd sense of connection and disconnection in this new suburbia, an infinite series of separate but identical homes, strung together like Christmas tree lights on a tract with one central switch. And that central switch was the growing communications complex through which people could keep their distance from the world but at the same time imagine that their domestic spheres were connected by a wider social fabric.[5]

When enacted live before the television public, the McCarthy hearings and the Senate investigations into organized crime lost the power to arouse partisan passions and became occasions for the construction of new cultural stereotypes. As they took place in daytime television alongside situation comedies, game shows, and old movies, these political events were redefined by a viewing public that had learned how to remove charged political situations from the public world and into their "extended television family," where they became events in a prolonged soap opera. Television enabled a public whose collective privacy had been violated by the National Security State to reclaim a private domain. The television set provided this extended family with a "monitor" on the actions of the state. Whereas the National Security State demanded, in a time of permanent war, the promotion of national values over private interests, television turned events construed as violations of the national interest (like Joe Cantwell's sex scandal) into opportunities to recognize the difference between private and public affairs. Unlike the National Security State, the television public preferred their private response to political scandals over explanations of them. When political scandals were subscribed to television monitoring, the public confirmed the superiority of their private values to the secret affairs of state. Political scandals entail conflicts between national and private interests. When they are adjudicated differently by the state apparatus and the television public, they clarify the differences between realms. The National Security State deployed the Cold War as a gigantic screen onto which it projected a spectacular public cover for covert operations, but the television public reduced the dimensions of the spectacle and uncovered the covert operations as a threat to their privacy. Once ethnic, class, and racial tensions were transferred into TV episodes, in such shows as *Molly Goldberg, The Life of Riley,* or *Amos 'n Andy,* they began to lose their threatening aspects and became occasions for the television family to prefer its conciliatory power over the state's covert operations. Like the charge of sexual impropriety leveled against Joe Cantwell in *The Best Man,* these intense public events underwent disarticulation into the separative connections binding together the television audience.

When Vidal ran unsuccessfully for Congress as representative of the twenty-ninth district of New York, he represented the political constituency educated in television values. Following his congressional campaign, Vidal imaginatively transformed his public persona into that of a ruler in political exile who understood how to construct ruling cultural narratives and how to change its rules. In refining this persona he ran a political talk show on television where he debated candidates for the presidency, delivered alternative accounts of the state of the union, and shuttled between homes in Europe and the United States.

In 1964 he returned from voluntary literary exile with the publication of his most popular novel since *The City and the Pillar.*[6] *Julian* is an historical fiction about a Roman emperor who considers Christian beliefs and the institutions confirmative of them—the Church, family, marriage—inferior to other ideologies available as agencies of imperial rule. While Julian finds Christianity a compelling narrative of self-sacrifice, he believes it to be an inadequate account of the intelligible world and (at a time when homosexuality and heterosexuality coexisted as more or less equivalent expressions of sexual appetite) unnatural in its denial of sexual gratification.

Having characterized the cultural agency regulative of sexuality as imperial rather than democratic, four years later Vidal designated the sex role resulting from those regulations—*Myra Breckinridge.*[7]

A transsexual who compulsively changes her gender identity to match her sexual activity—becoming a woman when attracted to men, a man when attracted to women—Myra Breckinridge quite literally cannot decide which sex she prefers. Myra's compulsion to become the normative sex role for the sexuality she practices results from her having internalized the sexual norms enforcing heterosexuality, and her apparently perverse sexual activities and gender-switching actually entail her scrupulous allegiance to those norms.

With his revisionist accounts of homosexuality in *Julian* and *Myra Breckinridge*, Vidal changed the nature of the event that had led to his banishment from Literature in the 1950s. Writing, moreover, from the antiwar culture of the 1960s, Vidal returned to that postwar period from two separate historical perspectives, the imperialist past of ancient Rome and the anti-imperialist present. Having subjected the psychosocial norms that had policed *The City and the Pillar* to critical scrutiny, Vidal returned to the postwar milieu in *Washington, D.C.* (1967), but this time as a cultural persona in imaginative possession of the social order to which he had previously been subjected. That public persona was a composite figure comprised of four different aspects and experiences: an imperial aspect developed out of Julian's recognition of the arbitrariness of ruling assumptions; a satirical aspect developed out of the exposure of Myra Breckinridge's compulsion to identify her subjectivity with her sexual activities; a political understanding developed out of the congressional campaign; and a historical consciousness developed out of the relations Vidal discerned between past events and the political controversies in which they are recalled. Altogether these aspects resulted in a flexible public figure who was able to understand past events as well as the larger sociopolitical contexts informing them.

In *Julian* Vidal conceptualized the difference between the Judeo-Christian values most Americans took for granted, and an emperor who chose not to believe in their social efficacy as ruling assumptions. By 1967, having internalized Julian's attitude toward ruling assumptions, Vidal was able to dramatize (in *Washington, D.C.*) the difference between the ordinary citizens positioned within the dominant social narratives and imperial subjects—like Roosevelt, Blaise Sanford, and Clay Overbury—who were able to construct such narratives. Following his dissociation of these ruling subjects from their constructed narratives, Vidal recorded the second-order social arguments among them over which narrative would predominate. These arguments produced a distinction between matters of fact and the narrative structure productive of those matters of fact that, in the 1960s, became a political resource in the struggle for social change.

An adequate understanding of the political consciousness Vidal had developed out of the antiwar controversy requires an explanation of Vidal's complex affiliation with the 1960s counterculture. Like Vidal, the student activists correlated U.S. imperialism with coercive psychosexual norms and believed the American literature of the postwar era to be an ideological apparatus of the National Security State. In a New Historicist account of her previous participation in the 1960s counterculture, Catherine Gallagher explained it as a reaction against the cultural politics developed in the late 1940s, "a politics that had already begun to transfer its hopes from the traditional agent of revolutionary change, the proletariat, to a variety of subversive cultural practices, the most prominent of which was aesthetic modernism. The transferral had started in the earlier belief that modernism was a support for revolutionary social change of an anti-Stalinist kind." We have already observed that the agent of those "subversive" cultural practices was empowered out of the substitution of "difficult" modern Literature for partisan politics and that both Vidal and the students experienced this substitution as an enforcement of dominant psychosexual norms. Vidal exposed these psychosexual norms as instruments of psychosexual imperialism, the internalization of which resulted in Myra Breckinridge, and the counterculture organized "love-ins" and "human be-ins" as cultural sites opposed to such internalization. On such sites, cultural activities (Gallagher continued her account of the counterculture) surrendered "their claim to separate status, [as] lived and symbolic experiences were consciously merged in guerilla theaters, in happenings, in attempts to live a radical culture."[8]

Instead of claiming for the literary self an immunity to political fragmentation, the selves student activists constructed out of their liberationist politics desublimated the energies previously contained within a separate cultural sphere. The students' demands for political arrangements organized around the fulfillment of libidinal drives resulted in part from the transference onto the political sphere of impulses and drives previously experienced in reading the Americanist canon. When they formulated demands within the political realm that Whitman and Melville, for example, had previously expressed from within the realm of American Literature, they broke down the barrier separating the American Literature they had internalized from the external norms of American realpolitik.

Because the desires student activists had internalized in reading American Literature were predicated on a collective denial of difference—of the ideal world American writers wanted in place of the one they had inherited—their politics was itself susceptible to the charge of imperialism. In *The Imperial Self*, a book published four years after Vidal's *Washington, D.C.*, Quentin Anderson conscripted the name that had united various oppositional political groups against U.S. foreign policy to describe the representative self produced within American Literature and proposed his rationale for this characterization in the following passage:

> I believe that the habit scholars have of calling Emerson misty or abstract, calling Whitman a successful charlatan, calling Henry James ambiguous, are but ways of referring to an inchoate perception of the absolutism of the self which is described in this essay. This absolutism involves an extreme passivity, which is complemented by, must be complemented by, the claim of the imperial self to mastery of what has almost overwhelmed it.[9]

In this passage Anderson reestablished the barrier between the realm of American Literature and political matters in the distinction he adduced between the imperial self and America's imperialist foreign policy. The cultural imperial ego is produced out of the urgent need to overcome an extreme passivity designed to "suffer" the unmastered materials of a world external to the creative imagination, following which the material so suffered ceases to remain external and turns instead into the fluent, circumambient energies of the creative self. Redefined as an unrealizable inner drive to master external matters, the imperial self ruled the difference between its inner America and the rest of the world. The imperial self *within* at once depended upon the opposition to U.S. imperialism for its definition, yet negated such a policy as antithetical to its authentic interests. Defined as self-ruled rather than interested in ruling others, Anderson's *Imperial Self* thesis condemned the need to realize that imagination in the political world as plain old U.S. imperialism.

After having analyzed the cultural preconditions for the construction of the Imperial Self, Anderson further identifies its literary activities as homosexual. "But the heterosexual force escapes [Henry] James," Anderson says, explaining his representative example of the Imperial Self. "Money, the unformed or excreted thing, the other end of the stick of consciousness has tremendous emotional weight for James. The notion of the penis in the vagina has none."[10] Presumably, Anderson's negative characterization of James' homosexuality accrues surplus cultural value for the "negative capability" of the liberal imagination to discriminate its values from a homosexual's imagination.

In *The Armies of the Night*, a nonfictional narrative about the student counterculture published in 1968, Norman Mailer corroborated Anderson's description of the difference between literary values and homosexuality. Instead of himself confusing literature with politics, Mailer substituted an account of his complex experience of the students countercultural activities that was acclaimed by most critics as his best work. The following reaction to writer Paul Goodman the day before they were to march together to protest the war is representative of the literary result:

> Goodman's ideas tended to declare in rough that heterosexuality, homosexuality, and onanism were equally valid forms of activity, best denuded of guilt. . . . [But] onanism and homosexuality were not to Mailer, light vices—to him it seemed that much of life and most of society were designed precisely to drive men deep into onanism and homosexuality; one defied such a fate by sweeping up the psychic profit which derived from the existential assertion of yourself—which was a way of saying that nobody was born a man; you earned manhood provided you were good enough, bold enough.[11]

As the concluding sentence in this passage (and the title of the book in which it appears) predicts, "Mailer" preserved the war-veteran-turned-hipster as the literary persona appropriate to encounter the counterculture. In the breathtaking trajectory of displacements the passage activates, Goodman's ideas about onanism and homosexuality give way first to Mailer's experience of them as primordial sexual drives, then onto the (profound) psychological resistance aroused within him along with those drives, penultimately to the "psychic profit" his mastery of those drives deposits and which Mailer finally cashes into the "existential assertion" of his "earned manhood." How his manhood can exist as at once a "psychic profit" he can expend yet be a living he must earn never becomes an explicit topic in a passage which instead tacitly borrows from the World War II mentality the ability to find homosexuality representative of the same alien imperialist power Mailer had previously struggled against.

Instead of justifying Mailer's imaginary usage, Vidal, in *Washington, D.C.*, explains the mythological role the composite figure of the communist-homosexual plays within the mentality constructed out of cold war anxieties. Peter Sanford provides that explanation in the following parody of the mentality:

> The communists offer a Utopian vision which is particularly attractive to two types: the ignorant and the degenerate. In fact since for statistical reasons all ignorant dupes and sexual degenerates are *ipso facto* Communists we may then assume that *any* sexual degenerate is by definition not only an ignorant dupe but a Communist or at the very least a fellow traveller.[12]

In this passage Vidal identifies the "psychic profit" Mailer accumulated in his encounter with Goodman's utopian sexual politics with the pervasive psychological mechanism developed in the early years of the Cold War. That psychological mechanism successfully confused a repressive political ideology with a repressed homosexual drive, and identified both with imperialism. Had he not substituted his literary experience of them for Goodman's sexual politics, Mailer implies, communism would have emerged in his psyche as an expression of his latent homosexuality. When Mailer earned his manhood instead of discovering his homosexuality, he described the result as a "psychic profit" rather than an effort because the psychological mechanism Vidal described was always already in place to earn his manhood for him. As Vidal offered an alternative explanation for this psychosocial mechanism, he also replaced Mailer's social imaginary with an historical understanding of the political norms enforcing heterosexuality.[13]

Throughout *Washington, D.C.*, Vidal supplemented the oppositional politics of the counterculture with an historical consciousness it otherwise lacked. Then, to secure a distinction from Mailer's cultural politics, he identified him with Aeneas Duncan, a character in the novel, whose "ten years of Freudian analysis" has prepared him only for symbolic enactments and whose writings are complicitous with the purposes of the National Security State. Throughout *Washington, D.C.*, real as opposed to symbolic enactments involve Vidal's characters in a confrontation with the complex mythological event which after World War II had taken the place of American history. "For the majority," Vidal observed, "history began with the New Deal, and any contemplation of the old Republic was downright antipathetic for those who wanted reform in the present and perfection in the future."[14] The complex mythological event enabling this amnesia cross-identified Columbus's discovery of the New World with America's successful war of Independence against the British Empire and then conscripted the composite to cold war politics. The mythological referents embedded within this complex event included "Nature's Nation," the "Virgin Land," the "Endless Frontier," and the "American Adam" and entailed the "liberation" of our "native land" from "foreign imperialism" as a permanent cultural enactment.

As long as World War II was understood as a collective effort to oppose foreign imperialism, it, as well as every subsequent war, became indistinguishable from that mythological event. From the epoch of its founding to the Vietnam era, the political doctrine of American Exceptionalism had supported the belief that events which officially took place in American History were structured out of the New World's opposition to the Old World's imperialist heritage. Any other account required an alternative to the doctrine of Exceptionalism. Instead of supplanting American Exceptionalism, the counterculture mistakenly established the ethical principles for its opposition to the Vietnam War on that doctrine. Because the doctrine of American Exceptionalism had predescribed all political opposition as the enemy of the United States, however, the students' opposition was itself subject to that description. Applying this doctrinal logic to events in the war resulted in the claim that it was not U.S. infantrymen who killed South Vietnamese villagers but Hanoi's resistance to the United States' anti-imperialist efforts. The doctrine of U.S. Exceptionalism and the political logic confirmative of its presupposition saturated the arena of political debate. Consequently, when revisionist historians like William Appleman Williams criticized the logic supporting these claims, their criticisms were removed from the public sphere and relegated to the cultural realm where the agency of imperialism was redesignated as mythological rather than actual. Unable to replace the doctrine of Exceptionalism with an alternative explanation of historical events, the counterculture passed out of American history along with the "imperialist war" it opposed.

Unlike the 1960s political activists, Gore Vidal had come of political age in the very era that had resulted in the "National Security State," whose relationship to the doctrine of American Exceptionalism Michael Paul Rogin described in the following passage:

> The 1950's vocabulary of American exceptionalism was thus a way of avoiding America. To take the vocabulary seriously exposes the European face of the decade, in immigrant consciousness, totalitarian traumas and cold war politics. But race was not the only subject elided by paranoid-style interpretation. In emphasizing mobility, interest conflict, immigrant rivalries, and status anxiety, 1950's social science avoided the major divisions that America shared with Europe— divisions of class, gender and institutional power. . . . It expatiates an alleged Populist anti-Semitism while burying the Red scares that swept throughout the country between 1877 and World War I; it discusses McCarthyism but not the development of a counter-subversive state apparatus; and it has nothing at all to say about women and Indians.[15]

If the historiography developed in the 1950s was structured out of these avoidances, the liberationist movements of the 1960s directly confronted questions of race, class, and gender. Acting out the psychic and political energies that cold war liberals had internalized as a permanent dialectical opposition (between U.S. freedom and Soviet totalitarianism), these new social persons liberated the psyche constructed in an era of political repression. They identified the social persons emerging within the counterculture as representatives of the peoples emerging from out of the capacious grasp of Cold War Imperialism. But without alternative histories within which to situate themselves, these different persons were "recontained" by one or another of the analytic frameworks inherited from the 1950s.

In *Washington, D.C.*, Vidal replaced the doctrine of American Exceptionalism with a representation of the United States as a settler society within the European capitalist World System. In refusing a distinction between New and Old World Imperialism, Vidal restored to American history representations of the class conflicts and the powerful state apparatus the consensus historians of the 1950s had denied existence. Vidal explained the doctrine of American Exceptionalism as a cover for an "American Imperium," a ruling class comprised of dynastic families, newspaper publishers, movie moguls, multinational corporations, and International Banks. From the eighteenth- through the twentieth-century American expansionism, Vidal argued, was a policy of imperialism more or less continuous with Great Britain's:

> After the French Revolution, the world money power shifted from Paris to London. For three generations, the British maintained an old-fashioned colonial empire, as well as a modern empire based on London's primacy in the money markets. Then, in 1914, New York replaced London as the world's financial capital. . . . All in all, the English were well pleased to have us take their place. They were too few in number for so big a task. As early as the turn of the century, they were eager for us not only to help them out financially, but to continue in their behalf the destiny of the Anglo-Saxon race: to bear with courage the white man's burden, as Rudyard Kipling not so tactfully put it. Were we not—English and Americans—all Anglo-Saxons, united by common blood, laws, language? Well no, we were not! But our differences were not so apparent then. In any case, we took on the job. We would supervise and civilize the lesser breeds. We would make money.[16]

Vidal tracks the progress of the colonial Empire from Britain to America in this passage with a matter-of-factness contemptuous of the outrage that it has provoked when applied to American history. In writing this account so matter of factly, he calls important attention to the difference between it and those that deny its central assumptions. When negotiated into the hard currency of official

U.S. history, the difference between these accounts determines what can count as a matter of historical fact.

When Vidal began the project that would become his American chronicle, he brought the narrative of an emerging American Empire into conflict with a counternarrative of an American Republic by following the rise to political power of an ambitious young politician who exploits both narratives. Clay Overbury begins his career as the protégé of James Burden Day, a United States senator who actually believes in the ideas of the early Republic. But Overbury later finds the newspaper empire of Blaise Sanford an environment more conducive to his ambitions.

After Overbury marries Sanford's daughter, he analyzes political actions in terms of their potential effect in the media. Actual historic events—Pearl Harbor, World War II, the death of Roosevelt, Hiroshima, McCarthyism, the Korean War—were emphasized and viewed differently in Senator Day's speeches and in Blaise Sanford's *Washington Tribune*. Senator Day subjects each event to the scrutiny of contending political principles: America's responsibility to the citizens of the Republic measured against his understanding of America's obligation to the international community. But when these same historical events are reported in the *Washington Tribune*, they become pseudoevents in a generalizable social narrative whose frame presupposes that complex mythological event which had taken the place of American history. Overbury constructs his public persona out of the mythological referents embedded within that national pseudoevent by becoming a war hero and then a political celebrity. In the following passage, Overbury reflects on the difference between his America and Senator Day's in terms that reduce this complex mythological event into its appropriate referents:

> Since the war began, Clay had come to admire the ravaged old President who continued to pursue, even as he was dying, the high business of reassembling the fragments of broken empires into a new pattern, with himself at center, proud creator of the new imperium. Now, though he was gone, the work remained. The United States was master of the earth. No England, no France, no Germany, no Japan (once the dying was done) left to dispute the Republic's will; only the mysterious Soviet would survive to act as other balance to the scale of power. Clay thought he understood the shape of this new

world. In any case, he did not regret the passing of the old America, unlike Burden, who truly believed his own rhetoric and was moved by his own sentimentality. Burden wanted to bring all of those without the law that sense of common dignity which was, he believed, America's peculiar gift to the world. But to Clay there was no dignity of any kind in the race of man. Nor was the United States anything more than just another power whose turn at empire had come, and in that empire he meant to wield power entirely for its own sake.[17]

Following the war the historical memory of most Americans was abbreviated to the span of attention required to misrecognize our imperialism as that of the mysterious Soviets. Whereas most Americans readily surrendered the facts to this interpretation, Overbury makes it his political business to enunciate this viewpoint while Senator Day dedicates himself to a contrary account. In the political struggle that ensues, Overbury threatens Senator Day with public exposure of the one occasion in which he compromised his principles and took a bribe. The bribe, which resulted in Indian land becoming available for public sale, also indirectly implicates Senator Day in the actual imperialist history—the United States' appropriation of Indian lands—he has opposed. Rather than face public exposure, Senator Day commits suicide.

Washington, D.C. constitutes something of a countermemory for Vidal's own lived experience of that period. Unlike his previous novels (*Williwaw, In a Yellow Wood, The City and the Pillar*), *Washington, D.C.* subsumes events described there to the larger goal of adjudicating between ruling national narratives. Returning to the past as an agent rather than an object of these ruling imperatives in *Washington, D.C.* enabled Vidal to discriminate the politically significant ways in which events happen differently according to different ruling narratives. In the novel, Vidal turned these differences into a stunning political resource in regard to the controversy over Vietnam. Political events from *Washington, D.C.* weirdly recall 1960s events: the death of Roosevelt in office prefigures Kennedy's; Truman's election seems reminiscent of Johnson's; the Korean War anticipates the war in Vietnam. By reexperiencing events of the 1960s in terms of a counterimperialist historical memory from the postwar era, Vidal fostered the recognition of the difference between historical narratives we can collectively choose against a political mythology whose enactments we are otherwise compelled to repeat.

In the historical narratives that followed *Washington, D.C.*, Vidal exploited similar linkages of past epochs with contemporary political controversies, to promote an awareness of the contrastive usages to which differing ruling narratives could put historical events. *Burr* (1973) and *1876* (1976) depended on debates over executive privilege, balance of powers, Nixon's Imperial Presidency, and the Watergate break-in for a contemporary consciousness responsive to the actions recorded in these novels. *Empire* (1987) and *Hollywood* (1990) addressed the troubling questions raised by a president who simply could not discriminate between his real-life policies in Nicaragua, Libya, or Iran and the fantasy world of the movies. *Lincoln* (1984) drew upon the public fear and political maneuvering that resulted from John Hinckley's attempted assassination of Ronald Reagan for its sustained meditation on the political mythology surrounding Lincoln's death.

As readers who engaged these contemporary political questions found them embedded within the events in Vidal's narratives, a more inclusive controversy was activated. Returning to the context of present political debates from contradictory historical narratives made those controversial questions historically consequential rather than merely topical. Or rather they became historically consequential after Vidal's reader recognized the difference between inherited political arrangements and the grand narrative structures supportive of them as an opportunity to revise those structures.

Throughout his chronicles Vidal included characters who, like the reader, experience themselves at a related intersection among competing narratives—not only Clay Overbury and Senator Day, but also Peter Sanford, the son of Blaise Sanford, who cannot recognize himself in any of his father's ideas for his future. When Peter Sanford reads the memoirs of his forefather Charles Schermerhorn Schuyler, he experiences the America inherited from him as if it were a power to alienate himself from what he has found most constrictive in present circumstances.

Burr's trajectory through Schuyler's memoirs dialectically reverses Clay Overbury's rise to political power. Unlike Overbury,

who exploits its media appeal, Burr repeatedly violates the mythological event that guaranteed the doctrine of American Exceptionalism. That mythological event conflated the nation's founding
with Columbus' discovery of the New World and required early
Americans to misrecognize the historical agency of their own imperialist wars—in Mexico, California, and the western territories—as
a result of some "foreign" power. Unlike George Washington and
the other founding fathers, who readily transcribed their own imperial ambitions onto this mythological coda, Aaron Burr freely expresses his wish to found an Empire in America and to expropriate
Native Americans' land in the name of the American Empire. A
historic representative of the imperialist agency Americans compulsively identify as the enemy, Burr enacts historical deeds—he
murders a founding father (Alexander Hamilton) and argues for the
constitutionality of secession—not conducive to mythological appropriation.

As a contemporary of the nation's founders who refused their
Americanist ideology, Burr occupies the intersection between the
founding father's real motives and the official historical explanations
of them. As an alternative consciousness of that period in American
history, Burr offers counter-explanations of their motives and events
that comprise an alternate American narrative coexisting within the
dominant narrative but internally distanced from its procedures.
Instead of finding them to be representative of American civic virtue
and American democracy, for example, Burr explains Washington's
belief in a strong central government as an effort to protect his vast
landholdings in Mount Vernon, and Thomas Jefferson's espousal of
states rights simply as a political strategy to win votes. Overall, Burr
estimates American democracy in the era of the nation's founding to
be a matter of "honest yeoman enjoying the fruits of black labor."

As a political figure who openly acknowledges his imperialist
ambitions, Burr represents a national history hidden by political
mythology. Without Burr to serve as ritual scapegoat for the contra-
dictions between their putative motives and actual deeds, the founders would have been subjected to a more severe critical scrutiny
rather than historical worship. Vidal rehabilitated Burr's character
during the intense scrutiny of the Nixon presidency. Burr's biogra-

phy legitimized the political critique of Nixon's imperialism but also recalled Vidal's banishment. Both Burr and Vidal were exiled for refusing to substitute mythology for political realities. As a result of their refusals, the dominant mythology labeled Vidal a homosexual and Burr a traitor. Like Julian, Burr did not believe in the civil religion that banished him. Burr's aspiration to found an American empire afforded Vidal a historical figure who could authenticate his imperialist counternarrative. Because Burr freely acknowledged political motives that other Americans relegated to a psychosocial censor, he also enabled Vidal to invent an entirely different psychological account of political motives. As a political motive that exerted homologous psychological resistance, imperialism became indistinguishable, in Vidal's chronicles, from repressed homosexuality. Their psychopolitical correlation therefore enabled Vidal to explain Theodore Roosevelt's imperialist foreign policy as being politically compensatory for his feared homosexuality.

In *Burr* Vidal's revisionist reading of an actual figure from political history emphasized what was significantly different in his understanding of the Revolutionary period. But *1876* is distinguished for Vidal's revisionist account of a figure from literary history. Throughout *1876*, Charles Schuyler contrasts Mark Twain's just-published *Adventures of Tom Sawyer* unfavorably with the work of literary figures lost to American literary history—Edward Eggleston and Edward De Forest. Schuyler's criticism of Twain is partially explained as his envy of Twain's popularity, but it is also the result of an acute insight into the social fate of Twain's humor:

> A nice paradox: although Mark Twain is himself one of those animals (otherwise, they would not worship him, for nothing truly alien can ever be popular), he hates them for all the right reasons and so must hate himself. Had he the character to be unpopular he might have been greater than Swift, another Voltaire, a new Rabelais. . . . Whatever he might have been, he is, for now at least, hurt Caliban, a monster who has had the ill-luck to see his own face mirrored in the composite looking-glass of a million adoring countrymen. By cunningly playing the fool, Twain has become rich and beloved; he has also come to hate himself, but lacks the courage either to crack the mirror or to change, if he could, that deliberately common face he so faithfully reflects.[18]

In this passage Schuyler reads Mark Twain as a dupe of the persona he has invented to delight his American readership with exposure of their pretensions. Because Twain crafted this persona to unmask only the pretensions of others, however, he could not recognize it as the mask for his own self-hatred. Schuyler's reading of Twain's self-delusion reflects his understanding of Aaron Burr's different social persona. Burr's candor and self-derision arms him against reinvention by the popular will but leaves him susceptible to ostracism. Twain's comic identification with the structure of the social relations he exposed defends him against ostracism but turns him into the object of Schuyler's more inclusive critique of the American character. Schuyler's voluntary exile in France distances him from the pretensions Twain comically acted out of the American character, enabling him to read Twain's comic act as affirmative of the pretensions in that character. By returning to America from the country in which Revolution had literally become Empire, Schuyler does not entertain misconceptions about identity, no matter whether national or personal. He believes Twain's humor to be deeply implicated with his American audience's collective need for self-delusion, and that Twain hated the self who gratified that need.

Vidal's expropriation of Burr and Twain from their official sites constituted a challenge to American Literature and American History. In *Empire*, he brought Henry James' mastery of the entire realm of Literature into competition with the imperialist aspirations of the politician Theodore Roosevelt and the historian Brook Adams. In the conversations among these characters, Vidal did not reproduce Jamesian Literature, but brought the imperial motives informing it into lively juxtaposition with the others' imperial ambitions. Because James' literary practices compete with these other forms of authorized imperialism, their composite effect undermines any belief in Literature as a substitute for political gratifications.

Most literary critics did not take either Vidal or his readings of Twain and James seriously, and most historians considered Burr a minor historical figure they could readily surrender to Vidal's fictional history. Vidal's revisionist account of Abraham Lincoln, however, did meet with strong resistance from both literary scholars and historians. In a review published in the *New York Review of Books*, Harold Bloom remarked the importance of Lincoln to American

Literature and American History succinctly, "Lincoln is to our national political mythology what Whitman is to our literary mythology: the figure that Emerson called our Central Man."[19]

In *Lincoln* Vidal indulged neither mythology. The myth of Lincoln involves the sacrifice of his person to suture a divided nation together with the founding principles (of liberty and union) holding it apart. Vidal's Lincoln is a political heretic who believes in none of the political instruments supportive of union (the Congress, the Courts, the Constitution) except insofar as they can supplement his will to absolute executive power, and he believes the emancipation of slaves entails their exportation to the West Indies or Liberia. Unlike the Lincoln of American History and American Literature, Vidal's Lincoln does not sacrifice his life for liberty and union but "had willed his own murder as a form of atonement for the great and terrible things he had done by giving so bloody and absolute a rebirth to his nation."[20] These words conclude Vidal's novel and thoroughly separate Lincoln's death from the nation-state founded upon his martyrdom. He does not give up his life for the good of the nation-state but wills the murder of a will that would otherwise become identified as the nation's will to world dominion. In place of the usual signs of self-sacrifice, Vidal found in Lincoln's assassination evidence that Lincoln (as well as his assassin) wished for the death of a tyrant, and characterized the need for the political mythology about Lincoln's assassination as the nation's justification for imperialism and racism. When construed as the terrible psychological expense of union, Lincoln's death, in Vidal's account, authorized the annexation of new American territories as compensatory for the loss of his person, and Lincoln's assassination resulted in an enduring political reaction against blacks, who were believed to be the indirect cause of his death.

Because the national identity was commonly understood as a recovery of the Union Lincoln died for, the mythology associated with Lincoln supported a related nationalist myth. And when remembered out of the broken body of Lincoln, the doctrine of American Exceptionalism accrued an equivalent mystical significance. But Vidal offered contrary representations of the martyr and his heritage. He replaced the Lincoln who sacrificed himself for the common welfare with a Lincoln interested mostly in self-aggrandizement, and replaced the martyr for Union from the popular mythology with a Lincoln who contracted syphilis from a prostitute and communicated this disease to his wife and children.

In discriminating Vidal's Lincoln from that of American History's, C. Vann Woodward used *Lincoln* to illustrate the distinction between a historical fiction and a fictional history. Whereas a historical fiction placed "fictional characters in a more or less authentic historical background," a fictional history, Woodward observed (in a review of *Lincoln* in the *New York Review of Book*), subordinated real historical figures to the inventive powers of the novelist. Fictional history did the greater mischief, Woodward explained, for "it is here that fabrication and fact, fiction and non-fiction, are most likely to be mixed and confused." For evidence of such mischief in *Lincoln*, Woodward quoted Richard N. Current, a leading Lincoln biographer who declared Vidal "'wrong on big as well as little matters,'" and Roy P. Basler, editor of *The Collected Works of Abraham Lincoln*, who testified that "'more than half of the book could never have happened as told.'"[21]

Vidal responded that his facts were accurate, his research sound, and characterized his critics as "scholar squirrels" who depended upon the Lincoln martyrology for the benefits that accrued to the hagiographer and upon inherited prejudices for their working assumptions. Vidal's rejoinder is significant for the more inclusive controversy he constructs out of it:

> In 1946 my first novel was published. A war novel, it was praised by the daily book reviewer of the *Times*, one Orville Prescott, whose power to "make or break" a book was then unique and now unimaginable. I was made. Then in 1948, two books were published within weeks of one another. First, *The City and the Pillar* by me; then *Sexual Behavior in the Human Male* by Dr. Alfred C. Kinsey, et al. In my novel I found the love affair between two ordinary American youths to be a matter-of-fact and normal business. Dr. Kinsey then confirmed [this]. . . . At the time Orville Prescott told my publisher, Nicholas Wreden of E. P. Dutton, that he would never again read much less review a book by me. The *Times* then refused to advertise either my book or the Kinsey Report.[22]

Having recorded this biographical fact within the context of his argument over the accuracy of his fictional history, Vidal brought the resulting historical context dramatically to bear upon his distinction between more or less agreed upon facts and the social narratives they verified. Richard N. Current rejected the claims that Lincoln was a racist who infected his wife and children with syphilis for reasons congruent with the *New York Times'* rejection of *The City and the Pillar*, Vidal argued. Both books violated the official social narratives which exclude homosexuals from the Republic of Letters and racism from the Great Emancipator's politics. Vidal believed that the myth of Lincoln the Emancipator was responsible for continued race hatred and that the denial of Lincoln's syphilis was supportive of the politics of sexual repression. Vidal did not substitute official Lincoln mythologies for these political realities, but recalled the effects of an analogous substitution in his personal life. Unlike Mailer, Vidal had not been able to return after World War II to American History. In *Lincoln*, he turned Americans to a different understanding of their history.

Vidal also used the dramatic context he constructed out of the controversy over *Lincoln* to clarify his understanding of Literature as a historical force. The "historical" characters he proposed for Current, Basler, and the other historians in his response are not significantly different from the "historical" characters in the American chronicles. Like Brooks and Henry Adams in *Empire*, these academic historians were unlike other Americans because of their ability to produce cultural discourses that discriminated facts from fiction. In the second-order cultural argument he conducted with these historians, Vidal constructed the narrative equivalent of a public sphere, a site of contestation over the significance of political significance to the future of the Republic.

Throughout his arguments with them Vidal refused the historians' criteria for their discriminations. In the distinction he drew between fictional *history* and historical *fiction*, Woodward located the culturally dominant term in the substantive of each category. Because Vidal is a novelist and not a historian he should not, Woodward asserted, have presumed authority over the historical record. In pursuing his argument, Woodward tacitly presupposed that Literature differed from History in that it substituted events the author imagined from the historical archive. Woodward assumed that historical facts were logically incommensurable with fictions and that novels and histories belonged to different orders of reality. History aspired to represent what actually happened, while Literature did not. Because Woodward insisted on the difference between historical evidence and literary invention, he faulted Vidal for inventing evidence. Vidal conceded there are "more or less agreed upon facts," but he strongly disagreed about the narratives in which they were taken so matter of factly. Culturally persuasive accounts of what happened in the past depended, Vidal argued, on the political consciousness constructed out of contemporary political controversies as well as the historical impediments to that construction.

After having refused to subordinate his fictional *history* to Woodward's account of a proper historical narrative, Vidal associated Woodward's strategy with Literature's subordination of *The City and the Pillar* to dominant psychosocial norms, and concluded that both acts of subordination presupposed a belief in Literature as a substitute for History but unable to effect historical action. But Vidal believed his fictional history to be a historical force as well as a literary artifact. Situated between previous accounts of Lincoln and the political controversy it aroused, *Lincoln* became a historical agency capable of producing social change. To make this point emphatic, Vidal situates it in a political context:

> It is my radical view that Americans are now sufficiently mature to be shown as close to the original as it is possible for us so much later to get. Since the race war goes on as fiercely as ever in this country, I think candor about blacks and whites and racism is necessary. [23]

In this passage Vidal has carried his argument over the historicity of *Lincoln* into a context where the "radical" consciousness it conveys exists as political resource, but without an identifiable social movement in which it can be exercised.

Having arrived at the point in this account where the political consciousness Vidal's project effected could not be situated within an available historical context, I want to recall the earlier relationship adduced between Vidal's fictional history and the 1960s counterculture, and fulfill my earlier promise to correlate Vidal's chronicles with the New Historicism.

With the publication of *Washington, D.C.* in 1967, Vidal constructed a historical context for the political consciousness of the

1960s antiwar culture. Because its members were unable to sustain a historical site for their politics, the counterculture passed out of American history with the Vietnam War. But when some of those active in the counterculture later became professors of American Literature, they recalled that earlier history lesson and refused to credit accounts of American literary culture as a realm apart from American History. Their literary criticism insisted on the importance of the historical context to the study of Literature. One academic result of the return of this suppressed context has been the emergence of a new academic discipline called the New Historicism.

In his succinct account of the difference between History and the New Historicism, Frank Lentricchia formulated the assumptions of the new field as if they were a reprise of Vidal's argument with the historians:

> So for a new historicist literature is no cool reflection on a "background" of stable and unified historical fact. It is at once part of the "fact" itself and what gives shape to what we know as the fact. The mainstream historicist must therefore practice a triple repression: first, of his own active participation in the creation of the history he thinks he objectively mirrors; second, of the interest-ridden complicity of the literature he studies in the shaping of what we are given as history; third, of the political conflict of dominant and subaltern social groups which presumably constructed literature's true shape and content. [24]

Unlike the literary critics who banished Gore Vidal, the New Historicists share his understanding of Literature as an historical force. The difference between them involves the sites on which they would exert this force. Because Vidal's work has never been a presence within the academy, his fictional histories are addressed to the larger public constructed out of the controversies accompanying his books. But the New Historicists have conducted all their fieldwork in the academy. Like their precursors in the counterculture, they have returned political categories—race, class, gender—to the study of literature, and thereby changed this field of academic study as well as the literary curriculum. But without widespread understanding of the historic significance of this change in literary understanding the New Historicists remain a marginal political force.

As the historical consciousness for the 1960s counterculture,

Vidal has been practicing the New Historicism since 1967. His fictional histories constitute a research archive for this emergent field as well as a broad public for its political concerns. As the heirs of the political imperatives of the 1960s counterculture, the New Historicists constitute an emergent political movement in which Vidal's chronicles can function as a valuable resource.

When construed as the historical consciousness missing from the counterculture, Vidal's chronicles can be understood to historicize the New Historicists' project. Those works undermine the assumptions constructive of Literature as a discipline separable from History as well as the ruling narratives corroboratory of their separation. In the arguments he has conducted with academic historians and literary critics, Vidal has produced an accessible context for understanding the new literary field. Because of the assumptions about Literature and History they share, Vidal's chronicles will become crucial to the development of this emergent discipline. But this relationship will not be a reciprocal one until the New Historicists include Vidal's works within the Literature courses from which they have been excluded for the last forty-five years.

21

An Interview with Gore Vidal

JAY PARINI

This interview with Gore Vidal took place at his villa in Ravello, Italy, in the summer of 1990. The villa, called "La Rondinaia," is a five-storied house that clings like a swallow's nest to a steep cliff overlooking the Mediterranean. It has a dizzying view of the Amalfi Coast, looking southward to Salerno. On a clear day one sees the faint outline of Calabria in the distance. Directly below, the little town of Amalfi—once a major port of call and commercial center—hugs the shore.

Vidal has been living in this part of Italy since 1972, and he obviously adores the situation he has created for himself: the writer in voluntary exile. And it's a splendid exile. One approaches the state grounds of "La Rondinaia" by following a long and winding path that proceeds through a grove of cyprus trees, past a deep-blue swimming pool (its color is meant to imitate the legendary "blue grotto" of Capri) through an old-fashioned loggia, down and up many stairs, to the villa itself. Above the door is a statue of Cybele with her wheel.

Inside "La Rondinaia," high ceilings and sweeping marble stairwells add to the spatial sense. Vidal lives much like a Roman emperor in exile, enjoying the fruits of his craft. Having written numerous best-selling novels, countless television and movie scripts, and several Broadway hits, he does not have to worry about money. What separates him from almost all other writers of commercially successful projects, of course, is the quality of his work. Vidal is a major writer, an intense and witty man who has thought deeply about many of the most difficult issues of our time.

We talked over a drink in his large study, surrounded by editions of Henry James, Turgenev, and dozens of other writers who have an important place in Vidal's continuously expanding universe. The shelves also boast a leather-bound set of Vidal—itself an amazing sight, and a wall of framed magazine covers featuring Vidal. On a table, one sees photographs of Vidal's father with Franklin Roosevelt, of Vidal grandfather, Senator Thomas P. Gore, and other celebrities, including Italo Calvino, whom Vidal considered a friend.

We talked about his craft, mostly, and about the reception of his work in academe. Critics—especially academic critics—have not always been kind to Gore Vidal, for many reasons. This is Mr. Vidal's own version of what has happened to him in four decades of creative work, with assorted comments on the nature of his own achievement and some thoughts on his contemporaries.

JAY PARINI: Your writing career seems to have elicited such a wide range of responses from critics, ranging from enthusiastic to downright mean. What's going on here?

GORE VIDAL: For a start, there's just so much of it. I've had one of the longest careers in American literary history. Very few writers who began publishing in the forties are still at it in the nineties. I don't think a lot of critics now working really know much about the war years, about my generation. Everything is so quickly forgotten, especially in the U.S., which I often call the United States of Amnesia. There is also the fact that I write in so many different genres: novels, screenplays, essays, stage plays, and so on. That seems to puzzle everyone. The general pattern isn't easy to work out, so I don't blame anyone for not trying.

JP: Are you talking about changes that have occurred in the critical aesthetic?

GV: No, just a lack of knowledge. The critics don't know an awful lot. They think that American literature began when, in 1969, they first happened to read *The Great Gatsby*.

JP: Is there some basic pattern in your own work that you'd want to point out?

GV: The novels fall into two categories: meditations on history and politics—book such as *Burr* and *Julian*—and what I call my "inventions"—such as *Myra Breckinridge* and *Duluth*. The second category of books are rather like satirical arias; nobody else seems to write that kind of thing.

JP: Quite a few writers, on the other hand, write historical novels, don't they?

GV: Yes, but my "meditations" deal with matters that most of the others ignore. The Good Novelists—as opposed to the trashy bestseller types—usually avoid topics such as the nature of society, the fate of the republic, or the origins of Christianity. Elizabeth Hardwick once said to me, after the publication of *Julian*, "Only you could have written that, Gore." I said, "Yes, and I'm the only American writer who would have *wanted* to write it. I may be the only American writer who would even *read* such a book!"

JP: It often strikes me that you're not really a writer in the American tradition. Your work harks back to the British satirists: Swift, Peacock, Evelyn Waugh. Is that fair?

GV: Yes, and P. G. Wodehouse, whom I adore. He was a very great influence on me, as he was on Umberto Eco. But my early novels were influenced by Mark Twain, Stephen Crane, and Theodore Dreiser—all Americans.

JP: At a certain point your work changed quite dramatically, didn't it?

GV: *The Judgment of Paris* was my turning point. After that, I no longer echoed the ancestral voices, I suppose. I found something like my "real voice."

JP: Let's talk about your early education. What authors did you read as a young man—before you started writing?

GV: As you know, I never went to college, so my reading was idiosyncratic. Unlike most American writers, I was never afflicted by The Tradition. The American canon, you know, doesn't compare to the English, French, or Russian. But American educators, desperate to have a literature equal to their empire, have tried hard to make Herman Melville into a major writer; the work, however, just isn't good enough. It won't bear that kind of examination.

JP: So who did you read?

GV: I worked my way through a shelf of Scott. I read all of Meredith and Henry James. When I was a bit older I read Flaubert, Proust, and George Eliot. And, of course, I loved Peacock, Huxley, Wodehouse—the satirists. I read Swift, I admired him, but he was not a very important influence. I'm not conscious of that, in any case. Mario Praz once pointed out that Voltaire had influenced my work, and he was right.

JP: I can't get Swift out of my head. The similarities are too great.

GV: As a polemical essayist, yes. I took Swift as a model. A better place to look is to the American pamphleteers of the Southwest. My grandfather loved them, and so do I.

JP: One senses that Mark Twain lurks in the background somewhere, not only in the essays throughout but in some of the novels, too.

GV: That was all pointed out by Leslie Fiedler in his famous essay "Come Back to the Raft Again, Huck Honey." He noticed that in *The City and the Pillar* I'd taken *Huckleberry Finn* a step further.

JP: Did the later Twain, which is so very dark, influence novels like *Kalki* and *Duluth?*

GV: Maybe so. What you mustn't forget is that Twain was always a great entertainer.

JP: And a public figure, like you.

GV: But unlike me, he was afraid of losing the favor of his audience. He would never have said, as I have, that he was an atheist. He was an atheist, of course, as the posthumously published work shows, but he was too frightened during his lifetime to admit it.

JP: What was he afraid of?

GV: His wife, certainly. And his public. They wouldn't have stood for Mark Twain the Atheist.

JP: Can we talk about your work as a scriptwriter? You've written endless television scripts and screenplays. Why?

GV: Contrary to legend, I did not inherit a great deal of money. I have supported myself from the age of seventeen. Perhaps I should say that the U.S. Army supported me between the ages of seventeen and twenty-one. After that, I supported myself as a writer. I've gone where I had to go to make a living. When I was blacked out by *Time* and *Newsweek* and the *New York Times*—back in the late forties and early fifties, in response to *The City and the Pillar*—I had no way to continue as a writer of novels. So I turned to television. Within a year or so, I was doing extremely well for myself. I went on to write for the theater, for the movies. I turned to politics for a while, and to writing essays and reviews. Then I returned to the novel, with *Julian*. Necessity is what drove me. The fact that I was versatile was simply good luck.

JP: If you had it to do over, what would you have done?

GV: Stayed with the drama, in whatever form it took—stage plays, movies. I understood the theater in the fifties and sixties, but Broadway is, of course, dead now.

JP: You've had at least two major hits on Broadway and a string of huge bestsellers. What accounts for your popularity?

GV: I have no idea. Perhaps it's because history is so badly taught in the schools, which means there's a real hunger for information of a certain kind. Americans want to find out about their past. There's also the fact that I deal with interesting subjects. Most writers today are not interesting because they're not interested. What concerns them is something called The Novel. But The Novel doesn't exist. There are only novels. And most of these are disguised autobiographies. Writers tell us about their marriages and mental problems. But who cares? If nothing else, by reading *War and Peace* you'll get a wonderful recipe for strawberry jam. Great books teach you lots of things. And then there's the delicate matter of class—a taboo subject in America. Most writers come from the middle classes, and they never venture outside their little realm. They don't even know that there *is* a class system in America. The myth is put forward that we have no ruling class. Anyone can become president of IBM, they argue. Sure they can. But who owns the majority of IBM's stock? The small number of families who actually own America are unknown to most people, especially writers. Nevertheless, they do exist.

JP: Does this lack of awareness of the class system lead to a certain naïveté in American fiction?

GV: Yes. Novelists ought to explore the issue of class and write for the society at large. But novelists today prefer to write for each other. They know very little about the way the country is governed or how society works. They imagine that if they sign a petition against South Africa that they've made a great political gestures. They have no idea about how the mayor of their city was elected, however. Or what that process says about their world.

JP: Have none of our writers dealt with class in a way that strikes you as mature?

GV: Louis Auchincloss has. He understands about the old families, and he knows how their interlocking trusts actually work. Only junk novels commonly deal with these subjects.

JP: You've been extremely hard on academics and university life. What's going on here?

GV: I don't take most academics as seriously as they take themselves. If I had known that the academics would absorb the novel in such a total way, I'd probably have been more polite. That took me by surprise. The academic novelists are the worst, however: Barth, Gass, Barthelme, and so on. For them, nothing exists but what is happening on campus. They're obsessed with theories of the novel, and they write to mirror those theories. It's all a vicious little circle, and it doesn't result in something anyone would like to read. These books exist to be put on a college syllabus or dissected by an academic critic. There is no sense of a genuine audience.

JP: What about reviewers? Has much changed in the four decades that you've been on the scene?

GV: The reviewers are all professors now. That wasn't the case in, say, 1950. I have nothing against professors as such. But the influence of the academy has been unfortunate for American fiction. Again, what gets left out of the equation is the "real" world.

JP: You've often said that Hollywood has taken over where literature left off, and that future generations will have lost all interest in books. All they'll want to do is watch movies. Isn't that partly true of your generation, too?

GV: Of course. I grew up in the Golden Age of talking pictures. The language of film is as natural to my generation as the language of fiction. When I turned to writing for Hollywood, I was already well prepared. I knew how the thing was done because I'd seen so many films. If you grew up in the thirties and forties, the movies were your world. It's one of the great things people of my age have in common: we've all seen the same pictures.

JP: Your novels seem consciously constructed along cinematic lines, which is to say they proceed by scenes. Reading them is like watching a film.

GV: I don't work so consciously. I prefer writing dialogue to description, I suppose. Description is usually boring. On the other hand, if you have a gift for pursuing narrative through dialogue, you can end up taking too many shortcuts. Your novel will look, in the end, like a movie script that was thinly adapted to the conventions of fiction. Ideally, the making of sentences creates a sense of kinetic energy that's different from the dialogue of scripts.

JP: Do you work from an outline?

GV: If I'm working on an historical novel, then history itself provides the outline. When I was working on *Lincoln*, for instance, it seemed quite natural to end with the assassination. There would have been no point in continuing with Mary Todd's story. That didn't interest me anyway. Historical novels seem to follow their own designs, their own self-limits.

JP: What about the fictional aspects of the historical novels? *Lincoln* is, after all, described as "a novel."

GV: I like to invent characters—fictional persons—who will then observe the "real" people. In *Lincoln*, I tell the story from about five different viewpoints—though I never pretend to get inside Lincoln's head, as such. I've always found first-person narrative the easiest, I suppose. Once you get the tone of voice, the book writes itself. That was certainly true of *Myra Breckinridge*, *Messiah*, and *Julian*—each of those novels is a form of acting. I just invent a character and let him or her talk. Dickens, you know, was marvelous that way. He conjured such a wide range of voice. He could act them all. That's pretty much what I'm trying to do.

JP: Did you discover a good deal about each character or "voice" as you went along?

GV: Myra didn't even know she'd been a *man* until halfway through her narrative. How's that for a little surprise? *Myra*, for me, was simply a case where the voice took over, took possession of me. The same thing happened with *Duluth*, which is my favorite of these books. "*Duluth! Love it or loathe it, you can never leave it or lose it.*" That sentence just came thundering into my head one day as I was walking down the street in Rome. What on earth is *that*, I thought. I sat down at the desk, and there it was: the whole novel just opened itself before me. It might interest you to know that this novel has been one of my most quietly popular books. I got a list recently from the British Public Library of my most popular books, and *Duluth* and *Creation* were the ones most frequently taken out.

JP: What about *Kalki*, which has a lot in common with *Duluth*? It's essentially what Anthony Burgess would call a "dystopian" novel. Did the voice come easily?

GV: That voice was much harder to get at. It betrayed me several times. The whole thing needed recasting.

JP: You wrote more than half a dozen novels in your twenties, including *Williwaw, The City and the Pillar, In a Yellow Wood, The Season of Comfort, A Search for the King,* and *Dark Green, Bright Red.* That's quite an array of books, though they seem so very different from the work of your later years. How do you think about those books now? Are they something of a lost continent? Or do you go back to them occasionally?

GV: I don't think about them. I never reread them. Oddly enough, they stay in print, especially in translation. *Dark Green, Bright Red*—a novel about CIA activity in Guatemala and other such things—is very popular in Brazil and Latin America. *The City and the Pillar* seems to have a life of its own. *Messiah*, written at the end of this "early" period, has always had a following.

JP: Going back to the novels about American history: Did you think of them as a sequence?

GV: Not at the outset. I suppose it was during the composition of *Burr* that I realized that a sequence could be made of that material. I had several references to Aaron Burr in *Washington, D.C.*, and of course my stepfather's family was related to Burr. Somewhere along the way I realized I was involved in a family history, that it could all be expanded from there. In *Burr*, I focused on the first thirty years of the Republic. I wanted to keep going, to see what would happen to these people and their descendents. Eventually, the story spanned two centuries. I suspect that few critics have really read the novels in sequence and understand what I was trying to do.

JP: Those novels are so full of data—historical information, period detail, the minutiae of politics from each era. Do you employ researchers or anything?

GV: I've simply got to do all of the research myself in order to *discover* what I want to know. The process occurs like this: I order boxes full of books from American booksellers. I may buy two or three hundred books for each novel. I read the books here, in Ravello, taking notes. After I've written the novel, I always get a professional historian to check the novels to see that I've not made any great gaffs. Writing these books has been my education. *Creation* was, for me, a crash course in comparative religion.

JP: *Creation* seems an odd book for you to have written, though it's full of fascinating material. I found the voice rather flat—at least compared to *Myra Breckinridge* or *Duluth*.

GV: Flat! I found the voice of Cyrus very interesting, full of biases of one kind or another. He's anti-Greek, pro-Persian by temperament. He thinks he knows the truth about things. But he gets hung up on the notion of creation—how it all began. As he goes farther and farther East, he sees that it's a non-question. It didn't ever begin. And it won't end. Finally, with the Buddha, he realizes it's not here at all. The world doesn't exist, as such. Life is a dream. What he comes to see is that he was asking the wrong questions. Western culture is always asking the wrong questions. It's our fatal flaw.

JP: How would you describe the goal of life as Cyrus—and perhaps Gore Vidal—have finally come to see it?

GV: To be free of desire is true knowledge, to break the repetitive cycles of birth and death and rebirth. That's the goal.

JP: Is the Buddha your philosopher of choice?

GV: No, I prefer Confucius. Confucianism isn't a religion at all; it's a system of education, of administration. It's the sanest approach to life that I know about.

JP: Your narrator in *Creation*—Cyrus—is certainly a type of philosopher and teacher. His blindness reminds me of your grandfather, Senator Thomas P. Gore, who was blind. Is there anything autobiographical about this novel?

GV: No, it's an objective book—if there can be such a thing. I'm tired of Romantic modernism and those autobiographical books like Joyce's *Portrait of the Artist*, a novel that gets written over and over. Many critics seem to believe it's the only novel worth writing, that it's The Novel. It is *not*.

JP: One critic, Frederick R. Karl, has complained that you have not taken modernism seriously. He seems to believe that you never really took on the modernist revolution, which means that you're stuck back in some premodernist limbo. You and George Meredith.

GV: Modernism was finished by the time I was born. All sorts of mediocre writers enjoyed playing at being "modern." They still do. But there's nothing in it.

JP: Italo Calvino once described you as a postmodern writer, like himself. I can see that, with your interest in "doubleness," the wittily self-conscious nature of your inventions. This label— and I detest labels as much as you do—would seem to work best with the satirical novels—*Myra*, *Duluth*, and so on.

GV: Yes. Calvino said that in a review of *Duluth* that appeared in an Italian newspaper. But it was Peter Conrad who, in the *TLS*, called me a "duplicitous" writer. I liked that, largely because it seemed to describe my work in a way that made sense to me. Fortunately, I don't have to teach literature, I only write it. So I don't need those categories.

JP: You've spent a great deal of time in Italy in the past three decades. Have any of the Italian writers—Calvino, Umberto

Eco, Moravia—influenced you in any way? I suppose this is a roundabout way of getting at the subject of living abroad generally. There must have been, must be, an effect.

GV: Living out of the country concentrates your mind wonderfully. You see your own country more clearly. I really can't say that I have ever been much influenced by Italian or European writers, at least not consciously, though of course I've read them all. Calvino I considered a friend, and I admired his books.

JP: And, of course, you introduced Calvino to the American public.

GV: A fact conveniently forgotten by many.

JP: What attracted you to Calvino's work?

GV: He was essentially a scientist, with a scientist's eye for detail. *Mr. Palomar* is the ideal example of this, the last novel published before he died. I admire any writer who has gifts that I don't have.

JP: How would you describe your own particular gifts?

GV: I can invent worlds that were not there before. That's the supreme task of a writer, isn't it? Swift did that, of course, but he was very different from me. We create such different kinds of worlds. *Duluth* is my best work in this regard.

JP: Critics often comment on your language, which is remarkably fluent and clear.

GV: It varies, depending on the voice of the novel. My essays are closest to my own actual voice, though I couldn't imagine doing *Duluth* in the tone of my essay on William Dean Howells. I do suppose that an ear for language is one of my strengths—and it's something unusual for an American writer. The language of the American novel is now a much diminished thing. The general vocabulary of fiction has shrunk visibly in my lifetime. The average educated person in my father's day had access to many more words than people do now. Even Tennessee Williams used to tell me that my novels were full of so many strange words that he couldn't read them. I once asked him for an example. "Solipsism," he said. "I had to look it up." I said, "Look, Tennessee. If there's any word you *need* in your vocabulary, it's solipsism!" Of course, Tennessee never read anything.

JP: What does a writer need to succeed—not only in the commercial or critical sense, but aesthetically?

GV: A writer needs energy most of all. Physical energy and imaginative energy.

JP: What are your weaknesses as a writer?

GV: If I could see them, I'd avoid them. What I do see is that nothing I've written has ever satisfied me. You can't really succeed with a novel anyway; they're too big. It's like city planning. You can't plan a perfect city because there's too much going on that you can't take into account. You can, however, write a perfect sentence now and then. I have.

JP: That reminds me of Randall Jarrell's famous definition of a novel as "a book that has something wrong with it."

GV: Exactly. Nobody can command it all. The minimalists have gotten onto something here. They half suspected there was no way they could write a good novel: they lacked the gift for language, and they had little in the way of knowledge of the world. You have to have those things to write a good novel. So they worked backward, eliminating things. The instinct was sound. Raymond Carver kept as safely as he could to the little he knew, though he knew that little bit of the world very well. Some of his writing is very good indeed—so well observed.

JP: What other writers do you admire—among current writers?

GV: William Golding is very fine. Saul Bellow I've known for years—we used to live near each other on the Hudson, near Bard College—and I admire his intelligence. His novels, however, don't interest me very much. I find them difficult to finish. I tried recently to read *Humbolt's Gift*, but my energy ran out after about a hundred pages. Or perhaps *his* energy ran out. I've had the same experience with most of his other novels, including *Herzog*. Nabokov I admire, except the later work. *Ada* is unreadable. Self-love on that level is difficult to respond to. I adore some of the early books, though, such as *Laughter in the Dark*. He was, as V. S. Pritchett once said, a grammarian of genius. I also like reading what I call "the girls"—Joan Didion, Diane Johnston, Alison Lurie. They operate so well in the diurnal world of marriage, teaching, jobs, children. They have such malicious eyes. And I love Jeanette

Winterson, a young English writer who is extremely funny. She's absolutely wonderful—the best thing to come out of England in the last twenty years.

JP: Would you say you're hopeful about the future of literary writing in America or, for that matter, anywhere?

GV: There will always be a certain amount of good writing, but what I have to wonder is who will read it? There was a time when only the poets read other poets. That's true of novelists now—serious novelists, as they're called. I notice myself much less interested in reading other writers—in fact. I've got an endless supply of old movies to watch on video. They're heavenly. On the other hand, I keep writing—novels, essays, screenplays. Again, it's simply what I do. I'm a writer.

NOTES

1. Parini—Gore Vidal: The Writer and His Critics

1. Frederick R. Karl, *American Fictions: 1940–1980* (New York: Harper and Row, 1983), p. 92.

2. Elizabeth Dipple, *The Unresolved Plot: Reading Contemporary Fiction* (New York: Routledge, 1988), p. 3.

3. Gore Vidal, *Empire* (New York: Random House, 1987), p. 3.

4. Gore Vidal, *Reflections upon a Sinking Ship* (New York: Little, Brown, 1969), p. 50.

5. The *Esquire* piece is reprinted in *Matters of Fact and Fiction (Essays 1973–1976)* (New York: Random House, 1977), pp. 264–85.

6. Reprinted in *The Second American Revolution* (New York: Random House, 1982), pp. 243–46.

7. See Robert F. Kiernan's discussion of this novel in "The Vidalian Manner," included in this collection.

8. The documentary appeared on December 13, 1959.

9. *New York Times* June 17, 1946, p. 19.

10. Vidal's immaturity as a writer here is oddly represented by the combination of emotional stress *and* coldness.

11. Claude J. Summers, *Gay Fictions: From Wilde to Stonewall* (New York: Continuum, 1990). pp. 112–29.

12. John W. Aldrige, *After the Lost Generation: A Critical Study of the Writers of Two Wars* (New York: McGraw-Hill, 1951).

13. Robert J. Stanton, *Gore Vidal: A Primary and Secondary Bibliography* (Boston: G. K. Hall, 1978).

14. Stanton, *Gore Vidal*, p. 52.

15. Stanton, *Gore Vidal*, p. 51.

16. Bernard F. Dick, *The Apostate Angel: A Critical Study of Gore Vidal* (New York: Random House, 1974).

17. Dick, *The Apostate Angel*, p. 67.

18. Gore Vidal, *At Home: Essays 1982–1988* (New York: Random House, 1988), pp. 241–42.

19. *New York Times*, February 8, 1957, p. 359.

20. Gore Vidal, *Homage to Daniel Shays: Collected Essays, 1952–1972* (New York: Random House, 1972), p. 34.

21. Ray Lewis White, *Gore Vidal* (Boston: Twayne, 1968).

22. There is an excellent documentary film about Vidal's California campaign for the Senate seat called *Gore Vidal: The Man Who Said No* (Mystic Fire Video).

23. Robert F. Kiernan, *Gore Vidal* (New York: Ungar, 1982), p. 8.

24. Cited by James Tatum in "The *Romanitas* of Gore Vidal," which appears for the first time in this volume.

25. *Newsweek*, June 15, 1964, p. 106.

26. London *Times*, October 15, 1964, p. 15.

27. *New York Review of Books*, July 30, 1964, p. 21.

28. *Spectator*, October 16, 1964, p. 518.

29. Gore Vidal, *Creation* (New York: Random House, 1981), p. 452.

30. Kiernan, *Gore Vidal*, p. 66.

31. A survey done by the British Library has shown that Vidal's two most popular books are *Creation* and *Duluth*. Who would have guessed?

32. Gore Vidal, *Myra Breckinridge* (New York: Random House, 1968), p. 1.

33. Gore Vidal, *Washington, D.C.* (New York: Random House: 1967), p. 27.

34. Edwin Morgan, "The Coil of Corruption," London *Sunday Times*, March 28, 1976, p. 40.

35. Peter Conrad, "Re-inventing America," *TLS*, March 26, 1976, pp. 347–48.

36. Joyce Carol Oates, *New York Times Book Review*, June 3, 1984, pp. 1, 36–37.

37. Harold Bloom, "The Central Man," *New York Review of Books*, July 19, 1984, pp. 5–8.

38. Two more recent examples of the genre are Gabriel García Marquez's novel about the life of Simon Boliver, *The General in His Labyrinth* (New York: Knopf, 1990), and my own novel about the last year of Leo Tolstoy's life, *The Last Station* (New York: Holt, 1990).

39. Joel Connaroe, *New York Times Book Review,* January 21, 1990, p. 38.

40. Michael Wood, "Improvisations on the Fact of Force," in *TLS,* November 10–16, 1989, p. 1243.

41. John Simon, "Vishnu as Double Agent," in *Saturday Review,* April 29, 1978, p. 33.

42. Angela McRobbie, "Sign Language," *New Statesman,* May 6, 1983, p. 24.

43. A typical example is the piece he wrote for *Newsweek* (July 3, 1987) on Oliver North during the Iran-Contra hearings. It is collected in Vidal, *At Home,* pp. 120–23.

44. Mitchell S. Ross, *The Literary Politicians* (New York: Doubleday, 1978), pp. 247–300.

45. Joseph Epstein, "What Makes Vidal Run," *Commentary,* June 1977, pp. 72–75.

46. Russell Jacoby, *The Last Intellectuals* (New York: Basic Books, 1987), passim.

3. Price—Williwaw: Gore Vidal's First Novel

1. See Robert J. Stanton, *Gore Vidal: A Primary and Secondary Bibliography* (Boston: G. K. Hall, 1978), pp. 41–42.

4. Summers—The City and the Pillar *as Gay Fiction*

1. See the "Terminal Note" to Forster's *Maurice* (New York: W. W. Norton, 1971; London: Edward Arnold, 1971).

2. Gore Vidal, *The City and the Pillar Revised* (New York: Dutton, 1965; New York: New American Library, Signet Books, 1965), p. 155. All subsequent quotations from the Afterword and from the revised version of the novel are from these editions.

3. Vidal, *The City and the Pillar* (New York: Dutton, 1948), p. 246. All subsequent quotations from the original version of the novel are from this edition. Vidal's 1965 revision substantially improves the novel's style and conclusion, but because my interests are historical as well as aesthetic, I refer throughout to the original version except where clearly indicated.

4. The arrest of Tilden, perhaps the greatest tennis player of all time, for homosexual offenses involving minors sent shock waves through the sports world and challenged the widely held assumption that athletes could not be homosexual. In January 1947, Tilden was sentenced to nine

months in jail for contributing to the delinquency of a minor. In 1949 he
was sentenced to one year in jail for a similar offense.

5. *The Diary of Anaïs Nin*, vol. 4, *1944–1947*, ed. Gunther Stuhlmann (New York: Harcourt Brace Jovanovich, 1971), p. 175.

6. The term is that of Bernard F. Dick in *The Apostate Angel:* A
Critical Study of Gore Vidal (New York: Random House, 1974), p. 38. But
because Dick does not recognize the homosexual myths that Vidal uses in
the novel, he seriously misleads by creating a false antinomy when he
remarks that Vidal's book is "important as a mythic novel, not a homosexual one." He is challenged on this count by Roger Austen, *Playing the
Game: The Homosexual Novel in America* (Indianapolis: Bobbs-Merrill,
1977) pp. 123–24, and by Stephen Adams, *The Homosexual as Hero in
Contemporary Fiction* (New York: Barnes and Noble, 1980), p. 18.

7. Dick, *The Apostate Angel*, p. 39 (the previous quotation is from
p. 31). For a challenge to Dick's thesis, see Adams, *The Homosexual as
Hero*, p. 18. In *Gore Vidal* (New York: Ungar, 1982), Robert F. Kiernan
links Jim Willard with George Willard of Sherwood Anderson's *Wine-
sburg, Ohio* and other "boy-men" of American literature (pp. 39–40).

8. Walt Whitman, "Song of Myself," line 200, in *Walt Whitman: The
Complete Poems*, ed. Francis Murphy (Harmondsworth, Middlesex, England: Penguin, 1975), p. 3. Among the late nineteenth-century homoerotic paintings of bathing scenes are "The Swimming Hole" by Thomas
Eakins and "August Blue" by H. S. Tuke. Austen explains the prevalence
of bathing scenes in gay American literature in practical terms: "Since the
one sensuous nude/near nude experience American society permits young
males to have with each other is related to some variation of 'the old
swimming hole,' it is not surprising that many of the more autobiographical novels contain swimming scenes. The traumatic shock of recognition that one is 'different' often goes back to some early and indelible
fascination with the naked body of a slightly older male . . . , and futher-
more it is not uncommon for the physical characteristics of this person to
serve as the ideal against which all later love objects are measured. . . .
Sharing some golden moments with an adored near-naked buddy is
the closest many gay males come to perfection during their pecu-
liarly troubled adolescence, and thus it seems that the appearance of these
poignant pool scenes can also be understood in terms of the novelist
recapturing the golden moments of his youth" (*Playing the Game*,
p. 141*n*40).

9. Austen, *Playing the Game*, p. 124; Adams, *The Homosexual as
Hero*, p. 18. The Hylas ritual is outlined and explained by Rictor Norton,
The Homosexual Literary Tradition: An Interpretation (New York, Revi-
sionist Press, 1974), pp. 1–27; see also his discussion of "The Love-Battle,"

pp. 56–74. It is unlikely that Vidal consciously intended to evoke the Hercules-Hylas myth, but he was certainly aware that wrestling is frequently a symbol or metaphor for homoeroticism.

10. See *The Symposium*, trans. W. H. D. Rouse, in *Great Dialogues of Plato*, ed. Eric H. Warmington and Philip G. Rouse (New York: New American Library, 1956), pp. 85–89.

11. Kiernan, *Gore Vidal*, pp. 42–43.

12. Kiernan, *Gore Vidal*, pp. 41–42.

5. Dick—Gore Vidal: The Entertainer

1. Gore Vidal, *A Search for the King* (New York: E. P. Dutton, 1950), p. 51. Subsequent references are to this edition and are given in the text.

2. Leslie Fiedler, *Love and Death in the American Novel*, rev. ed. (New York: Delta, 1966), p. 49. Subsequent references are to this edition and are given in the text.

3. Gore Vidal, *Dark Green, Bright Red* (1950; revised and reprinted, New York: New American Library, Signet Books, 1968), p. 23, Subsequent references are to this edition and are given in the text.

6. Kiernan—The Vidalian Manner: The Judgment of Paris, Two Sisters, Kalki

1. Gore Vidal, "Foreword," *Visit to a Small Planet and Other Television Plays* (Boston: Little, Brown, 1956), p. xv. Reprinted in Vidal, *Homage to Daniel Shays: Collected Essays, 1952–1972* (New York: Random House, 1972), p. 30.

2. John W. Aldridge, "Three Tempted Him," *New York Times Book Review*, March 9, 1952, p. 4

3. One of Vidal's remarks in the Mitzel and Abbot interview is relevant: "I think you will find it takes a long time to find your tone of voice. I didn't until *Judgment of Paris*. I published five or six books before I really got it. I wouldn't say I got it right, but I got it accurate." John Mitzel and Steven Abbot, *Myra & Gore: A New View of Myra Breckenridge and a Candid Interview with Gore Vidal. A Book for Vidalophiles* (Dorchester, Mass.: Manifest Destiny Books, 1974), p. 78. The interview appeared originally in *Fag Rag* (Winter–Spring 1974), pp. 1, 3–9.

4. See Gore Vidal's essay, "The Fourth Diary of Anaïs Nin," in Vidal, *Homage to Daniel Shays*, pp. 403–9, for Vidal's reaction to his appearance in Nin's diary.

5. "Jimmy" is probably James Tremble, to whom *The City and the Pillar* is dedicated. See Bernard Dick's study for an interesting speculation that James Tremble was something of a Bob Ford character in Vidal's life. Dick, *The Apostate Angel* (New York: Random House, 1974), pp. 36–38. References to boyhood lovers who die in battle also occur in *The Season of Comfort* ("Jimmy Wesson"), "Pages from an Abandoned Journal" ("Jimmy"), *Washington, D.C.* ("Scotty"), and *Two Sisters* ("Jimmy").

8. Neilson—The Fiction of History in Gore Vidal's Messiah

1. Page references are to Gore Vidal, *Julian* (St. Albans: Panther Books, 1972).

2. Cited in Robert J. Stanton, *Gore Vidal: A Primary and Secondary Bibliography.* (Boston: G. K. Hall, 1978), p. xii.

The revision of *Messiah* was not quantitatively substantial, but served in the main to reduce the narrator's tendency to verbosity and complicated syntax. Page references are to Gore Vidal, *Messiah* (St. Albans: Panther Books, 1973).

3. Cited in Robert F. Kiernan, *Gore Vidal* (New York: Ungar, 1982), p. 45.

4. "Most bad criticism stems from the desire to make a case that all of the work of a given writer repeats a single theme. The best writers (and critics) are various. After all, what was Shakespeare's theme? Making that noun singular makes the question silly." Gore Vidal as quoted in *Views from a Window: Conversations with Gore Vidal.* ed. Robert J. Stanton and Gore Vidal (Secaucus, N.J.: Lyle Stuart, 1980), p. 165.

5. "My real name is Eugene Luther Gore Vidal, so I've given him my name." Gore Vidal, interview with Heather Neilson in *Antithesis* (Melbourne, 1987), 1(2):41–5 (quote from p. 45) Vidal's papers are held in the archives of the State Historical Society of Wisconsin, Madison, Wisconsin. In its description of the contents of the Gore Vidal Collection, Vidal's original name is given as Eugene Louis Vidal.

6. Kiernan, *Gore Vidal*, p. 58.

7. "I never much liked the classical canon in American literature. I always thought that our great novelists were minor provincial writers. . . .

"No, I don't feel any particular kinship with the early American writers. . . . Since I do not write romances I was not influenced by Hawthorne & Co., who were all romancers rather than novelists." Vidal, as quoted in *Views from a Window*, p. 182.

8. See for example Lakshmi Mani, *The Apocalyptic Vision in Nineteenth-Century American Fiction: A Study of Cooper, Hawthorne, and Melville* (Washington, D.C.: University Press of America, 1981).

9. Nathaniel Hawthorne, *The Blithedale Romance* (first published 1852), ed. Seymour Gross and Rosalie Murphy (New York: Norton, 1978). "The one book of his . . . that I really like, is *The Blithedale Romance*, which is not a romance, but the only novel he wrote. It showed he had some humour. I could have written Zenobia. I'm glad he wrote Zenobia. Zenobia is always with us—a wonderful character." Vidal, interview with Heather Neilson, in *Antithesis*, p. 49.

10. William H. Shurr, *Rappacini's Children: American Writers in a Calvinist World* (Lexington: University Press of Kentucky, 1981), p. 2.

11. Norman O. Brown, *Life Against Death: The Psychoanalytical Meaning of History* (London: Routledge and Kegan Paul, 1959), p. 211.

12. Vidal, Interview with Heather Neilson, in *Antithesis*, p. 45.

13. More recently, Vidal has written with greater urgency of this aspect of Christianity in the essay "Armageddon?" in Gore Vidal, *Armageddon?: Essays 1983–1987* (London: Andre Deutsch, 1987), pp. 101–15. In this essay Vidal takes as his point of departure Grace Halsell's *Prophecy and Politics: Militant Evangelists on the Road to Nuclear War*, in which Halsell describes the belief of millions of Christian fundamentalists in the United States, among them possibly the then President Ronald Reagan, in the imminence of a nuclear apocalyse: "Only Fundamentalist Christianity in our century has got so seriously into the end-of-the-world game, or Rapture, as it is described by the Dispensationalists" ("Armageddon?" p. 106).

14. *Views from a Window*, p. 99. Eugene Luther reinforces this thesis in a reference to the fourth-century Donatists as detesters of life (*Messiah*, p. 105), which reads as a paraphrase of part of the relevant passage in Edward Gibbon's *The Decline and Fall of the Roman Empire*, ed. J. B. Bury, 7 vols. (London: Methuen, 1901), 2:412–13.

Vidal's quarrel is with the various systems developed in the name of Jesus of Nazareth, rather than with the historical figure's original message: "I doubt if even the most anti-Christian freethinker would want to deny the ethical value of Christ in the Gospels. To reject that Christ is to embark on dangerous waters indeed." Gore Vidal, "Two Immoralists: Orville Prescott and Ayn Rand," in Vidal, *Rocking the Boat* (London: William Heinemann, 1963), pp. 227–34) (quotation from p. 233).

15. As Robert Lane Fox points out, the Antonine age too has been characterized by scholars as an "age of anxiety" and the resurgence of paganism before its final defeat by Christianity attributed to a rise in irrationality. Fox himself doubts the validity or utility of such an attribution to a particular age. Fox, *Pagans and Christians* (New York: Viking Penguin, 1986), pp. 64–65.

16. In one interview Vidal, speaking of the ending of *Messiah*, professed to have superseded the dystopias in *Brave New World* (1932) and

1984 (1949): "I shuddered . . . knew awe, for I had knocked both Huxley and Orwell out of the ring" (*Views from a Window*, p. 94).

17. See, for example, Bernard F. Dick, *The Apostate Angel: A Critical Study of Gore Vidal* (New York: Random House, 1974): "Luther was closer to St. Luke, the most literary of the evangelists, who gave the words of Jesus a grace and rhetorical polish they obviously could never have had in their spoken form" (p. 97).

See also Robert F. Kiernan, *Gore Vidal*, p. 130. Even Theodore Ziolkowski assumes that the analogy is suggested by Luther's name. Ziolkowski, *Fictional Transfigurations of Jesus* (Princeton, N.J.: Princeton University Press, 1972), p. 255.

18. Ziolkowski, *Fictional Transfigurations of Jesus*. Under the heading "fifth gospel" Ziolkowski also examines Lars Gorling's *491*, Günter Grass's *Cat and Mouse*, and John Barth's *Giles Goat-Boy*.

19. Dick, *The Apostate Angel*, p. 101.

20. The irony behind this reference, presumably intended, is oblique. Socrates was held responsible by his enemies for the disastrous turn in the career of Alcibiades, his arrogant sometime-disciple who, severely provoked by political rivals, turned to treason. Cave was the monster of Luther's making, yet Luther would be constituted as traitor in Cavite legend.

Vidal's interest in Alcibiades as a character was more fully expressed in his script of the unproduced screenplay *The Golden Age of Pericles*, on which he worked between 1954 and 1963 (see Box 66 in the Gore Vidal Collection, Madison, Wisconsin).

21. Dick, *The Apostate Angel*, p. 100.

22. Vidal, in conversation with the author, in Los Angeles on December 7, 1985.

23. Cf. Vidal, *Messiah*, ch. 8, sec. 4, and *The Republic of Plato*, trans. Desmond Lee. (Harmondsworth: Penguin, 1955; rev. ed., 1974), pp. 236–52.

24. See, for example, *Views from a Window*, p. 293.

25. *Views from a Window*, p. 304.

26. Vidal, "Evelyn Waugh," in *Rocking the Boat*, p. 239.

27. *Plato's Phaedo*, trans. R. Hackforth (Cambridge: Cambridge University Press, 1955), pp. 58–65.

28. John W. Aldridge, *After the Lost Generation: A Critical Study of the Writers of Two Wars* (New York: McGraw-Hill, 1951; New York Vision Press, 1951), p. 183.

29. Vidal, interview with Heather Neilson, in *Antithesis*, pp. 46–47.

30. Ray Lewis White, *Gore Vidal* (Boston: Twayne, 1968), p. 93.

31. Gore Vidal [*Homage to Daniel Shays*], *Collected Essays, 1952–*

1972 (London: William Heinemann, 1974), pp. 67–74); the quotation is from pp. 73–74.

I am unsure as to when this essay was written. Vidal has said that it was "the beginning of [his] life as an essayist" but that no one would publish it until he included it in this volume. Vidal, interview with Heather Neilson, in *Antithesis*, p. 45.

32. See Gore Vidal, *Lincoln: A Novel* (New York: Random House, 1984), chapter 3, pp. xx.

33. Vidal, interview with Heather Neilson, in *Antithesis*, p. 45. It is possible that Vidal was also "having some fun" with the protagonist of Hemingway's *The Sun Also Rises* (1926). Jake Barnes, rendered impotent in the First World War, also hopelessly loves an unavailable woman and takes pleasure in swimming in the ocean. If the resemblance is intentional, Vidal has achieved a most delicate mockery of Hemingway the literary "great" who, in Vidal's estimation, never wrote a good novel (*Views from a Window*, p. 185).

34. *The Journals [Diary] of Anaïs Nin*, vol. 4, *1944–1947*, ed. Gunther Stuhlmann (London: Quartet Books, 1974), p. 196.

9. White—Vidal as Playwright: In Gentlest Heresy

1. Gore Vidal, *Three Plays* (London: William Heinemann, 1962), p. 253. Subsequent references are to this edition.

2. Vidal, *Three Plays*, p. 253.

3. Gore Vidal, *Rocking the Boat* (Boston: Little, Brown, 1962), p. 86.

4. Eugene Walter, "Conversations with Gore Vidal," *Transatlantic Review* (Summer 1960), p. 12.

5. Gore Vidal, *Visit to a Small Planet: A Comedy Akin to Vaudeville* [Broadway version] (Boston: Little, Brown, 1957). However, all textual references will be to *Three Plays*.

6. Vidal, *Three Plays*, p. 259.

7. Vidal, *Three Plays*, p. 258.

8. Vidal, *Three Plays*, p. 259.

9. Ibid.

10. Gore Vidal, *The Best Man: A Play About Politics* (Boston: Little, Brown, 1960). However, all textual references will be to *Three Plays*.

11. Vidal, *Three Plays*, p. 155.

12. Vidal, *Three Plays*, p. 156.

13. Vidal, *Rocking the Boat*, p. 300.

14. Unpublished. Manuscript available at the State Historical Society of Wisconsin.

15. Vidal, *Three Plays*, p. 87.

16. Ibid.

17. Gore Vidal, "In the Shadow of the Scales," *Reporter* (April 30, 1959), 20:40. Reprinted in *Rocking the Boat*, pp. 184–89.

18. Gore Vidal, *Romulus: A New Comedy, Adapted from a Play by Friedrich Dürrenmatt* (1962; reprint, New York: Dramatists Play Service, 1966), p. x. Subsequent references are to this edition.

19. Vidal, *Romulus*, p. x.

15. Stimpson—My O My O Myra

1. *Myra Breckinridge* was first published in 1968, *Myron* in 1974. In 1986, Gore Vidal put them out in one volume. In this essay, I refer to the 1989 British edition (*Myra Breckinridge and Myron*, London: Grafton Books; hereafter, *Myra and Myron*). For this new volume Vidal made some typographical alterations, substituted a new "Introduction" to serve both novels (replacing an untitled foreword to the 1974 *Myron*), and erased a sardonic political joke: In 1973, while he was writing *Myron*, the Supreme Court issued its infamous ruling on obscenity in *Miller v. California*. An obscene work, the Court declared, has three defining features: the average person, applying "contemporary community standards," would find that the work as a whole appealed to "prurient interest"; the work depicts or describes sexual conduct in a "patently offensive way"; and the work (again, taken as a whole) "lacks serious literary, artistic, political, or scientific value." In response to the decision, Vidal called for "massive civil disobedience" and said that he was modifying *Myron* in a surprising way "that would distress the Supreme Court" ("Broad Spectrum of Writers Attacks Obscenity Ruling," *New York Times*, August 21, 1973, p. 38).

Vidal's joke was to replace "bad" words (in the calculation of American puritanism, "bad" equals "dirty") with the names of the five Court justices who had concurred in the majority opinion (Rehnquist, Powell, Whizzer White, Blackmun, and Burger) as well as with "two well-known warriors in the battle against smut" (*Myron*, 1974, foreword, pp. ix–x). These two men were Father Morton Hill, S.J., and Edward Keating (who in 1989–1991 became a central figure in the savings and loans scandal in the United States).

Here are two examples of Vidal's ironic euphemisms: Too proud for self-pity, Myra nevertheless rages at the "private tragedy" of the last five years of her life, at "being trapped inside a Chinese caterer in the San Fernando Valley, with, admittedly, a big restructured rehnquist between his legs but no powells" (*Myron*, 1974, p. 7). In the 1986 revision, Myra is still too proud for self-pity, but now snarls at "being trapped inside a Chinese caterer in the San Fernando Valley, with, admittedly, a big restructured phallus between his legs but no scrotal sac" (*Myron*, 1989, p. 221). In another scene in the first version, Whittaker Kaiser challenges Myron, "My rehnquist is bigger than your rehnquist" (*Myron*, 1974, p. 19). In the rewrite, he now burbles aggressively, "My cock is bigger than your cock" (*Myron*, 1989, p. 231). Frankly, I miss the original, but perhaps the rewrite does purge *Myron* of an excessive topicality. However, many other topical jokes remain. Moreover, the first version shows the giddy ease with which we can rename parts or functions of the body as well as a host of sexual terms, indeed the *variousness* of the linguistic codes for these words. The phallus *can* become a rehnquist.

2. Thomas A. Sebeok, "Zoosemiotic Components of Human Communication," in Sebeok, *The Sign and Its Masters* (Austin and London: University of Texas Press, 1979), pp. 35–60.

3. Even Robert Mazzocco, who reads *Myron* shrewdly, writes that it is a "vampiristic vaudeville, baroquely cadenced and cleverly done . . . nevertheless, no match for the ineffable ease and raunchy simplicity of its predecessor." Robert Mazzocco, "The Charm of Insolence," *New York Review of Books* 21 (November 14, 1974), pp. 13–15; quotation is from p. 13.

4. In Vidal's *Hollywood* (1990), Caroline Sanford has plastic surgery in order to become more youthful and gain more power in the movie business. Although Caroline's surgery is less extreme, her ambitions less cosmic, her self-willed passage through the theater of the operating room in order to control the theater of the collective unconscious mimics Myra.

5. Vidal, in Michael S. Lasky, "His Work, His Work Habits, His Workings," *Writer's Digest* (March 1975), pp. 20–26 (see p. 25); and Vidal, *Myra and Myron*, p. x.

6. Francis Wyndam, "Hooray for Hollywood," *Times Literary Supplement*, April 11, 1975, p. 389.

7. In 1969, the Stonewall Riots in New York City marked the formal beginning of the Gay Liberation Movement, a political event that *Myra* and earlier Vidal novels helped to make possible through the clarity of their confrontations with homophobia.

8. Several critics have discussed the relationships between *Myra* and Parker Tyler's criticism. See Bernard F. Dick, *The Apostate Angel: A Critical Study of Gore Vidal* (New York: Random House, 1974), pp. 144–48; Robert F. Kiernan, *Gore Vidal* (New York: Ungar, 1982), p. 98; Gerald Mast and Marshall Cohen, eds., *Film Theory and Criticism* (New York: Oxford University Press, 1974), p. 4; and Richard Schickel, "Introduction" (1970) to Parker Tyler, *The Hollywood Hallucination* (1944; reprint, New York: Simon and Schuster, 1970), p. vi.

A rule-of-thumb judgment is that the more solemnly devoted a reader is to Tyler, the more he or she will resent Vidal and find him a crude thief of Tyler's wisdom—an attitude that Tyler's own responses to *Myra* might initially seem to encourage, e.g., "It is slanderous to assume that I ever indulged in anything like the simple-minded, extravagant, mock-serious stuff which both Vidal's novel and the film script put on Myra's lips" (Parker Tyler, "Letter" in "Movie Mailbag," *New York Times*, July 19, 1970, p. 4). Tyler's rhetorical assault, however, has echoes of Myra's campiness. "Why can't . . . Mr. Vidal take me at my own, virile enough, words rather than tilt at me as if I were a trans-sexualized windmill in the mind of some sex-mad Don Quixote of a film buff?" (ibid.).

The presence of these echoes makes the Vidal-Tyler textual exchange more than an outraged victim's identification of the man who mugged him. The exchange also shows, I believe, a mutual appreciation of stylistic flair. To be sure, *Myra* does parody Tyler's alliance of brilliant generalization and precise detail, aphorism and enthusiasm. However, the motive for parody can be respect as well as contempt. Something or somebody is *worth sending up*. Vidal had praised a pornographic piece that Tyler wrote with Charles Henri Ford as a "pioneer work [that] . . . reads surprisingly well today." Gore Vidal, "On Pornography," *New York Review of Books* 6–7 (March 3, 1966), pp. 4–10; quotation from p. 5.

9. Brigid Brophy makes this point as well. Like Vidal, Brophy not only condemns censorship of sexual materials, but sees the connection between sexual and political censorship: "The images lodged in citizens' imaginations are part of the socio-political character of of a country." Brigid Brophy, "The Tang of Uncertainty," *Listener* 80 (September 26, 1968), p. 412.

10. Vidal, "On Pornography," p. 8.

11. In 1990 Vidal wrote, "The tragedy of the United States in this century is not the crackup of an empire, which we never knew what to do with in the first place, but the collapse of the idea of the citizen as someone autonomous whose private life is not subject to orders from above." Gore Vidal, "Notes on Our Patriarchal State," *Nation* 251 (August 27–September 3, 1990) pp. 185, 202–4; quotation from p. 202.

12. William Arrowsmith, "Introduction" to Petronius, *"The Satyricon* (Ann Arbor: University of Michigan Press, 1959), p. x.

13. Purvis E. Boyette was among the first to treat *Myra* seriously as prose satire, tracing its lineage to Sterne and Swift, the picaresque novel, and the antinovel (especially Nathanael West's *A Cool Million*). Interpreting satire as a moral genre in which the satirist seeks to reform the object of his attack, Boyette finds the America that Vidal is exposing "ahistorical, empty of traditional values . . . artistically shallow" and spiritually sterile. Purvis E. Boyette, *"Myra Breckinridge* and Imitative Form," *Modern Fiction Studies* 17 (Summer 1971), pp. 229–38; quotation from p. 235.

So far, so plausible, but Boyette resists Vidal's sexual anarchy and radicalism. He insists that "transexual Myra is . . . the . . . figure of our cultural impotence. . . . As the archetypal pervert she is the image of a debased and debauched society" (ibid., p. 236). Quivering with fears of castration and anal penetration, Boyette blames Rusty Godowski for allowing himself "to be raped by a woman wearing a dildo" (ibid., p. 236). Rusty "could . . . have escaped the event had he fought hard enough" (ibid., p. 236). Protecting phallic power, Boyette unwittingly echoes the language that blames female rape victims for their misery.

14. Peter Conrad also reads *Myron* through "On Pornography," stressing more than I would the separation of sex, "playfully experimental and unfaithful," from "the craven attachments of love." Peter Conrad, "Look at Us," *New Review* 2 (July 1975), pp. 63–66; quotation from p. 65. Promiscuity, then, is "the final conversion of sex into art" and Myra "a feminine Don Giovanni" (ibid., p. 65).

15. Brophy, "The Tang of Uncertainty," p. 412.

16. Vidal, "On Pornography," p. 8.

17. Vidal, "On Pornography," p. 6.

18. Ibid.

19. From the advance review in *Publishers Weekly* 193 (February 5, 1968), p. 63. Dennis Altman wryly describes his vain efforts to prove to Australian authorities that *Myra* is not obscene when he brought a copy back from America: Altman, "How I Fought the Censors and (partly) Won," *Meanjin Quarterly* 29 (Winter 1970), pp. 236–39. Kiernan, *Gore Vidal*, pp. 99–100, analyzes Vidal's skittish treatment of fetishism and the rhetoric of pornography, especially for gay men.

20. Dick, *The Apostate Angel*; and Kiernan, *Gore Vidal*, pp. 98–99.

21. In 1969, a year after *Myra*, Philip Roth, whom Vidal admires, published *Portnoy's Complaint*, another study in sexual excess and the exploitation of the analyst's office as fictive setting.

22. One review of *Myron* mourned that, in the 1974 Camp Sweepstakes, it had to take second place to Rona Barrett's autobiography, "a rags-to-riches Queens-to-Hollywood saga, with plenty of wretchedness along the way . . . told in a headlong no-holds-barred style that . . . would have done Myra proud." Eliot Fremont-Smith, "Second Prize in the Camp Sweepstakes," *New York* 7 (October 21, 1974), pp. 90–91; quotation from p. 91.

23. Kiernan, *Gore Vidal*, p. 106.

24. Dick, *The Apostate Angel*, p. 170.

20. *Pease—America and the Vidal Chronicles*

1. John W. Aldridge, in *After the Lost Generation: A Critical Study of*

the Writers of Two Wars (New York: McGraw-Hill, 1951), gives a broad-ranging account of the new postwar novelists, with the following characteristic assessment: "The final effect [of] *Williwaw* is similar to that of *The Naked and the Dead*—utter futility. But where the parts of Mailer's story anticipated a protest in the conclusion, *Williwaw* moves logically through the futility of its parts to the climaxing futility at its end" (p. 172).

2. To date there are three books on Vidal: Ray Lewis White, *Gore Vidal* (Boston: Twayne, 1968); Robert F. Kiernan, *Gore Vidal* (New York: Ungar, 1982); and Bernard F. Dick, *The Apostate Angel: A Critical Study of Gore Vidal* (New York: Random House, 1974). Of the three books only Dick's moves beyond plot summary. A scattering of articles and book reviews also engages single novels.

Aldridge's reaction to *The City and the Pillar* is again characteristic: "But when we have explored all the flaws of the novel, we have still not really arrived at the basis of its total failure, which is that it is at bottom a thoroughly amoral book—not immoral in the conventional sense that it deals with homosexuality, but amoral in the purely ethical sense, because there is no vitality or significance in the view of life which has gone into it" (*After the Lost Generation*, p. 148).

3. Gore Vidal, *At Home: Essays 1982–1988* (New York: Random House, 1988), pp. 274–75.

4. Norman Mailer, *Cannibals and Christians* (New York: Dial, 1966), pp. 340–71.

5. Lynn Spiegel, "Installing the Television Set: Popular Discourses on Television and Domestic Space, 1948–1955," *Camera Obscura: A Journal of Feminism and Film Theory* 16 (January 1988), p. 14.

6. From 1948 to 1954 he published four novels and a book of short stories that received little public notice. Although he revised earlier novels (including *The City and the Pillar*, whose ending he changed to rape instead of murder) and began work on *Washington D.C.*, the novel *Julian* marked his real return to the world.

7. In *Julian*, Vidal took possession of the Judeo-Christian tradition as a manipulable social narrative; in *Myra Breckinridge*, he dispossessed himself of the psychosocial assumptions of the ruling sexual narrative.

8. Catherine Gallagher, "Marxism and the New Historicism" in H. Aran Veeser, ed., *The New Historicism* (New York: Routledge and Kegan Paul, 1989), p. 38.

9. Quentin Anderson, *The Imperial Self* (New York: Random House, 1971), pp. ix–x.

10. Anderson, *The Imperial Self*, p. 210.

11. Norman Mailer, *The Armies of the Night* (New York: New American Library, 1968), pp. 24–25.

12. Gore Vidal, *Washington, D.C.* (New York: Ballantine, 1967), p. 320.

13. Two essays, "Sex Is Politics" and "Pink Triangle and Yellow Star," originally published in *Playboy* and *The Nation*, draw out some of the political implications of a society formed out of the ritual scapegoating of homosexuals. The shellacking he gave Midge Decter in the latter essay resulted in a bitter controversy between Vidal and Norman Podhoretz whose "The Hate That Dare Not Speak Its Name" contrasted Vidal's supposedly explicit anti-Semitism unfavorably with Decter's putative homophobia. Both of Vidal's essays are reprinted in *The Second American Revolution and Other Essays* (New York: Random House, 1982), pp. 149–84. Podhoretz's response is in *Commentary*.

14. Vidal, *Washington, D.C.*, p. 334.

15. Michael Paul Rogin, *Ronald Reagan: The Movie* (Berkeley: University of California Press, 1987), passim.

16. Vidal, *At Home*, pp. 105–6. The essay from which this quote is taken, "The Day the American Empire Ran Out of Gas," also first appeared in *The Nation* in November 1985 and also resulted in a controversy with Podhoretz (and many others) in the Letters to the Editor pages for many weeks. Vidal's *Empire* depended on the political consciousness this controversy produced for much of its power.

17. Vidal, *Washington, D.C.*, p. 240.

18. Gore Vidal, *1876* (New York: Ballantine, 1982), pp. 344–45.

19. Harold Bloom, "The Central Man," *New York Review of Books*, July 19, 1984, p. 5; see also essay 16 in this volume.

20. Gore Vidal, *Lincoln* (New York: Random House, 1984), p. 657.

21. C. Vann Woodward, *The Future of the Past* (New York: Oxford University Press, 1989), p. 238.

22. Vidal, *At Home*, p. 288.

23. Vidal, *At Home*, p. 286.

24. Frank Lentricchia, "Foucault's Legacy: A New Historicism?" in *The New Historicism*, Aram Veeser, ed. (New York: Routledge, 1987), p. 234.

SELECTED BIBLIOGRAPHY

I. Works by Gore Vidal

At Home: Essays 1982–1988. New York: Random House, 1988.

Armageddon? Essays, 1983–1987. London: Andre Deutsch, 1987.

The Best Man: A Play About Politics. Boston: Little, Brown, 1960.

Burr: A Novel. New York: Random House, 1973.

The City and the Pillar. New York: E. P. Dutton, 1948. Rev. ed., New York: E. P. Dutton, 1965.

Creation: A Novel. New York: Random House, 1981.

Dark Green, Bright Red. New York: E. P. Dutton, 1950. Rev. ed., New York: New American Library, 1968.

Death Before Bedtime [Edgar Box pseud.]. New York: E. P. Dutton, 1953.

Death in the Fifth Position [Edgar Box pseud.]. New York: E. P. Dutton, 1952.

Death Likes It Hot [Edgar Box pseud.]. New York: E. P. Dutton, 1954.

1876: A Novel. New York: Random House, 1976.

Empire: A Novel. New York: Random House, 1987.

An Evening with Richard Nixon. New York: Random House, 1972.

Hollywood: A Novel. New York: Random House, 1990.

Homage to Daniel Shays: Collected Essays, 1952–1972. New York: Random House, 1972. London: William Heinemann, 1974.

In a Yellow Wood. New York: E. P. Dutton, 1947.

The Judgment of Paris. New York: E. P. Dutton, 1952. Rev. ed., Boston: Little, Brown, 1965.

Julian: A Novel. Boston: Little, Brown, 1964.

Kalki: A Novel. New York: Random House, 1978.

Lincoln: A Novel. New York: Random House, 1984.

Matters of Fact and Fiction (Essays 1973–1976). New York: Random House, 1977.

Messiah. New York: E. P. Dutton, 1954. Rev. ed., Boston: Little, Brown, 1965.

Myra Breckinridge. Boston: Little, Brown, 1968.

Myron: A Novel. New York: Random House, 1974.

On the March to the Sea: A Southern Tragedy. Evergreen Playscript Series. New York: Grove Press, n.d.

Reflections Upon a Sinking Ship. Boston: Little, Brown, 1969.

Rocking the Boat. Boston: Little, Brown, 1962.

Romulus: A New Comedy, Adapted from a Play by Friedrich Dürrenmatt. New York: Dramatists Play Service, 1962.

A Search for the King: A Twelfth-Century Legend. New York: E. P. Dutton, 1950.

The Season of Comfort. New York: E. P. Dutton, 1949.

The Second American Revolution and Other Essays (1976–1982). New York: Random House, 1982.

Sex, Death and Money. New York: Bantam Books, 1968.

A Thirsty Evil: Seven Short Stories. New York: Zero Press, 1956.

Three: Williwaw, A Thirsty Evil, Julian the Apostate. New York: New American Library, 1962.

Three Plays. London: William Heinemann, 1962.

Two Sisters: A Memoir in the Form of a Novel. Boston: Little, Brown, 1970.

A View from the Diners' Club: Essays 1987–1991. London: Andre Deutsch, 1991.

Views from a Window: Conversations with Gore Vidal. Edited by Robert J. Stanton and Gore Vidal. Secaucus, N.J.: Lyle Stuart, 1980.

Visit to a Small Planet: A Comedy Akin to Vaudeville [Broadway Version]. Boston: Little, Brown, 1957.

Visit to a Small Planet and Other Television Plays. Boston: Little, Brown, 1956.

Washington, D.C.: A Novel. Boston: Little, Brown, 1967.

Weekend: A Comedy in Two Acts. New York: Dramatists Play Service, 1968.

Williwaw. New York: E. P. Dutton, 1946.

II. Works About Gore Vidal

Dick, Bernard F. *The Apostate Angel: A Critical Study of Gore Vidal.* New York: Random House, 1974.

Kiernan, Robert F. *Gore Vidal.* New York: Frederick Ungar, 1982.

Mitzel, John, and Steven Abbot. *Myra & Gore: A New View of Myra Breckinridge and a Candid Interview with Gore Vidal. A Book for Vidalophiles.* Dorchester, Mass.: Manifest Destiny Books, 1974.

Stanton, Robert J. *Gore Vidal: A Primary and Secondary Bibliography.* Boston: G. K. Hall, 1978.

White, Ray Lewis. *Gore Vidal.* Boston: Twayne, 1968.

III. Selected Essays About Gore Vidal

Aldridge, John W. "Gore Vidal: The Search for a King." *After the Lost Generation: A Critical Study of the Writers of the Two Wars,* pp. 170–83. New York: McGraw-Hill, 1951.

Armstrong, I. D. "An Old Philosopher in Rome: George Santayana and His Visitors." *Journal of American Studies* (December 1985), 19:349–68.

Barton, David. "Narrative Patterns in the Novels of Gore Vidal." *Notes on Contemporary American Literature* (September 1981), 7(4):3–9.

Bargainnier, Earl P. "The Mysteries of Edgar Box (aka Gore Vidal)." *Clues: A Journal of Detection* (Spring–Summer 1981), 2:45–52.

Boyette, Purvis E. "'Myra Breckinridge' and Imitative Form." *Modern Fiction Studies* (Summer 1971), 17:229–38.

Buckley, William F., Jr. "On Experiencing Gore Vidal." *Esquire* (August 1969), pp. 108–13.

Clarke, Gerald. "Petronius Americanus: The Ways of Gore Vidal." *Atlantic* (March 1972), pp. 283–311.

Clemons, Walter. "Gore Vidal's Chronicle of America." *Newsweek* (June 9, 1984), 103(24):74–75, 78–79.

Conrad, Peter. "Hall of Mirrors: The Novels of Gore Vidal." London *Sunday Times,* March 27, 1977, p. 35.

———. "Look at Us." *New Review* (July 1975), 2:63–66.

———. "Re-inventing America." *Times Literary Supplement,* March 26, 1976, pp. 347–48.

Epstein, Joseph. "What Makes Vidal Run." *Commentary* (June 1977), 63:72–75.

Fletcher, M. D. "Vidal's *Duluth* as 'Post-Modern' Political Satire." *Ihalia: Studies in Literary Humor* (Spring–Summer 1986), 9:10–21.

Hollinghust, Alan. "Imperial Dope." *London Review of Books*, June 4–17, pp. 13–14.

Krim, Seymour. "Reflections on a Ship That's Not Sinking at All." *London Magazine* (May 1970), pp. 26–43.

LaHood, Marvin J. "Gore Vidal: A Grandfather's Legacy." *World Literature Today* (Summer 1990), 64:413–17.

Mitzel, John et al. "Some Notes on Myra B." *Fag Rag* (Fall 1973), pp. 21–25.

Nin, Anaïs. *The Diary of Anaïs Nin*. Vol. 4, *1944–1947* (pp. 106, 113, 121). Edited by Gunther Stuhlmann. New York: Harcourt, Brace, 1971.

Oates, Joyce Carol. "The Union Justified the Means." *New York Times Book Review*, June 3, 1984, pp. 1, 36–37.

Ross, Mitchell S. "Gore Vidal." *The Literary Politicians*, pp. 247–300. Garden City, N.Y.: Doubleday, 1978.

Simon, John. "The Good and Bad of Gore Vidal." *Paradigms Lost*, pp. 105–10. New York: Clarkson N. Potter, 1980.

Summers, Claude J. "'The Cabin and the River,' Gore Vidal's *The City and the Pillar*." *Gay Fictions: Wilde to Stonewall: Studies in a Male Homosexual Literary Tradition*, pp. 112–29. New York: Continuum, 1990.

Wilhelm, John F. and Mary Ann Wilhelm. "'Myra Breckinridge': A Study of Identity." *Journal of Popular Culture* (Winter 1969), 3:590–99.

Ziolkowski, Theodore. *Fictional Transfigurations of Jesus*, pp. 250–57. Princeton, N.J.: Princeton University Press, 1972.

CONTRIBUTORS

LOUIS AUCHINCLOSS is a New York lawyer as well as a prolific novelist and critic.

HAROLD BLOOM is Professor of the Humanities at Yale University and the author of numerous ground-breaking studies, including *The Anxiety of Influence* and *A Map of Misreading*.

ROBERT BOYERS is Professor of English at Skidmore College and editor of *Salmagundi*. Among his many books are *Atrocity and Amnesia: The Political Novel Since 1945* and critical studies of F. R. Leavis, Lionell Trilling, and R. P. Blackmur.

ITALO CALVINO was an Italian novelist of international fame. He wrote the essay included here in praise of Vidal when he was made an honorary citizen of Ravello, Italy.

ALAN CHEUSE is Professor of English at George Mason University and the author of many books of fiction, including *The Grandmothers' Club*. He is also a regular fiction reviewer on National Public Radio.

BERNARD F. DICK is Professor of English at Fairleigh Dickinson University. He published *The Apostate Angel: A Critical Study of Gore Vidal* in 1974. He has written widely on modern fiction.

THOMAS M. DISCH is theater critic for *The Nation* and one of America's most versatile writers: poet, novelist, playwright, and essayist.

ROBERT F. KIERNAN has written widely on modern literature. His book-length study of Gore Vidal, published by Frederick Ungar in 1982, has been widely admired. He is Professor of English at Manhattan College.

HEATHER NEILSON recently was awarded a D.Phil. from Oxford University for a critical thesis on Gore Vidal. She is from New Zealand.

JAY PARINI, the editor of this volume, is a poet and novelist. Professor of English at Middlebury College, his books include *Anthracite Country, Town Life,* and *The Last Station.*

DONALD E. PEASE is Professor of English at Dartmouth College and the author of *Visionary Compacts,* an influential study of mid-nineteenth-century American writers. He has written widely in the field of literary theory.

SAMUEL F. PICKERING is Professor of English at the University of Connecticut. A well-known essayist and literary critic, he has published over half a dozen books, including *Continuing Education, May Days,* and *Still Life.*

RICHARD POIRIER is Professor of English at Rutgers University and editor of *Raritan.* His numerous books include *The Performing Self* and *Robert Frost: The Work of Knowing.*

DAVID PRICE is Professor of English at Middlebury College and a specialist in modern poetry and fiction.

WILLIAM H. PRITCHARD is Professor of English at Amherst College and the author of many critical books and innumerable articles and reviews. He has written biographical studies of Robert Frost and Randall Jarrell.

STEPHEN SPENDER is a poet and critic of international renown. He has taught at many universities in England and America.

CATHARINE R. STIMPSON is Dean of the Graduate School at Rutgers University and was until recently President of the Modern Language Association. Her pioneering work in feminist studies has established her as one of America's leading critics. She has also written a novel, *Class Notes.*

CLAUDE J. SUMMERS is Professor of English at the University of Michigan at Dearborn. In addition to a recent study of gay fiction, he has written books on E. M. Forster and Christopher Isherwood.

JAMES TATUM is Professor of Classics at Dartmouth College and the author of several important books on Roman literature, including *Apuleius and The Golden Ass.* He has translated several plays by Plautus and most recently edited a symposium on the ancient novel.

RAY LEWIS WHITE published the first full-length critical study of Gore Vidal in the Twayne's United States Authors Series in 1968.

INDEX

Library of Congress Cataloging-in-Publication Data

Gore Vidal : writer against the grain / edited by Jay Parini.
    p.   cm.
    Includes bibliographical references and index.
    ISBN 0-231-07208-2
    1. Vidal, Gore, 1925–   —Criticism and interpretation.
I. Parini, Jay.
PS3543.I26Z67   1992
818'.5409—dc20   91-45312
                                                            CIP

Casebound editions of Columbia University Press books are
Smyth-sewn and printed on permanent and durable acid-free
paper.